# IMAGE AN
# IMAGINATION

# IMAGE AND IMAGINATION

## ESSAYS AND REVIEWS

BY

## C. S. LEWIS

Edited by

Walter Hooper

# CAMBRIDGE
## UNIVERSITY PRESS

University Printing House, Cambridge CB2 8BS, United Kingdom

Published in the United States of America by Cambridge University Press,
New York

Cambridge University Press is part of the University of Cambridge.

It furthers the University's mission by disseminating knowledge in the
pursuit of education, learning and research at the highest international levels
of excellence.

www.cambridge.org
Information on this title: www.cambridge.org/9781107639270

© 2013 C. S. Lewis Pte Ltd

First published 2013

Printed and bound in the United States of America

*A catalogue record for this publication is available from the British Library*

ISBN 978-1-107-63927-0 Paperback

Cambridge University Press has no responsibility for the persistence or
accuracy of URLs for external or third-party internet websites referred to in this
publication, and does not guarantee that any content on such websites is, or
will remain, accurate or appropriate.

# CONTENTS

# PREFACE
*Walter Hooper*

C. S. Lewis would not have published anything he was not satisfied with, but his overflowing bookshelves contained few of his own books and writings. We can only wonder at what he'd make of this new book, which gathers up all his book reviews, forty-two in total, covering thirty-five years. These have never been collected and will be new to most readers. In addition, the book includes four major essays unavailable in print for over half a century ('The idea of an "English School"', 'Our English syllabus', the preface to *Essays Presented to Charles Williams*, 'The English prose *Morte*'), two essays that Lewis drafted but never published ('Image and imagination', 'Lucretius'), two obituaries (on Oliver Elton and Charles Williams), his preface to *A Faith of Our Own* by his friend, the theologian Austin Farrer, the foreword to *Smoke on the Mountain* by Joy Davidman, the woman he eventually married, and his introduction to an edition of Laȝamon's *Brut*, which he thought he might, one day, translate.

For ease of reference and as a guide through so broad an array of topics, I have presented the different essays and reviews under six broadly thematic sections, rather than chronologically. The first section contains general discussions of literature and literary history. The second includes Lewis's formal, published assessments of the work of his friends in the Inklings circle. A section reflecting on aspects of Christianity follows, and then the rest of the book considers, in turn, specific issues regarding Classical literature, Medieval and Renaissance literature, and, finally, Milton and later English literature. Within each section, material is arranged chronologically by subject (and so, for example, a discussion of Homer precedes one on Aristotle), and more general topics appear before those more narrowly focused. Readers should remember however that Lewis's mind was especially adept at forging unexpected connections. It was part of his genius to recognize that rationality and religion, the material and the metaphorical all inform one another. An essay or review in one chapter, therefore, may have – probably will have – implications for arguments expressed elsewhere.

This book will appeal principally to anyone with general interests in literature and religion, as well as those who have a particular regard for the academic work of C. S. Lewis or who simply like good English prose style. Taken together, the essays and reviews present some of his best literary criticism and religious exposition. Many were composed with the general reader in mind, having been written originally for popular newspapers and magazines such as *The Listener*, the *Observer*, the *Spectator*, the *Sunday Telegraph*, *Time and Tide*, *The Times*, and the *Times Literary Supplement*. As ever, I am grateful to the C. S. Lewis Estate for permission to reproduce this material.

I owe an immense debt to Dr A. T. Reyes, the Classical scholar, best known to Lewis readers for his magisterial edition of C. S. Lewis's translation of *The Aeneid – C. S. Lewis's Lost Aeneid: Arms and the Exile* (2011) – and to my godson, G. E. M. Lippiatt of Hertford College, who supplied, besides much good advice, the translation of Lewis's

French piece, 'What France means to me' in Chapter 20 (see pp. 143–6). I am very grateful to both.

Finally, I would like to thank the Syndics of Cambridge University Press for agreeing to publish this book. Dr Linda Bree, the editor in charge of its production, has been helpful and kind throughout. In 1969, I edited for Cambridge Lewis's *Selected Literary Essays*, to which I hope this new collection of writings will serve as a worthy companion and pendent.

# LIST OF ABBREVIATIONS

The following abbreviated references have been used:

| | |
|---|---|
| AV | Authorized Version (The King James Version) of the Bible |
| *Collected Letters I* | Walter Hooper (ed.), *The Collected Letters of C. S. Lewis*, vol. I: *Family Letters 1905–1931* (London: HarperCollins, 2000). |
| *Collected Letters II* | Walter Hooper (ed.), *The Collected Letters of C. S. Lewis*, vol. II: *Books, Broadcasts, and War 1931–1949* (London: HarperCollins, 2004). |
| *Collected Letters III* | Walter Hooper (ed.), *The Collected Letters of C. S. Lewis*, vol. III: *Narnia, Cambridge, and Joy 1950–1963* (London: HarperCollins, 2006). |
| 'On Fairy-Stories' | J. R. R. Tolkien, 'On Fairy-Stories', *The Monsters and the Critics and Other Essays*, edited by Christopher Tolkien (London: George Allen and Unwin, 1983), pp. 109–61. |
| RSV | Revised Standard Version of the Bible |

# PART I
## REFLECTIONS ON LITERATURE

~

*C. S. Lewis's pre-eminence as an author, academic and apologist is such that we often forget he was, for the most part, a teacher. At Oxford, every term, for eight weeks, he lectured and gave tutorials in English literature to undergraduates, aside from fulfilling other duties, decanal or administrative, on behalf of the University and the residents of his College. The first two long essays here, from the collection* Rehabilitations and Other Essays *(1939) reveal how important this facet of his life was to him. In both, he discusses the importance of academic rigour and intellectual exploration, not only in universities, but also in schools. The third long essay, 'Image and imagination' appears here for the first time. It is a philosophical analysis of the way an 'image' may inspire 'imagination' and vice versa. In a way, 'Image and imagination' is analogous to Tolkien's famous story 'Leaf by niggle'. Both are conceptual treatments of what is happening when an author creates an imaginary world. The other articles display the range of Lewis's literary interests, casting light on the smallest matters of bibliography, as well as more weighty problems of translation and interpretation.*

# I

## The idea of an 'English School'

~

Non leve quiddam interest inter humanae mentis idola et divinae
mentis ideas, hoc est inter placita quaedam inania et veras signaturas
atque impressiones factas in creaturis, prout inveniuntur.[1]

Bacon, *Novum Organum*, i.23

The title of this paper is unfortunate in recalling that of
Newman's best book.[2] It is doubly unfortunate in so far
as it not only suggests, on my part, an arrogant intention
of pitting myself against so great a writer, but also carries
with it an omen of failure on the practical side; for none of
the things which Newman advised has come to pass. Yet
some such title is unavoidable. I intend, it is true, to talk
a good deal about the Final Honour School of English as
it actually exists at Oxford. But I am concerned with that
School not as an historical fact but as an approximation
to an ideal. What we are doing at Oxford is of universal
interest only as an indication of what, on my view, we are
trying to do or ought to do. We are doubtless full of faults
and do not shun criticism, provided such criticism is based
on an understanding of our aims. You may not agree with
these aims – though I hope that you will – but do not

Published in C. S. Lewis, *Rehabilitations and Other Essays* (London: Oxford
University Press, 1939), pp. 57–77; originally read to a joint meeting of
the Classical and English Associations (date unknown).

blame a man for making slow progress to the North when he is trying to get to the East.

We are under no illusions as to our reputation in the outer world. What our enemies think of us is vigorously enough, if not always very lucidly, conveyed by the expressions they use – by their references to 'the Germanic jungle', 'all this philology', 'Verner's law', 'Anglo-Saxon', and (most damning of all) 'Gothic'. When we listen attentively to this buzz of condemnation, we think that we can distinguish two strains in it. The confusion between 'Germanic' or 'Anglo-Saxon' on the one hand and 'philology' or 'Verner's law' on the other, is made, we believe, by two classes of people. In the first class we find the man who is still living in the Renaissance, the belated Ascham,[3] who is quite sure that literature he cannot translate must be bad literature – must be 'Gothic' in the classical sense of the word. He does not like the poetry of the Dark, and Middle Ages (*ignoti nulla cupido*)[4] and he uses 'philology' simply as a term of abuse. He is not really thinking of philology at all. In the second class we find a much more respectable opponent, probably a real scholar who knows that he does not know any medieval language. His objection is not to the unknown literatures – in such a man it could not be – but to comparative philology. He has in his mind the picture of a promising academic discipline, in which the young might have been guided to a systematic study of our English classics, not without some subsidiary Greek and Latin to steady their judgement, perverted and thwarted by irrelevant excursions into Germanic philology; he sees the interest which ought to have been concentrated on Shakespeare and Johnson dissipated on mere comparisons between English and cognate languages; and he wonders why English should have been selected to carry this purely scientific and unliterary burden which might, with equal propriety or impropriety, have been bound on the back of several other subjects.

To this second, and reasonable, type of critic, our reply is a simple one. His information is out of date. No undergraduate at Oxford is obliged to know a single word of Gothic, old High German, or Old Norse, or to study the relations between these languages and his own. The English student can choose between three alternative courses, all of which can conduct him to the highest honours. One of these is frankly medieval, and if a student chooses it he does so because he is interested in early English and its immediate relatives. The second is a halfway house – a complicated affair that need not now concern us. The third is the literary course proper, which the vast majority of our students take.

But here comes the rub. This third and literary course, I must confess, contains three papers which the enemy will be tempted to describe as 'philological'. The first is on Modern English, and deals mainly with the history of meaning, whether in syntax or vocabulary. The second is on Anglo-Saxon texts, and the third on Middle English texts. I do not imagine that the critic I have in view will object very strongly to the first of these. If he does, the official voice of our English School will reply with the very pertinent question, 'Do you wish students to understand what they read or not?' For the fact is that those who have had no experience in the teaching of English are living a fool's paradise as regards the ability of the average undergraduate to *construe* his mother tongue. Again and again curious statements in the essays of our pupils can be traced back to an original failure to make out the sense of Milton or Johnson or Coleridge, as a schoolboy fails to make out the sense of Caesar or Xenophon. And with this answer I expect that the critics will be satisfied. But the other two papers – the Anglo-Saxon and Middle English texts – I fear he will regard as *vestigial*, as relics of that philological period in which, admittedly, English studies at Oxford began – *ein Theil des Theils, der anfangs alles war.*[5] He will be in danger of looking upon them as a rearguard which has not yet been defeated but whose defeat may be hourly expected. His hopes are vain; and it is at this point that I must join issue with him. If any of the three papers is really vestigial, it is the paper on Modern English. I have just stated the official defence for it; but it would be disingenuous not to confess that this paper is a subject of dispute among ourselves. I am, in fact, one of those who disapprove of it. But that is not our present concern. I mention it only to emphasize the fact that this paper is incomparably the most philological of the three, and that the other two, so far from being vestigial, are essential to the idea of an English School as I see it.

Before I attempt to explain why, I must remove two possible misconceptions. One is the belief that Anglo-Saxon is a language other than English, or even, as used to be said, that English is a third language born from the union of two earlier languages, Anglo-Saxon and French. This is an error so gross that six weeks' study would remove it from the minds of the most prejudiced. You might as well say that Latin was a new language born from the union of Roman and Greek. Anglo-Saxon is simply early English. Norman-French is simply one of the foreign languages which, from time to time, have enriched our vocabulary.

Most of the changes which separate what we call Anglo-Saxon from what we call Middle English had begun before the Normans landed, and would have followed much the same course if no Conquest had ever occurred. Brevity compels me to be dogmatic; but it is not really a subject that admits of discussion.

The second misconception turns on our old friend 'philology'. There is no philology in the papers on Anglo-Saxon and Middle English. They are papers on texts, consisting of a core of passages for translation surrounded by questions on archaeological, textual, cultural, or historical matters relevant to the texts. The student is asked to know about *Beowulf* or *Pearl* just those things which the classical examiner demands that he should know about Virgil or Sophocles. Philology is absent, unless you call grammar philology. Before some audiences I should feel it my duty to insist rather strongly on the value of grammar. I am told that there have been critics of Chaucer who perpetrated serious blunders in translation, and built up formidable aesthetic superstructures on a purely intuitive, and sometimes erroneous, conception of their author's meaning. But I presume that every one present agrees that if you are going to read a book at all, it is desirable to be able to tell which words are in the Nominative and which are in the Accusative.

We are now, at last, in a position to come to grips with the main question. Granted that these old books are written in what is unmistakably English, and granted that we do not set philological questions on them, still, it will be asked, why should we read them? What relevance has the study of *Beowulf* for the man who wants to read modern English literature? If we are looking for sheer

7

poetical merit, are there not many poems greater than *Beowulf* and no more difficult? Why not the *Iliad*, or the *Aeneid*? If, on the other hand, we are looking for the origins of Modern literature, shall we not find them in Rome and Greece? None of our great poets could read Anglo-Saxon: nearly all of them could and did read Latin, and some knew Greek.

I will take the second question first, and before I attempt to answer it, let me protest that I am no enemy of the classics. I have read the *Aeneid* through more often than I have read any long poem; I have just finished re-reading the *Iliad*; to lose what I owe to Plato and Aristotle would be like the amputation of a limb. Hardly any lawful price would seem to me too high for what I have gained by being made to learn Latin and Greek. If any question of the value of classical studies were before us, you would find me on the extreme right. I do not know where the last ditch in our educational war may be at the moment; but point it out to me on the trench-map and I will go to it. At present, however, we are only asking whether it is true that the origins of English literature are to be found in the classics. And perhaps if 'the origins' here means 'all the origins' no one, however, ignorant, would answer Yes. At most our critics can only mean that of the innumerable debts which our literary tradition owes, the debt to Rome and Greece is the greatest and most important. I do not think this is true.

The first step in an inquiry into its truth is to rule out the greatest Greek poets and philosophers. Except on a few isolated writers such as Milton and Gray,[6] these have no influence worth talking about before the nineteenth century. Chapman's Homer, and even Pope's,[7] might almost have been written to prove that Homer was invisible to Englishmen until the Romantic Revival had cleared their eyes. In drama, Seneca is of far more importance than all the Greek tragedians put together. The real Plato counts for less in our tradition than that strange theosophy which Ficino[8] and others called 'Platonic theology'. Aristotle, I admit, in a slightly Thomized form, bit deeply into the minds of the Middle Ages; but where are the literary results of this? On seventeenth-century criticism we can trace his influence at every step, but it is an influence almost wholly mischievous.

Having got rid of these august but irrelevant names, it may be well to remind ourselves of the authors who have really affected us deeply and over long periods. Of the Romans those naturally come first who enjoyed the same degree and nearly the same kind of prestige both before and after the Renaissance – the great Kings whose reign had begun before *Beowulf* was written and has not ended yet. I mean, of course Boethius, Ovid, and Virgil – and I would put them roughly in that order of importance. Immediately below these, in length and security of reign, we might put Juvenal, the moral works of Cicero and Seneca, Horace, Statius, Claudian, and a few others. Apuleius and the elder Pliny would come a good deal higher than they do in our modern scholastic tradition. Of the Greeks, the great gossiping authors, the repositories of anecdote, like Plutarch and Diogenes Laertius, would stand at the top of the list. Second to these we should find, indistinguishably blended, the joint influence of Theocritus and the novelists – Longus, Heliodorus, and the like; and perhaps – but I am doubtful about my facts here – the influence of the *Anthology*.[9]

Having identified the influential authors it remains to consider what their influence really was. It is clear, in the first place, that our literature is not greatly indebted to them for its forms. We are apt to forget that Milton's classical epic and classical tragedy are lonely exceptions. Most attempts to transplant an ancient form into English literature have failed. Milton is the single survivor in a forlorn hope where Cowley, Blackmore, and Glover fell: *Samson* lives, but *Gorboduc*, *Cato*, and *Caratacus* do not. A list of our best narrative poems would contain *Troilus*, *The Faerie Queene*, *The Prelude*, *Don Juan*, and *Endymion*, and would leave out all our classical epics save one. A list of our greatest dramas would give an even more striking result. Our lyric poetry is, no doubt, richly decorated in certain periods with borrowings from ancient Latin and Greek, though they are not more numerous than its borrowings from medieval Latin, from Italian, and from old and modern French. Its chief serious attempt to adopt an ancient form, however, has left behind it only one or two successes by Gray amidst a ruinous waste of 'Pindarique Odes'; and in the very nature of things formal similarities between quantitative lyric and rhymed accentual lyric must be very superficial. Already in *Summer is icumen in* we are basing our lyrical poetry on discoveries in music which the Greeks never made. The novel, born from the marriage of the periodical essay and the romance, or the sonnet, descending from the Provençals, are even farther removed from ancient literature. The Satire and the Pastoral are more instructive, for in them we can see side by side the unhappy attempts to adhere to the classical form and the happy departures from it. The Roman model – the static, rambling diatribe – is preserved by Donne, Hall, Marston, and Churchill, and by Pope in his inferior works; our great satires, deserting this in favour of extravagant satiric fiction and owing something, perhaps, to Lucian and the *Margites*, but much more to Rabelais and Cervantes, have given us *Hudibras*, *Absalom*, *The Rape*, *The Dunciad*, *Gulliver*, *Don Juan*, *Erewhon*, and *Brave New World*. In the Pastoral we can trace both developments in the same writer (and that, not only in English) as we gratefully lay aside Sannazaro's tedious *Piscatory Eclogues* and open his *Arcadia* or turn from the fussy futility of the *Shepherd's Calendar* to the sixth book of *The Faerie Queene*. The little drop of Theocritus properly mixed with northern romance and Provençal love poetry improves the drink: offer it neat, and our stomachs turn. We can read Sidney and William Browne, but who, unbribed, would open the pastorals of Mantuan, Barclay, or Googe?

But perhaps I have argued too long on a point that is obvious. No one can really be maintaining that the best and most characteristic English work is deeply indebted to the classics for its form. We are more likely to be told that something subtler than a form – a spirit or temper or attitude – has been transferred. And, of course, I have no wish to deny that many individual English authors have in this way been deeply affected by their classical reading. We cannot even imagine Chapman without the Stoics, Burke without Cicero, or Tennyson without Virgil. It is equally true, however, that we cannot imagine Chaucer without Guillaume de Lorris, or Spenser without Ariosto, or Morris without Froissart and the *Edda*. Of tracing such individual affinities there would be no end. What the argument requires is to show that the spirit of our literature, or our best literature, or most of our best literature, is closer to that of the classics than to that of other cultures. And this, I think, has never been shown.

Ovid's erotic poetry, received by our culture, becomes the poetry of Courtly Love; his mythological poetry becomes the wonder of Chaucer and Gower, the allegorical and astrological pantheon of Fulgentius and Lydgate, the gods of Botticelli, Titian, and Tintoretto, the emblematic deities of masque and ballet and pantomime, and the capitalized abstractions of eighteenth-century verse. The tale of Troy wears casque and habergeon in the fourteenth, lace and periwig in the eighteenth, century. The Pastoral, snatched from those realistic Sicilian slopes, is carried into the depths of an Arcadian golden age and there enchanted. The change which the classics undergo when we take them into our own imagination is precisely a change of spirit or temper. Names and myths remain, but all is romanticized, darkened here and softened there, filled with new shadows and assimilated to our needs. There is no question of new wine being poured into old bottles: rather, a little new wine is poured into a lot of old wine. We were not an emptiness which the classics filled, nor a patient on which they acted. We had our own idiosyncrasy. We also were a spirit, an ancient, complex, and intensely active spirit. We let in what we could turn to our own substance, and the process of digestion was thorough. *Quidquid recipitur, recipitur ad modum recipientis.*[10] Of this *recipiens*, the real English Muse, the mother of us all, I shall have more to say in a few moments. She is, you will notice, the person who has hitherto been left out of the story.

My present duty, however, is to answer the question I set myself: what did the influence of the classics really amount to? And already, I fear, it may seem to you that I have proved too much. If they gave us neither form nor spirit, then what, in heaven's name, is this debt to them which even I acknowledge? The answer to that is a very simple one. They gave us Matter: not a new way of writing and feeling, but new things to write and feel about – theories, histories, facts, myths, anecdotes, people. That is why the gossiping or encyclopaedic authors, like Plutarch, Pliny, Diogenes Laertius, Aulus Gellius, and Macrobius are so important. This is the real impress which classical education has left on our literature. You can read English poetry for days on end without coming across classic form or classic feeling; but you will have been inundated with references to how Acteon died or what birds saved the Capitol, what Agesilaus said or Pompey did, the constitution of Sparta, the matrimonial troubles of Socrates, and some one's witty reply to Alexander. It is this kind of influence that lies on the surface of our literature and meets every one's gaze; and it is of this that most people are really thinking when they say that our origins are in Greece and Rome.

But a source of matter is a very different thing from a source of inspiration, a real influence on form and spirit. The difference becomes clear if we compare the effect of the Classics upon us with the effect of a force that reached us a few centuries before the Renaissance. I promised, a minute ago, to say something more of our mother, the English Muse – the *recipiens* who receives everything in her own fashion. It is now time to remind you that long before this mother of ours met with Greek literature, she had already had a lover – a much more masterful lover whom she has never yet been able to forget. I mean, of course, Old French. I have said that you can read English poetry for a long time without coming across classic form. You cannot read one verse, unless it is *vers libre*, without meeting Old French form. It was Old French that overthrew our native prosody: we have been singing an old French tune ever since. It was Old French that taught us those species of sentiment and refinement which we still use. Whenever you think of a rhyme for a limerick, or accept fictitious prose narrative as an obvious form of serious literature, or offer a chair to a lady, or build a castle instead of a villa in the air, you are being Old French. You can choose, to some extent, how classical you will be; you cannot choose how Old French you will be. The thing is in our system, bred in the bone. This is a real influence. Compared with it the influence of the classics is recent, superficial, almost negligible.

You will have noticed that this casts a disquieting light on our educational problem. If we are to seek the true sources of our own literature, then the serious rival to Anglo-Saxon is not the classics, but Old French. If we abandon *Beowulf* we must put in not Homer but the *Romance of the Rose*, and that for two reasons. In the first place, as I have said, the Old French influence is incomparably greater in degree. But secondly, it is of a kind that cannot be studied at second hand. A real transfusion of spirit involves intangibles: to study it is to study things that can only be known by long and sympathetic reading of originals. But the matter, which is what we have mainly borrowed from Greece and Rome can be quite adequately learned from Classical Dictionaries, historical text-books, and translations. Do not misunderstand the word 'adequately'. I do not mean that we shall thus have an adequate knowledge of the classics, but that we shall have an adequate preparation for the study of English. We shall have learned what our authors learned and often in the same way. A great deal of the classical ornament in English poetry was learned from text-books like Natalis Comes and Lemprière, and from translations like North's *Plutarch*. Pope found that he could very comfortably make a version of Homer without seriously learning Greek.

The real choice, then, is between Anglo-Saxon and Old French (or, perhaps, medieval Latin[a]), and if I choose the former it is again in virtue of the principle *Quidquid recipitur*. Our mother surrendered more to Old French than to the classics, but she did not surrender completely: even in the eleventh century she had a spirit of her own capable of transforming and assimilating what she received, modifying its gallantries with a homelier affection, hardening its heroisms, neglecting its ironies, broadening its humour, deepening its pathos, shading its marvels with a more awe-inspiring obscurity, and accentualizing its syllabic verse. And so, in the end, I am driven back to our ancient alliterative poetry. There for the first time I find a prosody based on the speech rhythms that I hear in conversation to-day. I find a sense of language so native to us all that the phrases which hit the eighth-century audience hard, hit me hard too as soon as I have learned to understand them; I see at once that words like *gold* and *wolf* and *heart* and *blood* and *winter* and *earth*, had the same overtones for them as for me. Everything is already unmistakably English. This mere Englishness is usually called

---

[a] On further consideration I should regard the claims of medieval Latin as almost equal to those of Old French. It would not, at present, be easy to put the relevant texts in the hands of students, and they are hard to translate.

Romanticism by those who do not know Anglo-Saxon. They are fond of tracing it to the French Revolution or even to the Celtic strain in our blood. They bring far-fetched explanations why the English wrote melancholy poems about ruins in the eighteenth century, not knowing that the English had begun to do so in the eighth. When they read of remote wanderings upon strange seas in Morris or Coleridge they think the emotion in which such things are steeped by these poets essentially modern, and contrast it with the unambiguous simplicity of the *Odyssey* where the wanderer desires nothing but to get home. The contrast is just; but the English mood is not modern. The same thing is to be found in Anglo-Saxon poetry, associated, too, as Wordsworth might associate it, with the call of the cuckoo. Indeed the *Odyssey* is everywhere instructive as a contrast to our oldest poetry; Grendel and the Cyclops[b], at the very beginning of the two literatures, symbolize their difference – the one so dark, so mysterious, so fitted to be the central symbol of evil in a great poem; the other so matter of fact, so accidental, so blasphemously tracing his descent from a god though he is the enemy of man. Virgil, as in space, so in temper, is the middle point between Homer and *Beowulf*, holding out his left hand to the colour and clarity of the Greek, his right to our English poet whom he so resembles in melancholy without pessimism, in half-articulate piety, and, above all, in his sense of the past. I doubt if Homer would really have appreciated *horrendum silvis et religione parentum*[11] or the whole conception of Latium as Lurkwood (*quia*

---

[b] See, on this point, J. R. R. Tolkien's indispensable *Beowulf: the Monsters and the Critics*.

*his latuisset in oris*)[12] as any Englishman of any period must do.

If, then, we are concerned with origins, Anglo-Saxon must keep its place in any English syllabus – nor is it improper, at this stage, to add that the majority of the students like it. In the old philological days they did not; now they do. But, of course, continuity is not everything, and we have not yet considered the man who says: 'The origins of English literature may be as you say. All I know is I had rather my boy read Homer than *Beowulf*.' This is a very legitimate preference, and of course the most natural way of gratifying it is to persuade the young man to take up classics instead of English. We are to suppose, however, that this is for some reason impossible: what the father wants is not classics instead of English but classics somehow included in English.

I would like to pass over all the practical difficulties of such a proposal, great as they are, because the question of principle involved goes right down to the roots of a man's educational theory. The English School as it stands has chosen unity and continuity: that is to say, taking a given area of reality, it has chosen, so far as possible, to explore it thoroughly, following the natural structure of that area, and neglecting all the interesting and delightful things over the frontier. The alternative school which is suggested, with Greek, Latin, and perhaps French classics side by side with the greatest English writers would be based on a different principle – the principle of selection. In the one you turn the young out into a single, untidy country to make what they can of it; in the other you take them to what their elders think the five or six most interesting places in a whole continent. It is the difference between knowing, say, Worcestershire inside out, while remaining ignorant of the rest of the world, and knowing four or five European capitals while striking no roots in any single European soil. The choice is a very difficult one. On the one hand we have Arnold's ideal – 'the best that is known and thought in the world';[13] on the other *Spartam nactus es*.[14] Embrace the latter and you may become insular and provincial; embrace the former and you may be a mere tourist, glib in all countries and rooted in none. Which is the more deeply ignorant, the shepherd who has never left the Cotswolds, or the Peripatetic millionaire – the taproom of the 'Red Lion', or the lounge of the Palace Hotel?

Where a final choice is so difficult I would recommend a compromise. I think that the high lights chosen by his elders and the wide area of ordinary country explored on his own, are both necessary elements in a man's education. But I feel very strongly that the place for the selected high lights is the school, and the place for the other is the University. It is natural and necessary that we should begin by giving a boy the keys to some four or five chambers of knowledge which we think the best, but it is equally natural to let a man choose which he will to live in. The true nature of this change is obscured if we say that we believe in 'increasing specialization': for specialization suggests narrowing and narrowing suggests confinement. Now there is, of course, an obvious sense in which the specialist is narrower than the man reading a selection of 'great literatures'. But is there not a sense in which he is freer? Any balanced course of English and Classics which we could draw up would bear the imprint of cultural ideals peculiar to an age and a class much more unmistakably than a school of mere English need do. 'English', including Anglo-Saxon and Middle English along with modern English, including what we ordinarily call the 'dull' periods as well as the 'great' ones, is an object more or less presented to us by nature: the balanced course would be *our* selection, a selection which, in obedience to our local and momentary ideals, would cut across the joints, or veins, or grain of reality. The one is given, the other a construction. And it must be our construction, not the student's. We are doing for him one of the things he ought to do for himself. Our wild, rough English course has already thrown up interesting discoveries: the dull and difficult periods which any one working on the selective principle twenty years ago would have omitted to make room for foreign dainties, are turning out not to be dull at all, and Anglo-Saxon technical influences have appeared in the work of our younger poets. In other words, having kept our eye on the object and not on our own preconceptions, we are learning; we know more than we did. But this would have been quite impossible if we had begun with a syncretism of the 'best' in two or three different literatures. 'The best' could only have meant what a committee of four or five dons, brought up in a particular tradition, happened to think the best. We should have been dictating the course of future knowledge and taste on the authority of our existing taste and ignorance. A discipline so formed would be incapable of growth. No more would come out of it than had been put into it; and real advance in our knowledge of English would be made, if at all, by real scholars working privately in country rectories and London lodging-houses in contemptuous independence of us.

Such is my idea of an English school, and that is why the classics find no place in it. Need I say that I should like English students to know Greek and Latin? But they must not come to an English school to learn them. If they have not learned them before they come to me, I should like them to learn them after they leave me. Any proposal which enables them to do so in those postgraduate years which are increasingly spent at the university will always have all the support I can give it; and to that end I am ready to sacrifice any amount of what is called 'Research'.[15]

# 2

# Our English syllabus

~

'I do not like her name.'

'There was no thought of pleasing you when she was christened.'

SHAKESPEARE[1]

Schoolmasters in our time are fighting hard in defence of education against vocational training; universities, on the other hand, are fighting against education on behalf of learning.

Let me explain. The purpose of education has been described by Milton as that of fitting a man 'to perform justly, skilfully, and magnanimously all the offices both private and public, of peace and war'.[2] Provided we do not overstress 'skilfully' Aristotle would substantially agree with this, but would add the conception that it should also be a preparation for leisure, which according to him is the end of all human activity. 'We wage war in order to have peace; we work in order to have leisure.'[3] Neither of them would dispute that the purpose of education is to produce the good man and the good citizen, though it must be remembered that we are not here using the word 'good' in any narrowly ethical sense. The 'good man' here means

Published in *Rehabilitations and Other Essays* (London: Oxford University Press, 1939), pp. 79–93; originally read to the English Society at Oxford (date unknown).

the man of good taste and good feeling, the interesting and interested man, and almost the happy man. With such an end in view education in most civilized communities has taken much the same path; it has taught civil behaviour by direct and indirect discipline, has awakened the logical faculty by mathematics or dialectic, and has endeavoured to produce right sentiments – which are to the passions what right habits are to the body – by steeping the pupil in the literature both sacred and profane on which the culture of the community is based. Vocational training, on the other hand, prepares the pupil not for leisure, but for work; it aims at making not a good man but a good banker, a good electrician, a good scavenger, or a good surgeon. You see at once that education is essentially for freemen and vocational training for slaves. That is how they were distributed in the old unequal societies; the poor man's son was apprenticed to a trade, the rich man's son went to Eton and Oxford and then made the grand tour. When societies become, in effort if not in achievement, egalitarian, we are presented with a difficulty. To give every one education and to give no one vocational training is impossible, for electricians and surgeons we must have and they must be trained. Our ideal must be to find time for both education and training: our danger is that equality may mean training for all and education for none – that every one will learn commercial French instead of Latin, book-keeping instead of geometry, and 'knowledge of the world we live in' instead of great literature. It is against this danger that schoolmasters have to fight, for if education is beaten by training, civilization dies. That is a thing very likely to happen. One of the most dangerous errors instilled into us by nineteenth-century progressive optimism is the idea that civilization is automatically bound to increase and spread. The lesson of history is the opposite; civilization is a rarity, attained with difficulty and easily lost. The normal state of humanity is barbarism, just as the normal surface of our planet is salt water. Land looms large in our imagination of the planet and civilization in our history books, only because sea and savagery are, to us, less interesting. And if you press to know what I mean by civilization, I reply 'Humanity', by which I do not mean kindness so much as the realization of the human idea. Human life means to me the life of beings for whom the leisured activities of thought, art, literature, conversation are the end,[a] and the preservation and propagation of life merely the means. That is why education seems to me so important: it actualizes that potentiality for leisure, if you like for amateurishness, which is man's prerogative. You have noticed, I hope, that man is the only amateur animal; all the others are professionals. They have no leisure and do not desire it. When the cow has finished eating she chews the cud; when she has finished chewing she sleeps; when she has finished sleeping she eats again. She is a machine for turning grass into calves and milk – in other words, for producing more cows. The lion cannot stop hunting, nor the beaver building dams, nor the bee making honey. When God made the beasts dumb He saved the world from infinite boredom, for if they could speak they would all of them, all day, talk nothing but shop.

---

[a] The natural end. It would have been out of place here to say what I believe about Man's supernatural end or to explain why I think the natural end should be pursued although, in isolation from the supernatural, it cannot be fully realized.

That is my idea of education. You see at once that it implies an immense superiority on the part of the teacher. He is trying to make the pupil a good man, in the sense I have described. The assumption is that the master is already human, the pupil a mere candidate for humanity – an unregenerate little bundle of appetites which is to be kneaded and moulded into human shape by one who knows better. In education the master is the agent, the pupil, the patient.

Now learning, considered in itself, has, on my view, no connexion at all with education. It is an activity for men – that is for beings who have already been humanized by this kneading and moulding process. Among these men – these biologically simian animals who have been made into men – there are some who desire to know. Or rather, all desire to know, but some desire it more fervently than the majority and are ready to make greater sacrifices for it. The things they want to know may be quite different. One may want to know what happened a million years ago, another, what happens a million light-years away, a third, what is happening in his own table on the microscopic level. What is common to them all is the thirst for knowledge. Now it might have happened that such people were left in civil societies to gratify their taste as best they could without assistance or interference from their fellows. It has not happened. Such societies have usually held a belief – and it is a belief of a quite transcendental nature – that knowledge is the natural food of the human mind: that those who specially pursue it are being specially human; and that their activity is good in itself besides being always honourable and sometimes useful to the whole society. Hence we come to have such associations as

universities – institutions for the support and encourage-
ment of men devoted to learning.

You have doubtless been told – but it can hardly be
repeated too often – that our colleges at Oxford were
founded not in order to teach the young but in order to
support masters of arts. In their original institution they
are homes not for teaching but for the pursuit of knowledge; and their original nature is witnessed by the brute
fact that hardly any college in Oxford is financially dependent on the undergraduates' fees, and that most colleges
are content if they do not lose over the undergraduate.
A school without pupils would cease to be school; a college without undergraduates would be as much a college
as ever, would perhaps be more a college.

It follows that the university student is essentially a different person from the school pupil. He is not a candidate
for humanity, he is, in theory, already human. He is not
a patient; nor is his tutor an operator who is doing something to him. The student is, or ought to be, a young
man who is already beginning to follow learning for its
own sake, and who attaches himself to an older student,
not precisely to be taught, but to pick up what he can.
From the very beginning the two ought to be fellow students. And that means they ought not to be thinking about
each other but about the subject. The schoolmaster must
think about the pupil: everything he says is said to improve
the boy's character or open his mind – the schoolmaster
is there to make the pupil a 'good' man. And the pupil
must think about the master. Obedience is one of the
virtues he has come to him to learn; his motive for reading
one book and neglecting another must constantly be that
he was told to. But the elder student has no such duties

*ex officio* to the younger. His business is to pursue knowledge. If his pursuit happens to be helpful to the junior partner, he is welcome to be present; if not, he is welcome to stay at home. No doubt the elder, of his charity, may go a little out of his course to help the younger; but he is then acting as a man, not as a student.

Such is the ideal. In fact, of course, Oxford has become in modern times very largely a place of teaching. I spend most of the term teaching and my tutorial stipend is part of my income no less important than my fellowship. Most of you, perhaps, have come here with the idea of completing your education rather than with the idea of entering a society devoted to the pursuit of knowledge for its own sake. What do these changes mean? They mean, I think, that a temporary immersion in the life of learning has been found to have an educational value. Learning is not education; but it can be used educationally by those who do not propose to pursue learning all their lives. There is nothing odd in the existence of such a by-product. Games are essentially for pleasure, but they happen to produce health. They are not likely, however, to produce health if they are played for the sake of it. Play to win and you will find yourself taking violent exercise; play because it is good for you and you will not. In the same way, though you may have come here only to be educated, you will never receive that precise educational gift which a university has to give you unless you can at least *pretend*, so long as you are with us, that you are concerned not with education but with knowledge for its own sake. And we, on our part, can do very little for you if we aim directly at your education. We assume that you are already human, already good men; that you have the specifically human virtues and above all the great virtue of curiosity. We are not going to try to improve you; we have fulfilled our whole function if we help you to *see* some given tract of reality.

I dare say some of you are wondering by now what all this has to do with the English syllabus. I am just coming to that. From what I have said, it follows that on my view a freshman hesitating over the choice of a Final School is quite on the wrong track if he is asking himself, 'Which gives me the best general education?' He may be compelled to ask, 'Which qualifies me for the best jobs when I go down?' for unfortunately we have to make our livings. The necessity which thus limits his choice is, as it were, an external necessity: poverty will prevent one man from becoming an astronomer as blindness may prevent another from becoming a painter. But to ask for the best 'general education' is to ask for one's school-days over again. The proper question for a freshman is not 'What will do me most good?' but 'What do I most want to know?' For nothing that we have to offer will do him good unless he can be persuaded to forget all about self-improvement for three or four years, and to absorb himself in getting to know some part of reality, as it is in itself.

The qualification 'as it is in itself' is here important. At first sight it might seem that since the student cannot study everything he should at least study a bit of every-thing; that the best Final Honour School would have a composite syllabus – a little philosophy, a little poli-tics, a little economics, a little science, a little literature. There are many objections to such a discipline, but I will mention that one only which is central to my argument. The composite school, as its very name implies, has been composed by some one. Those little bits of various subjects are not found lying together in those quantities and in that order which the syllabus shows. They have been put together in that way artificially by a committee of professors. That committee cannot have been following the grain and joint of reality as reality discovers itself to those actually engaged in the pursuit of learning. For the life of learning knows nothing of this nicely balanced encyclopaedic arrangement. Every one of the suggested subjects is infinite and, in its own way, covers the whole field of reality. The committee would in fact be guided by their idea of what would do the students good – that is, by a purely educational idea. In reading such a school, therefore, you would not be turned loose on some tract of reality as it is, to make what you could of it; you would be getting selections of reality selected by your elders – something cooked, expurgated, filtered, and generally toned down for your edification. You would still be in the leading strings and might as well have stayed at school. Your whole reading in its scope and proportions would bear the impress neither of reality nor of your own mind but of the mind of the committee. The educational ideals of a particular age, class, and philosophy of life would be stamped on your whole career.

The objection will naturally be clearest to us if we consider how the subject we know best would fare in such a school. There would be a little bit of literature. What would it consist of? Obviously, of great works, for we should have to make up in quality what we lacked in quantity. Perhaps a few great 'classics' each from French, German, and English. As a curriculum for a schoolboy, nothing could be more liberal and edifying. But you see at once that it has very little to do with a knowledge of literature as it really grows and works, with all its ups and downs, in any actual country. It may train your mind and make you in the Aristotelian sense a better man; but are you not old enough now to cease being trained? Is it not time for you to venture to look on reality in the raw?

If this objection to the composite school is accepted, we may summarily reject certain proposals for the reform of the English School. When people ask, 'Why not a little philosophy?' 'Why not Italian literature?' 'Why not some psychology?', they are usually hankering after the composite school. But they may have better motives than that. They may want philosophy and Italian not because these are educational but because English writers have in fact been influenced by philosophical speculation and by Italian literature – because these things, in fact, *are* parts of the piece of reality we have set out to study.

They are quite right. So is the history of the Romance and Germanic languages from the earliest times, the history of all the literatures that have affected us, the history, political, social, and economic, of all Europe, and even the flora, fauna, and geology of Great Britain. A perfect study of English would involve all this; nay, as Hegel saw, a perfect study of anything requires a knowledge of everything. But

The lyf so short, the craft so long to lerne[4]

forces us to be content with less, and you, who are with us for only four years, to be content with less still. Thus I admit that some limitation is necessary; the whole literary reality cannot be embraced by any Final Honour School. But there is a difference between arbitrary selection and a curtailment which obediently follows the joints of the real as they are, not as we choose to pretend they are. Thus if a man has not time to learn the geography of the world, we might teach him that of Great Britain, a land mass given to us by nature. There are facts about England which he would be unable to understand because he did not know Europe; we should have to put up with that. The other, the arbitrary, alternative would be to give him selected high lights from all over the planet – the Grand Canyon, the Rhine, a glimpse of a South American forest, the Bay of Biscay, and the Gobi Desert. The first would give him a real though limited knowledge of nature – would teach him how one country smelled, looked, lived, and died. But the second might make him a mere globe trotter.

In this spirit, then, we approach our vast subject of English literature, admitting that we cannot study it whole, but determined to neglect outlying provinces and remote connexions rather than to break up the central unity. The first thing to do, obviously, is to cut off some years from this end. The reasons for choosing this end are, I suppose, obvious. In the first place, we naturally wish to help the students in studying those parts of the subject where we have most help to give and they need help most. On recent and contemporary literature their need is least and our help least. They ought to understand it better than we, and if they do not then there is something radically wrong either with them or with the literature. But I need not labour the point. There is an intrinsic absurdity in making current literature a subject of academic study, and the student who wants a tutor's assistance in reading the works of his own contemporaries might as well ask for a nurse's assistance in blowing his own nose. Again, things are understood by what precedes them rather than by what follows them. It may be disappointing to stop a story in the middle, but you can understand it as far as you have gone; you cannot understand it if you *begin* in the middle. I can indeed imagine a man denying this and maintaining that the nineteenth century can be understood only in the light of the twentieth. But if that is so, then the twentieth can be understood only in the light of the twenty-first and all succeeding centuries. We are therefore doomed to an equal misunderstanding wherever we stop, and may just as well stop where we find it convenient.

We begin then by cutting off a hundred, or two hundred, or any reasonable number of years from this end, and still we have too much left. If we picture our subject as a tree we have first of all the soil in which it grows: that is, the history of the English people, social, economic, and intellectual. I imagine that neither you nor I wish to draw attention to this; for if you look in the statutes you will find that examiners are at liberty to set questions on it, and it is always possible that if we talk much about it they may wake and really do so. Let us keep quiet about the soil, and go on to the roots. The great central tap-root is old Germanic developing, as we pass above the ground-level, into Old English. A second root, not quite so big and important as this is Old French. A third, noticeably smaller, strikes farther away into Latin. But all these are pretty tough and more or less essential to the tree. Then come the little ones – the tiny, much advertised, and attractive Greek root, the modern Spanish, modern Italian, modern French, German, etc. Our problem is to find which of these we can neglect with least violence to the nature of the tree.

Well – the little ones must go. We have not time, in four years, for Greek, Spanish, Italian, French, and German. If one could be saved, it would have to be modern French. Of course if we were considering which is the most interesting in itself I should unhesitatingly choose the Greek; but that would be to fall back from naturalism to arbitrary selection, from learning to education. Certainly Greek literature is better than French; but certainly English and French lie together in reality as English and Greek do not. But even French we can hardly save, for we have the three great roots to consider. The tap-root, Anglo-Saxon, can never be abandoned. The man who does not know it remains all his life a child among real English students. There we find the speech-rhythms that we use every day made the basis of metre; there we find the origins of that romanticism for which the ignorant invent such odd explanations. This is our own stuff and its life is in every branch of the tree to the remotest twigs. That we cannot abandon. Old French and Latin we have reluctantly given up: if you want them, I am the last man to deny you.

With these limitations, then, we hand you over our tract of reality. Do not be deceived by talk about the narrowness of the specialist. The opposite of the specialist, as you now see, is the student enslaved to some one else's selection. In the great rough countryside which we throw open to you, you can choose your own path. Here's your gun, your spade, your fishing-tackle; go and get yourself a dinner. Do not tell me that you would sooner have a nice composite *menu* of dishes from half the world drawn up for you. You are too old for that. It is time you learned to wrestle with nature for yourself. And whom will you trust to draw up that *menu*? How do you know that in that very river which I would exclude as poisonous the fish you specially want, the undiscovered fish, is waiting? And you would never find it if you let us select. *Our* selection would be an effort to bind the future within *our* present knowledge and taste: nothing more could come out than we had put in. It would be worse; it would be a kind of propaganda, concealed, unconscious, and omnipotent. Is it really true that you would prefer that to the run of your teeth over the whole country? Have you no incredulity, no scepticism, left?

# 3

# Image and imagination

≈

*The title 'Image and Imagination' is the editor's, not Lewis's. The essay appears untitled in a ruled school-notebook of the sort that Lewis typically used for his drafts. It is possible that the title Lewis intended is one of those mentioned in a letter of 2 June 1931 that he sent to T. S. Eliot, asking about the possibility of publishing some of his work in* The Criterion, *which Eliot founded and edited.[1] Lewis wrote:*

The essay ['The Personal Heresy in Criticism'] does, as you have divined, form the first of a series of which I have all the materials to hand. The others would be

2. Objective Standards of Literary Merit
3. Literature and Virtue . . .
4. Literature and Knowledge
5. Metaphor and Truth.

The whole, when completed, would form a frontal attack on Crocean aesthetics and state a neo-Aristotelian theory of literature (not of Art, about which I say nothing) which inter alia will re-affirm the romantic doctrine of imagination as a truth-bearing faculty, though not quite as the romantics understood it.[2]

*A draft of 'Objective Standards of Literary Merit', but titled 'Objective Value of Poetry', appears in the same notebook as 'Image and Imagination', which is probably,*

34

*therefore, part of the extensive argument re-affirming 'the romantic doctrine of imagination' Lewis planned.*

\* \* \*

Many people think that literature is one *species* of a *genus* called Art. This seems to me doubtful. But the doctrine which I am going to develop does not depend on this doubt, and it will be possible for a consistent reader to agree with what follows and still to think that literature and art are to one another as *species* is to *genus*. But many people who think this, draw from it a conclusion which I not only doubt but which I claim to refute. It is held that if anything appears in literature other than those characters which are common to all art, then that thing belongs to the book or poem in question *per accidens* and is foreign to its poetical nature. This would be supported by analogies.

A particular triangle may be blue; but as colour is not included in the definition of all triangles, the blueness of this one is foreign to its triangularity. It is blue not *quâ* triangle but *quâ* something else; change its colour and its triangular qualities remain as they were. In the same way, it cannot be denied that a particular poem may tell a story which is in fact historical, or a particular painting may resemble a real man; and if this is so we may, if it so happens, derive knowledge from both. But music cannot thus convey facts, and the enjoyment of music cannot be knowledge. But music is an art. Therefore 'conveyance of fact' or 'knowledge' cannot be included in the definition of Art. Therefore, wherever it occurs in a given work of art, it occurs *per accidens*. The poem gives knowledge, or

35

possesses truth, not *quâ* poem, but *quâ* something else: and the knowing cannot possibly form part of our appreciation of the poem as a poem.

Fortunately we need not inquire into any of the *facts* underlying this argument, for it can be refuted on logical grounds. It depends on an exploded view – what may be called 'the L. C. M. view' – of universals, on which we may consult any formal treatise, such as Joseph's *Logic*.[3] To take an example from that work, we need only point out that locomotion cannot be included in the definition of 'engine'. But in the case of a given locomotive engine, we cannot say that locomotion is foreign to its engine-character, for 'being a locomotive' makes it precisely the engine which it is. In the same way, though truth cannot be included in the definition of Art, it might well be (for all the present argument shows) that *all* literature was true, and true *quâ* literature, and that the definition of literature was 'that species of Art which is true'. Thus, again, if we were dealing with Beauty instead of Art, we certainly could not include truth in our definition; but this could not prevent a particular poem from being true, nor could it prevent the truth from being intrinsic to the beauty. For neither could we include in our definition of Beauty such things as 'a spondee in the fifth foot' or 'a sequence of back and front vowels': yet in a given line the spondee or the sequence might *be* the beauty. In other words you cannot find which of the characters of a given poem, or animal, or engine, are accidental and which are intrinsically poetic, animalic, and mechanic, by the easy process of looking up your definition and finding which are common to the whole *genus*. Rule of thumb will not help, and we have to think instead. Hasty deductions from a highly abstract conception of Art, formed by leaving out all the concrete characters of all the poems and pictures we know, are one of the prime sources of critical error. It is not surprising that 'Art' should be amoral, alogical, a-this and a-that, when you have arrived at Art by sheer subtraction.

Having got rid of the logical blunder, we are now in a position to devote ourselves to literature and explore the characters it really has – undeterred by the false theory that anything which literature does not share with the other arts must be accidental and unliterary. Now the obvious differentia of literature is that it uses language. And language means words combined so as to have meaning. No doubt we can derive a certain degree of pleasure from hearing a poem read in a language we do not understand – at least, if the language is melodious. But in so far as the reader, by his voice and eye, gives us an inkling of the meaning, the language is language and not mere sound to us. If he does not, then the pleasure is simply a low form of *musical* pleasure and does not concern us here.

Literature, then, uses language. And language is language to us only when it has a meaning. It is true that we may find it difficult to say what the meaning of a given sentence in a poem is – though Dante, by the way, has a relevant comment on this point. But the demand is perverse. If it means that all significant language can be translated without loss, we can only reply 'Why should it?' If it means that all significant language has a meaning restatable in the same language, in different words, we can point to such words as 'if', 'but', and the like, which are significant but cannot be paraphrased. If it means that 'the significant' must coincide with 'the logical' – i.e., with that which can be represented by pure conceptual symbols – then this is sheer dogma. I am speaking of meaning in the most elementary sense; and in this sense all literature uses significant language, and to enjoy it involves a knowledge of the meaning – as for example, you could not enjoy the lines in Keats' 'Ode' if you thought that a *casement* meant a kind of case, or that *opening on* meant 'opening on top of'.[4] Whatever difficulties there may be about the 'meaning' of poetry in some more ultimate sense, we clearly need to know 'what it means' in that lowest sense whereby a schoolboy knows or fails to know 'the meaning' of a bit of Caesar. You cannot have even a fairy tale unless the reader and writer understand what a castle, or a stepmother, or a giant *is*.

Now I have used the word 'is' advisedly. To read the fairy-tale we must know what a castle is; and that would seem to be a bit of knowledge about the real world. It will be objected, of course, that you may also need to know what a fairy 'is'; and this does not seem to be equally a bit of knowledge about the real world. It would, therefore, seem safer to emend 'know what a castle is' and say 'know what the author means by a castle'. That is (apparently), we do not need to know about things: we need only know of what imaginations in the author's mind each word is the name. But this substitution, which seems so reasonable, does not really help us at all; and the exposure of its illusory offers of assistance will occupy us for the next few pages.

Let us suppose that the narrator begins: 'Once upon a time there was a princess, who lived in a tower.' Suppose, again, that we interrupt him by asking 'What is a tower?'. 'Aha!', replies he, 'You are not going to catch me that way. The tower *is* not any thing *in rerum natura*, it is only the name of something in my imagination.' – 'Very well. Of what thing in your imagination is Tower the name?' – 'Oh, a tall kind of building, you know, with five or six stories and battlements on the top.' – 'It is one kind of building, then. And what about the word Building? Is that also the name of something in your imagination?' – 'Certainly. I mean a thing made out of some hard substance – stones or brick or wood – with empty spaces inside, where people can live.' – 'Dear me, this gets more and more difficult. We have now a whole host of things: stones, brick, wood and people, not to mention "substance". Are these the names of realities, or of things in your imagination?' – 'Of things in my imagination. But don't let us have any metaphysical nonsense about substance. I mean matter.' – 'Which again is the name of something in your imagination. And this imaginary matter is doubtless not merely a series of coloured shapes, but solid and resisting like the matter in the real world?' – 'Certainly.' – 'Then it has an "inside" no doubt. Between the surfaces of each bit there is something – whether continuous stuff, or discrete atoms, or forces?' – 'I suppose so.' – 'And this is all present in your imagination?' – 'I am not sure.' – 'And again, this matter occupies space, which, no doubt, is also the name of something in your imagination.' – 'Go on.' – 'And I suppose any particular piece of this imaginary space has other pieces surrounding it; as, for example, there is more space (filled or empty) to the left and right of the space which the tower occupies, and above it and below it?' – 'Naturally.' – 'Very well. Does this space in your imagination go on for ever or does it come to an end somewhere?' – 'It goes on forever.' – 'Then the space you imagine is infinite.' – 'Yes.' – 'Then an infinite is present to your imagination?' – 'I don't know.' – 'And if you turn to the princess,

I suppose you will say that she has parents, though only in your imagination?' – 'Well?' – 'And grandparents and remoter ancestors, back to the beginnings of human life, and beyond that to the beginnings of organic life? And all these exist in your imagination.' – 'I don't know.' – 'But surely you *do* know that there must be some flaw in the original position. For if the words in your story are really the names of things in your imagination, it will follow that in every sentence, and more than once in every sentence, a complete universe in all its detail must be present to your imagination. But that is impossible. We must have made some sort of mistake.' – 'I suppose we must.'

And with this the argument collapses. If the words used in literature name only *imaginata*, then, since any one object implies an infinite series both in time and space, every single *imaginatum* implies an infinite imagined series. For the *imaginata* are not in the same position as real objects. A real object, no doubt, demands a context reaching away on every side to infinity: but just because it is an object in the real world that context is provided for. It is there, *in fact*, whether we think of it or not. But the whole contention about literature was that it referred to objects existing only in imagination; and imagination cannot provide (as reality can) the necessary context. It is clear, therefore, that we shall have to allow some sort of interplay, or overlapping, between the imagined and the real, for only in the real can *imaginata* find the context they need. Monadism, even if it were true of the other arts, must be untrue of literary art. What we are really doing is to call the monadists' bluff: they are ready enough to talk of a tale or poem as presenting 'a world of its own': but we can show them that the word 'world' will have to be taken more seriously than they ever intended. To get a single blade of grass growing in that imaginary world you must make it a world indeed – a real universe, self-sufficing in space and time. But only one author can do that sort of stage-set. On this view only God can tell stories.

It will be objected that I am driving poets and story-tellers into a quite unreal difficulty by forcing on their imaginary worlds just that logical connection and recip-rocal implication which it is their privilege to neglect. A real tower, you say, needs stones, matter, gravity, space and time, but an imaginary tower does not. That is the whole point about an imaginary tower. But what does this defence really mean? If it means that we do not imagine the infinite series, I agree that we do not and cannot. But does that mean that we can dispense with it? For, of course, if we need it, and yet do not imagine it, the conclusion will be that we are using the *real* world to provide a context for our imaginary tower. Let us, then, inquire how we would get on with no context.

Let the narrator take up a new position. 'I see where I went wrong', he may begin, 'I should never have admitted that what I meant by a tower was a building etc. I grant you that once you let that in, you let in the whole universe. All I was really imagining was the gleam of its white pinnacles above the trees, and the cool, dark pit of its doorway, and the moss in the crevices.' – 'I see', returns the tormentor, 'In fact Tower, in your story, is the name of an image – or rather of a group of images, visual, tactual and what not.' – 'Yes, exactly.' – 'And that is all you need for your literary (or perhaps you would rather say "aesthetic") purposes?' – 'Yes. I have already admitted that.' – 'I suppose, now, that in a certain story, you could have a man wandering in an enchanted country where the mere *appearances* of buildings were constantly meeting him; things, I mean, that looked just like towers, but which he found he could walk through.' – 'I suppose I could if I wanted to.' – 'And again, you could have, in a story of a different kind, say a novel, a man encountering a real tower?' – 'Of course.' – 'Is there any reason why the mere *image* of the phantasmal tower should be any different from that of the real tower?' – 'I can't tell you without writing both stories.' – 'Well, at any rate, as far as *a priori* grounds go, you can't foresee a necessary difference?' – 'Perhaps not.' – 'Yet they would differ aesthetically wouldn't they? I mean they would be suitable to quite different *genres*?' – 'Well, of course a story of magic would be different from a realistic novel.' – 'Yes. But I do not mean merely that the actual walking through the Tower, and thus proving it to be phantasmal, would be different from any episode in the novel. I mean that whenever the phantasmal tower turned up, whether the hero walked through it or not, it would affect the reader differently, strike a different note, from a real tower. And that would be simply because he had learned to *take* it as a phantom: not from any fresh imaginary experience of its insolidity.' – 'I suppose so.' – 'And, yet, what he was visualising, the mere images, might be just the same as the images he would have if you had offered him a "real" tower?' – 'All right.' – 'So that precisely the same image may play different roles – aesthetically different.' – 'Well, as I said before, I doubt if they would be the same. It is a very far-fetched hypothesis: quite a marginal case.' – 'Perhaps it is. But what would you say to the two Florimels in Spenser. The whole point is that they are to *look* just the same. That is the poet's hypothesis. But you will admit that the two are aesthetically distinct. They affect us quite differently. And that is because, while the images remain indistinguishable, the one is "taken to be" a mere phantom, and the other is "taken to be" a woman who could have parents and children and could love and so forth. I say "taken to be" because, of course, we don't make the parents and children etc. actually present to the imagination.' – 'I don't know why we shouldn't.' – 'Because if we do (don't you remember the princess?) we get landed in the whole universe.' – 'Oh damn! So we do. All right.' – 'It seems then that aesthetic differences are not necessarily differences in images. Or take another example: "Childe Roland to the dark tower came."[5] Surely you just take it for granted that it is a "real" tower – I mean a solid tower, with an inside, and all that? You are not in any doubt?' – 'Well, I don't know. The poet might have gone on to make it a tall ogre in disguise. In a certain kind of poem that might work rather well. The moment of discovery would give an agreeable shock.' – 'Yes. But it would give no shock at all if it didn't surprise you: and it would not surprise you if you had not begun by taking it as something else. And "to take it as something else" means to have something more than an image. For, by hypothesis, the mere image is the same, whether it's going to turn out a tower or an ogre.' – 'Look here. I am getting very bothered about this everlasting harping on the "image". I'm not sure that I have these distinct images at all when I am telling or following a story. I think you are assuming that every one is an extreme visualist.' – 'No, that is what you are assuming. For on your view, in order to get rid of the infinite series, the naked image is all that you want for literature. The image is what counts aesthetically.

But if so, a bad image means imperfect appreciation of the story. On your view only visualists can be poets or readers of poetry.' – 'Remember, my tower wasn't only visual. There was coolness: and in fact there would be smells and all sorts of things.' – 'That makes no difference. I have used the word "visualist" for brevity; but if you like I will go through images of all the senses in turn.' – 'God forbid! I'd rather give in than that.' – 'We agree, then, that identical images can differ aesthetically, and, in general, that the aesthetic difference between two situations is not in proportion to the difference of the images? And, perhaps, now that we have raised the question of the visualist, you will admit that the images actually present to a reader matter very little to his appreciation. In fact, the image is not what counts. But this surely means that the words in a story cannot be simply names for images in the teller's imagination.' – 'Have it your own way.'

The attempt to do without a context for the *imaginata* thus collapses. Take away from the imagined tower all its implications and it ceases to be an imagined thing and becomes merely an image. But images are not enough: for the way in which they affect us depends, not on their content as images, but on what they are taken to be. Mention a tower, or a king, or a dog, in a poem or tale, and they come to us not in the nakedness of pictured form and colour, but with all the associations of towerhood, kinghood, and doghood. And there is this further defect in the image theory, that it throws an altogether artificial stress on the function of explicit psychological imagery in literature. What sort of blotch or blur is my 'image' of the dark tower to which Roland came? I hardly know. I know only that it is different every time I read the line, and that there is no proportional difference in my poetical experience. On this point I speak with some authority, having been born an extreme visualist, and having learned that this unruly power – in truth not the ally of imagination, but a mere nuisance to it – must be corrected and restrained in dealing with literature. Our imagination uses our images for poetical purposes, much as a child uses material objects for its games. An imaginative man can make of very scanty and crude images all he needs for appreciation of the greatest books, as a child worth its salt can make a liner or a railway station out of the first two or three bits of furniture it finds in the nursery. It is not the children with the costly toys who play best: or if they do, they do it in spite of the toys.

We now know that the words which occur in literature are not the names of mere images; and if they are the names of things, then these things demand a context which imagination cannot supply, and therefore these things are not, in any unequivocal sense, 'things in the imagination'. They seem, in the most troublesome way, to be half in the imagination and half in the real world; and this, however troublesome, is precisely the view we shall have to come to. When a fairy tale mentions a tower, it refers us to some rudimentary image which is just 'taken to be' a tower, and therefore affects us as a tower, though the infinite series involved in towerhood is not, and cannot be, present to imagination. There is always some tacit assumption, some taking for granted, about the words used in literature, whereby a 'girl' or 'storm' in a poem is enabled to let in on us the whole meaning of girlhood or of rough weather.

It is convenient, at this point, to remind ourselves of the situation as it exists, not in literature, but in ordinary life. In ordinary life we never see a 'tower'. We see a coloured

45

shape, which we take to be a tower, because we believe that it has another side, and is solid, and hollow, and fulfils all the other conditions of towerhood, which, however, are not given in the experience of seeing it. In other words, we turn a mere sense-datum into a tower by attributing to it a context. We link up the present experience with other actual and inferred experiences in one determinate way, and this fixes the present experience as a 'tower': if we had linked it up differently, or failed to link it up at all, it would not be a tower. In the case of sense data, then, in taking any sense datum as a 'thing', we assert categorically certain connections between it and the rest of our real world. Our problem is to find the parallel process whereby we take a mere image as an imagined 'thing'. Or, if there are some who do not visualise *at all*, how do we make a non-visual idea into an imagined 'thing'? For, of course, a non-visual idea, even a highly intellectual conception, can no more contain all the necessary conditions of thinghood than an image can. We can no more think the infinite series than we can picture it. In either case, something immediately present has to be treated as, or taken as, a thing, though in itself it cannot give us thinghood. In a sense, no doubt, this has to be done not only when we listen to a story, but whenever we listen to speech of any kind. But no other speech is in the same unhappy position as imaginative literature, for all other speech claims from the outset to deal with a real world. If you mention the Parthenon, I cannot furnish its context in my own mind: but then the real Acropolis and the Balkan Peninsula and the solar system *can*. But if you speak of Valhalla, and I cannot furnish the context, and without the context it is a mere image, who or what comes to our aid?

In a very rough and ready sense we may reply that this context, though not explicitly present to the imagination, is assumed. But we must find out what this means. We must not, for instance, interpret it by supposing that what is not explicitly present can be 'implicit', as unexpressed stages can be implicit in a chain of reasoning. For the character of reasoning is that every judgment rigidly determines and is determined by others: but the character of imagining is that it is free – at least within very wide bounds indeed. If you imagine a tower, even a solid tower, foundations and builders are not necessarily implied: for you are at perfect liberty if you choose to suppose that it was produced by the fiat of a magician and is supported by four buried Jinns. In conceptual thought, if more is meant than meets the eye, you can tell what that 'more' must be, because it must be related thus and thus to what does meet the eye. But in imagination, if there is any more, you cannot tell what it is, for it might be related to the explicit imagery in almost any way. It is like the difference between a mirror and a picture. If you ask what the invisible parts of the looking glass room are like, you can give an answer – *pace* Alice. You know where all the lines go to beyond the frame. But if you ask where a road in a landscape goes to when it passes into the frame, we can only reply either that it does not exist, and therefore goes nowhere, or that it may go anywhere: for it might turn sharply the moment it was out of sight. Similarly, of that which is not consciously present to imagination, we must say that perhaps it does not exist, and that if it does it might be almost anything. That it exists at all appears to me a rash assumption. To say that we imagine that of which we are unconscious, seems to set up with imagination itself a distinction, reality and appearance, which is all but meaningless. Surely here, if nowhere else, *esse* is *percipi*?[6]

The 'assumptions' or 'things taken for granted', then, which supplement the images or ideas actually present and convert them into imagined objects, cannot be, in the strict sense, 'implicit'. And yet they must exist. There remains only one possible explanation. If we asked the teller what he meant by a tower, he would, after the tortures to which he has been submitted, reply: 'I was imagining the sort of thing which you *could* walk all round, in which you *could* find stones and mortar, which would have foundations etc. – which *would* in short fit into a whole spatio-temporal system in one way and not in another.' This reply makes a great advance. The context does not actually exist: it is hypothetical. But all hypothesis rests on some actuality. Every conditional sentence has an 'if'-clause, concealed or expressed. 'I could do this' means 'I could do this if I liked.' We must therefore find the hidden protasis in the sentence: 'I was imagining the sort of thing which you could walk all round.' Clearly the protasis 'If you liked' will not serve. For, short of direct spatio-temporal inconsistency, you could do anything you chose in imagination; and to enumerate one or two of the myriad incompatible possibilities, therefore, will not determine your imagined thinking. It remains, then, to supply the only protasis which is left, namely 'If it were real'. When I imagine a tower I imagine a sense-datum which, if it were given in sense, would be connected thus and thus with the real world. The same conclusion can be reached in a different way. What we require in order to turn mere images into imagined things is something that can be assumed without being explicit or present. Here, as in all cases where an appearance is to be treated as a thing, more must be meant than meets the eye. But in imagination, *either* there *is* no more than meets the eye, *or* if there is, we do not know what it may be and therefore cannot assume it. Therefore imagination cannot yield the 'something more'. Therefore reality must yield it. But since reality does not actually give it, it must be given hypothetically. That is, what is really implicit in imagination is *hypothetical assertion*: and all hypothetical assertion is about reality. The statement 'I am imagining that, if it were real, would have the properties X Y Z' is a statement concerned just as much with the real world as with imagination; for it can be easily converted into the form 'The universals X Y Z, in the circumstances P Q R, would yield the appearance which I am imagining.' And this is a statement of exactly the same kind as any of the statements we meet in the works of science.

What we do when we imagine, then, is to suppose (with or without the support of explicit images) a reshuffling of universals taken from the actual world. When we imagine Britomart we take our idea of 'a girl', which is part of our general knowledge, and our idea of 'medieval knight', which is another part of our general knowledge, and put them together. To get into imagination itself what we mean by either of the two terms is impossible. They are not imaginations: they are summarised knowledge of the real. Always the real world is the bank on which the poet draws his cheques; and though a metaphysical lyric may be a fine and private place, all the meanings embraced within it are but passengers who come there from the public, eternal, objective world of reality and haste thither again. Aristotle was right. Poetry presents οἷα ἄν γένοιτο, things

49

that might be – it recombines elements which belong to the real, and to appreciate poetry involves at every moment a knowledge of those elements and therefore of the real.

What obscures this truth is the fact that we may find fairies as well as towers in our story. If all literature were realistic the doctrine which isolates 'art' from human experience as a whole would not be even plausible. The sort of monadism which I am rejecting may be regarded as one of the many attempts to explain the marvellous in literature: parallel to the allegorisations with which our ancestors excused their pleasure in Ovid, and equally shallow. In fact, the wildest passages of Italian or Indian epic conform to Aristotle's definition as easily as one of Thackeray's novels. Let us try the experiment. Disturb the realism of Roland's dark tower a little. As Roland approaches, let the bells within the tower begin to ring. But instead of sounds let them give forth great birds: and yet we understand somehow that the birds *are* the sounds. This seems a far cry from the real world. Yet even these birds affect us only because of their hypothetical connection with reality. For example, 'bats' would have a different poetical value from birds. Yet the images will scarcely be distinguishable: and neither their bat nature or their bird nature will be explicitly imagined. It is enough to give them the one or the other name and they will affect us accordingly: and this because we know what bats and birds are in the real world, and therefore what *these* would be in the real world. And however we vary the fantasy we shall find the same result. Let these bell-born birds be no common birds but the souls of dead men whose blood was used to temper the bells: and let them fly out singing with human voice *Justorum animae.*[7]

Does any one suppose that the imaginative value of such fantasies can be divided for a moment from our knowledge of death, and blood, and Christianity? You may say, indeed, that it is not our crystallised *knowledge* of these things that counts, but the *emotions* which have gathered about their names. But it is easy to answer that where a reader depends merely on the associations roused by the words, he will be right only by accident: as many a young reader has found to his cost. Good reading implies, and good writing demands of its readers, that the emotion should depend not on the name alone, but on the name understood. The name, indeed, rouses emotion, but rouses it through the memory of the thing; that is, through knowledge. And we have seen that no degree of unrealism in the imagination impairs this principle a whit. We can cut the bells off from the sound which they would really have and substitute birds; but then the quality of such a marvel depends on our having expected sounds, and we expected them because of our knowledge of real bell-hood. The birds again affect us by their hypothetical connection with real zoology: cut this off, and the whole process is repeated with the dead men. In other words, we can sever any number, one by one, of those connections which our imagined objects would have in reality, but for every one we sever we set up a new one. The monadist is fighting with a hydra. If A were real it would imply B. We can remove B and substitute C which A could not have in reality. But if C is to have any poetic significance for us, then C in its turn will be determined by its hypothetical connection with the real: C will imply D. You can change D if you choose, and D again will have meaning for us in virtue of its hypothetical E. Remove E and it will be the same again. You must stop somewhere: and wherever you stop you will find reality waiting for you. You may change, as much as you please, the character which your objects would have in reality: but reality furnishes both that which is changed and that by which you change it.

If this is true of a fairy tale, it is more obviously true of a tragedy, a novel, or an epic. A single image, a break in the rhythm, a 'Prithee undo this button' becomes the key to a whole situation. But these things can have no meaning to us which is separable, even in idea, from our knowledge of what they would mean in the real world. It is not the words, taken as mere sounds, that enlighten us. They reveal, as we are told, the character's [emotions]. Lear's speech shows what Lear felt. But then there is no Lear, and he never felt anything, if by Lear you mean something other than the words and, at the same time, actually present: the attempt to get Lear – as opposed to what Lear says – inside the imagined, ends in the infinite series. When we know Lear through the play, we know that if such things were said and done and suffered in the real world it would be by a man of such and such a kind. And this is a bit of knowledge about human nature, differing not at all from that knowledge of human nature which we use in our daily life.

Some will say that I am confusing 'aesthetic experience' with the cognitive experience which may lead up to it and merely forms its basis. But this is untrue. When one experience is merely the support or external *prius* of another, it does not survive in it. A comfortable chair may be the *prius* of appreciating a poem: but the sense of comfort has vanished from consciousness before appreciation begins. A knowledge of Greek grammar is the *prius* of enjoying

Aeschylus: but we are not aware of paradigms when we enjoy – nay, how many of us, if we are not schoolmasters, could write out, in answer to a grammar paper, those very forms which we understood as we read? But knowledge of human nature is not thus externally related to our imaginative apprehension. The character of Lear and the process by which we know it are one. The words, the rhythms, and the architectonics of the play are not separable from some 'subject' or 'content' which we reach through them. Form and matter – data and conclusion – are abstractions. What we have is matter informed, form incarnate: the tragic situation, or character, embodied in these words and no others.

And so an argument in which I have deliberately chosen the wildest fancies for my illustrations brings us back into line with the grand orthodox tradition of European poetics. Poetry imitates the universal, and when we read poetry we are engaged in knowing. Thus said Aristotle, thus the Neo-Platonists. To this Rymer[8] and Voltaire commented, though in a crude and vicious fashion, misconceiving the 'general' as the socially, or politically normal. On this Johnson based his disagreement with Rymer and Voltaire, returning like the saner Aristotelian he was, to 'just conceptions of general Nature'. This was the same orthodoxy to which Wordsworth returned, for Wordsworth also is in the true line of descent and agitated repeal rather than revolution. He would have us return 'to eternal nature' and leave those arbitrary idiosyncrasies which 'though they may have prevailed hundreds of years, a philosopher will look upon as accidents'.[9] It is not the romantics, but the Croceans, who are the heretics.

# 4

## Arundell Esdaile, *The Sources of English Literature* (Cambridge University Press, 1929)

~

Mr Esdaile, deserting the precedent of his predecessors in the Sandars Lectureship, has addressed himself to the young and inexperienced, and has produced an outline sketch which will be of service to students of English literature who are entering upon what is sometimes called 'postgraduate research.' They will not, of course, find him full enough, for he divides bibliographies into twelve classes, to the description of which he can give only 100 pages; but he has the merit of mentioning a great many works of importance, and of never praising a bad book (unless, perhaps, when he is complimentary to that pretentious, incomplete and irritating manual, Mr. de Ricci's *Book Collector's Guide*). His position at the British Museum has enabled him to give useful hints on such matters as the Museum system of cataloguing anonyma, the indexing of the Thomason Tracts, and other domestic matters, though sometimes a small addition would add much to the value of the information; it is mentioned, for instance, that Charles Burney's collection of old newspapers is bound up in order of date, but the period concerned is not stated, and, incidentally, Nichols' similarly arranged files

Review published in *The Oxford Magazine*, vol. 47 (16 May 1929), p. 633.

are ignored. And is it true that the Lamport books obtained by the British Museum were all duplicates of copies in the Britwell collection? Some of them have been described as unique.

In other libraries, Mr. Esdaile is less safe; to say that the library of John H. Wrenn, in Texas, is 'catalogued by Wrenn and Wise' is at best highly misleading, and the reader who finds, among the 'chief dramatic collections', that 'The Malone and Kemble copies have every leaf separately mounted', may reasonably doubt whether Mr. Esdaile has ever even handled a Malone play. The reference to the well-known Irish bibliographer, Mr. E. R. McClintock Dix, as 'Mr. E. R. McCraken Dix', is also unfortunate. But the student who has chosen an English Literature subject for a BLitt thesis will do well to read this book with care; it contains much useful information, concisely given, together with such valuable cautions as that on publishers' advertisements in the eighteenth century, and such occasional hints as the recommendation (which we heartily endorse) of Sayle's[1] use of the broken square bracket, or of Mr. Esdaile's own method of tabular indexing.

# 5

## W. P. Ker, *Form and Style in Poetry*: *Lectures and Notes*, ed. R. W. Chambers (London: Macmillan, 1928)

~

In this volume Mr. Chambers has gathered together a very valuable collection of Professor Ker's *opuscula*. The main body of the book consists of the University College lectures of 1914–1915, the text being arrived at through the collation of the verbatim report of Dr. Hitchcock's with the note-books of others who were present. (In a book of less absorbing interest than this, one could hardly refrain from discussing the extreme value of this process merely as a textual experiment.)

Similar to these, and in part overlapping them, there are some lectures on the Forms of English poetry delivered at Cambridge in 1912, the Clark lectures on Chaucer, a paper on Ballads reprinted from the Proceedings of the British Academy, and, above all, some ninety pages of Appendix, gathered from various sources, in which the very titles (*De superbia Carminum . . . Rhythmorum Exampla*) should whet the appetites of good men.

Such a collection however heterogeneous it were, would deserve the warmest thanks. No scrap of Ker's writing does not embody the quality of his mind as a whole, and

Review published in *The Oxford Magazine*, vol. 47 (6 December 1928), pp. 283–4.

no scrap therefore is negligible. What that quality was we shall perhaps appreciate more fully the longer we study it. No writer in modern times approached so nearly to that critical ideal of being 'like God – easy to please and hard to satisfy.'[1] No beauty was too small to escape his attention: none so enchanting as to hurry his critical sanity into excess. Almost alone among the critics who have lived since the Romantic movement, he never forgot that while one thing might be good, another might be better, and that better did not cancel the good.

This is well brought out in the very interesting letters which Raleigh wrote to him after the publication of *Epic and Romance*,[2] where one can guess Ker's answer from Raleigh's second letter, and where Raleigh, though a strong man himself, shows like a schoolboy.[3] With Raleigh, to see the epic for a moment as Ker saw it habitually meant to be unfair to Romance. Ker looks at both and will not be carried away; his blood and judgement are too well commingled. Of such a man's mind the least gleanings are venerable. Even if they lay ill together, we should be glad to have them. In point of fact, however, the present collection displays a singular unity of theme. The connecting link is the doctrine of the pure Forms – the abstract pattern of the epic, the abstract tune of a stanza – which will not be strange to any reader of the preface to Dryden's *Essays*.[4] It is this critical 'realism' which is the true topic of all these papers.[5]

The Forms are abstractions but they are not nonentities, for we see that they are operative. Among the many influences pressing upon the poet, we must leave room for these spectral and impersonal forces: we cannot reduce the whole thing to those more personal and passionate motives that tempt the biographer. When once we have understood the Forms we shall be free from many crudities of literary history: we shall cease to talk of the ballad of Orpheus as a stage in the decay of the romance of Orfeo. We shall learn that metres have a life of their own and beget of themselves the moods that seem to create them. There is, of course, far more than this in the book: admirable chapters on *Poetical Logic* and on *The Similie*: a cooling card here and there for those who believe too intemperately in the Renaissance: and the wonderful feast of metrical types in the appendix which no one but Ker could have given us, or would if he could. But it is in the development of the doctrine of Forms – a great and sorely needed act of justice to the impersonal – that I find the backbone of these works: though, to be sure, you must read them for the digressions even if you don't care about Forms.

# 6

## Denis de Rougemont, *Poetry and Society*, trans. Montgomery Belgion (London: Faber and Faber, 1940); Claude Chavasse, *The Bride of Christ* (London: Faber and Faber, 1940)

~

For the present writer to criticize Mr Belgion as a translator from the French would be impertinent, so we may proceed at once to consider his original. M. de Rougemont's book consists of a moral thesis coupled with an historical thesis. As they are of very unequal value, the purpose of this review is to deter readers either from neglecting the moral because they perceived the weakness of the historical, or from debauching their sense of evidence by accepting M. de Rougemont's history because they approve his ethics; that is, to counteract the effect of the exciting sentences with which Messrs Faber and Faber have adorned the jacket of the English version.[1]

The historical thesis is that the earliest medieval literature of Courtly Love was not really an expression of sexual passion at all, but the exoteric and symbolic expression of a wish for death and pain, itself the product of a widespread pagan Eros-mysticism, mediated to the Provençal poets through the Catharist heresy. The very best that can be said for this theory is that it is not formally

Review published in *Theology*, vol. 40 (June 1940), pp. 459–61.

impossible. The fatal principle of the author's method is quite frankly stated on p. 109 of the French text (though not, oddly enough, on the corresponding p. 122 of the English). It is that, since the Cathari were suppressed, documents are *naturally* lacking, and in their absence *toutes les hypothèses sont permises*. In fact, no hypothesis is permissible except that which covers the facts with the fewest possible assumptions, and M. de Rougement is falling into what I call the Gyges Fallacy (If there were an invisible man in the room it would look empty – The room does look empty. Therefore there is an invisible man in it).[2]

He lays enormous stress on certain unmotivated partings of the lovers in the *Tristan* romance; but loss of motivation easily occurs in stories through misunderstandings of the original, and the vast superstructure which M. de Rougemont builds is at the mercy of Occam's razor. He traces the lover's dislike of dawn in the Provençal *Alba*[3] to some Manichean doctrine of the duel between Day and Night – which would make Ovid a Manichean. When a lover prefers his mistress to the Papal and the Imperial thrones, this seems to M. de Rougemont 'to display the unmistakable demeanour of negative mysticism' (p. 103); but the same argument would find the *via negativa* in the song from the *Misanthrope* (*j'aime mieux ma mie*)[4] or even in the English 'I have a thirst I wouldn't sell for a thousand pounds.' The whole argument is maintained only by the continual predisposition to suppose every bush a bear.

But there is an even deeper objection. The author bases his thesis time after time on the existence of delays and obstacles in all love stories, which, for him, illustrate a secret desire for suffering and death, in seeming oblivion

of the fact that delays and obstacles play an equally important part in stories that have nothing to do with love –
in *Treasure Island* or the *Philoctetes* or *Beowulf*. The total
absence from M. de Rougemont's thought of any general
theory of story as such leads him to mete hard measure
to story-tellers. If they end unhappily, that is a death-
wish. If, after delays and obstacles, we reach a happy ending, this is a compromise between the 'romantic' and the
'middle-class' wishes (p. 238). The author hardly seems
aware that the formula 'obstacles followed by a happy ending' includes the *Odyssey*, *Aeneid*, *Gierusalemme Liberata*,
*Tempest*, *Pilgrim's Progress* and nearly every *märchen* in the
world; indeed, he seems unaware of the very existence of
literature which is not erotic.

Nevertheless this book is indispensable. Its moral thesis
can easily be separated from its historical, provided that we
do not equate origins with values. Romantic passion may,
or may not, have originated as M. de Rougemont maintains. But God can bring so much good out of evil, and
Satan so much evil out of good, that to know its origins
would help us little in estimating its present value. On
this problem M. de Rougemont writes one of the most
cleansing and penetrating sermons I have read for a long
time, and maintains with eloquence the incompatibility
between the Christian conception of marriage and the
modern notion according to which every marriage must
have 'falling in love' as its efficient, and world 'happiness'
as its final, cause. An English reader, bred on Patmore,
Chesterton, and Mr Charles Williams, may sometimes
wonder whether Romanticism has not a greater internal
power of shedding its own errors than M. de Rougemont

supposes; but all of us need to learn, almost daily, that Eros ceases to be a demon only when he ceases to be a god (p. 321).[5]

Mr Chavasse's short book – I wished it longer – traces the Nuptial Idea in theology from Old Testament times down to Alexander Cruden. Its main theological thesis, which I am too ignorant to criticize, is that the true conception of the Church as Bride has been largely obscured by misconceptions which assign that high position to the individual Christian soul or to the Blessed Virgin; but that it was recovered in its purity by the Anglican Reformation. An extremely interesting Appendix, entitled 'The Marriage in the Mission Field', discusses how far the *Hieros gamos* found in many contemporary mythologies can be used as a preparation for the true Nuptial Idea, but will be dangerous to pagans who, like the Hindoos, already have the idea of the soul bride. Mr Chavasse seems to me to have successfully avoided the dangers inherent in his subject and produced an edifying book.

# 7

## Oliver Elton (1861–1945): an obituary

~

'Carlyle and Mill had different ideas of justice . . . and a real divergence on such a point wrecks any friendship worthy of the name.'[1] That is one sentence from Oliver Elton. Here is another: 'I for one would sooner, any time, read a good book on what I think the wrong side than a bad one on my own.'[2] The two together give us roughly the measure of the man. The first was written in 1920, during the very nadir of kittenish antinomianism, when every-one almost was desperately concerned to be unacademic, not to be a prig. Of a hundred writers then chosen at random, perhaps ninety would have made the opposite point. One can easily imagine all the breezy, or flippant, or cynical, or 'full-blooded' declarations that a friendship worthy of the name would *not* be troubled by 'academic' quibbles about 'abstract' justice. Against that background Elton's sentence stands out like a rock of granite. But it is balanced by the other. He holds dogmas without being 'dogmatic' in the popular sense of the word. His sensibil-ity is not in the least hampered by his integrity: he can be as catholic and sensitive as the pococurantists without having paid their price. The range of his learning was so

Published in *The Oxford Magazine*, vol. 63 (21 June 1945), pp. 318–19. Elton had been Professor of English at Liverpool University and was best known for his six-volume work *A Survey of English Literature (1730–1880)* (London: E. Arnold, 1912–28).

wide that few men – certainly not the present writer – can speak adequately of him: but I am inclined to think that it is by his great *Surveys* that he will live. Literary history is a difficult, almost an impossible, art. If written by a mere critic it ceases to be history, and becomes merely a series of appreciations arranged in chronological order. If written by one whose main interest is in the 'becoming' it may lose sight of those aesthetic standards which are, after all, the chief reason for studying literature. No man held the balance better than Elton. The *Surveys* are equally satisfying whether you sit down fairly to follow the story or open them for half an hour to sharpen your vision of a favourite novelist or poet. Chesterton (or was it Raleigh?) once defined a German as 'the opposite of an Englishman.'[3] In the same way, we might almost describe Elton as 'the opposite of Saintsbury',[4] thus setting off one good thing by another. He had none of Saintsbury's mischievousness and perhaps little of his brilliance. He was at once more serious and more cheerful; and – it is rarer praise than it should be for literary historians – he never wrote of what he had not well and truly read. We have never had work in this kind which is more reliable, more manly, and, after repeated readings, more satisfying. He recalled literary history to the dignity it had in Warton.[5] Clio[6] was approached with proper piety and accepted the offering 'deliberately pleased.'[7]

# 8

## Howard Rollin Patch, *The Other World, According to Descriptions in Medieval Literature* (Cambridge, Massachusetts: Harvard University Press, 1950)

≈

This book is not, as I expected from its title, a study of medieval imaginations about the fate of the soul after death. Mr Patch is concerned with texts that describe strange regions or wonderlands: an island in the *Odyssey* or in an Irish *imram*, a place in a hollow hill, an allegorical garden, even the Green Chapel, are all, in his terminology, 'other world.'

His work obviously springs from a long and deep love of his matter. He is well aware that the genre continues to our own day and that it gives rise to many psychological and even philosophical questions. He is therefore quite free from any attitude of provincial superiority; he would not deride, though he declines, the question which Matilda answers in *Purgatorio* XXVIII, 139–141. For the purposes of his book, however, he limits himself to a single question: how far the medieval pictures of 'other world' depend upon folk-lore?

His study, therefore, resolves itself into a search for recurrent 'motifs' – the island, the river, the perilous bridge, the descent into the earth, the flight through the

Review published in *Medium Aevum* 20 (1951), pp. 93–4.

air. In order to disengage these, a prodigious number of texts are presented in abstract and quotation. The method is, inevitably, very hard on the texts as literature. 'Motifs', as Professor Tolkien has reminded us, are mere products of analysis. They do not, as 'motifs', occur in concrete imaginative experience.[1] If the text really captures us, we have, not an instance of 'the perilous bridge motif' but this individual bridge.

The search for 'motifs' forces upon our attention in each text precisely what mattered least to the story-teller and his audience. Hence, as Mr Patch sees (p. 320), no method could more effectively kill the interest in which his own labours began. 'Nothing' (to adopt Lowell) 'is beyond its power to disenchant.'[2] But this is no criticism of Mr Patch. Aesthetic appreciation was not his aim, and 'none can compass more than they intend.'[3] It would be a good reason for keeping his book, if possible, out of the hands of a beginner who was threatening to study literature before he had learned to enjoy it. That does not mean that the book will not be of real use to scholars.

Mr Patch well understands the danger of mistaking for common 'motifs' what are only accidental coincidences. I am not quite sure whether he is equally on his guard against the possibility of resemblances which result neither from chance, nor from a common origin in folk-lore, but from the exigencies of the narrative art itself.

The story-teller, after all, must make it clear why we do not walk into 'other world[s]' every day. This means that he must locate it far away or put it behind some barrier: seas, rivers, caves with small entrances, the wastes of the sky, are obvious expedients. I think that if Mr Patch sat down to write an 'other world' story himself he would soon find that it needed no folk-lore to make him put it under the earth, or in the sky, or on a remote island. There are also passages where, I think, he has put undue pressure on the individual image to bring it into conformity with the ideal 'motif': notably on p. 199. I doubt if we understand either folk-lore or the *Roman de la Rose* better by making the stream at l. 104 into an instance of 'the river barrier.' But such instances are the exception.

Only a deeply and curiously erudite reader will rise from this book without having learned much that is new to him.

# 9

# Werner Schwarz, *Principles and Problems of Biblical Translation* (Cambridge University Press, 1955)

~

The idea which provides the structure of this very useful book is that those two different approaches to Biblical translation which are represented by Erasmus and Luther can be traced through the history of Biblical translation as a whole.[1] Thus at the outset we get opposed accounts of the origin of LXX[2] from pseudo-Aristeas[3] and Philo *De Vita Mosis II*.[4] In pseudo-Aristeas the translators are chosen by examination and secure agreement by comparing their versions and discussing their differences. The result is approved by a larger assembly. In Philo the translators, apparently without communication among themselves, produce versions which were word for word the same. A new miracle had, in fact, been performed. The translation was as inspired as the original, so that LXX and the Hebrew text can be regarded, not as daughter and mother, but as 'sisters.' Here we have implicitly what Dr Schwarz calls the 'philological' and the 'inspirational' principles.

He finds them (pp. 28–44) exhibited once more by St Jerome and St Augustine. That St Jerome is 'philological' he very fully convinced me. But it might be doubted

Review published in *Medium Aevum*, vol. 26 (1957), pp. 115–17.

whether St Augustine is merely 'inspirational' in the same sense as Philo. He certainly holds an 'inspirational' theory; but is it an inspirational theory of translation? For he does not seem to me to be saying that LXX, by inspiration, always renders the Hebrew correctly, but that, whether it does or no, it is equally divine and oracular. His point is, not that it is always correct, but that when it is not, it is something quite as good, or better. If any rival (and correct) translation does not agree with it, this should only set us looking for the hidden sense peculiar to LXX: *si non congruere videtur, altitudo ibi prophetica esse credenda est.*[5] Thus in Jonah iii, 4 there is no doubt, for St Augustine, that 'forty days' is what the prophet actually said; the seventy, *longe posterius interpretati,*[6] are certainly (in the ordinary sense) wrong when they give 'three days.' But this mistranslation serves to raise the reader's mind from the history to seek those higher truths for whose sake the history was written. Thus all idea of translation disappears. The Holy Spirit *unum per Ionam prophetam alterum per septuaginta interpretum prophetiam . . . dixit.*[7] This, in one way, out-Luthers Luther. LXX is not a revealed version but a new revelation.

Chapter III ('The Traditional View') exhibits, with just the right amount of quotation, that close interlocking of medieval exegesis with the text of the Vulgate, which brought it about that so much should hang on the matter of re-translation. All this part is really very well done.

After this I became a little doubtful whether the antithesis of 'philological' and 'inspirational' could fully contain the richness of Dr Schwarz's matter. In his scheme Reuchlin[8] and Erasmus have to be lined up together as 'Philological' and contrasted to Luther as 'inspirational.'

Colet[9] does not fit in very comfortably. The Fifth Chapter deals at unexpected length with the history of Erasmus's thought before he became a Biblical translator; here, and here only in this book, I felt a certain *longueur*. I would gladly have bartered for some of these pages a little more detailed work (such as the author explicitly disclaims on p. 143) about the actual renderings of Reuchlin and Erasmus. I got the impression that the author was anxious to diminish the gulf which, in my opinion, divides Erasmus from Reuchlin and Colet no less than from Luther. One can see, of course, the sense in which the first three are all 'philological.' But is that the most significant grouping? Colet's pietism, his belief that Scripture can be understood 'only by grace', lines him up in one way with Luther, and indeed with Latomus,[10] against Erasmus. And Reuchlin's feelings about the Hebrew, linking him with Pico and a whole movement which was mystical, syncretistic, and even magical in its tendency, seems to me a radically different thing from the literary, enlightened, aesthetic approach of Erasmus – all that side of the man which made Luther call him a prattler.

Some of the problems raised in this section seem to me to admit of a psychological solution. The friendship (across fundamental differences) of Erasmus and Colet can surely be explained by the hatreds they shared (see p. 115). All the opponents of an established order will at one stage make common cause. It is only victory that sets them belabouring one another. As for Erasmus's repeated statement that mere *belles lettres* had now lost all savour for him, is it any more mysterious than a man's repeated statements that he has finally given up smoking?

The most obvious defect of this book is, fortunately, one which will not much impair its utility; I mean, the imperfections of its English. On p. 15 'God's direct intercession', though etymologically defensible, is very harsh according to modern English usage. Dr Schwarz means 'intervention.' On p. 19 'origin by God' is not English. On p. 66 'transcriptions' appears to mean 'transliterations.' On pp. 82, 154, and 165, 'apexes' is odd. Why not 'tittles' (κεραίαι)? On p. 156 'inspirational method' ought surely to be 'inspirational theory'; how can there be an inspirational *method*? On p. 168 (in the translated quotation) 'virtue' should be 'power.' On p. 196 'unlike Erasmus's view' should be 'unlike Erasmus.' On p. 170 Luther's *ich mich wohl hätte mügen . . . einen Knecht und Evangelisten rühmen und schreiben*[11] is rendered in words that do not really make any sense at all. What is more dangerous is the statement (p. 59) that 'Sir Thomas More was opposed to all modern Bible translations.' Dr Schwarz is far too well informed to be in error about the facts. He means that More was hostile to the vernacular versions actually made in his own day. I am afraid he will be taken to mean that More opposed the making of any version: which is of course false.[a] A strange storm in a teacup – *fluctus in simpulo*[12] – is stirred up about a not very extraordinary Latin sentence at the bottom of p. 147.

These are from one point of view trifles. The book is welcome. Despite its brevity it contains a great deal of information and will give many readers who are scholars

---

[a] See *The Apologye of Syr Thomas More*, ed. A. I. Taft, Early English Text Society (1930), p. 13.

without being specialists in this field pretty well what they want. If it reaches (as it deserves to do) a second edition, I hope the index will be fully revised. (Try looking up *Vetus Latina*.)[13]

Though it does not concern Dr Schwarz more than a hundred modern writers, I venture to put in here a plea against the growing, and now almost universal, practice of mentioning Renaissance scholars by their vernacular names (e.g., Dorp for Dorpius). It is hard to see how this originated if not in a silly ostentation of irrelevant erudition, or how it has been continued except by fashion. Why should every beginner in these subjects have to learn a number of names by which the old authors were never known in Europe in their own day, and which he will not find in the text or index of even a nineteenth-century authority?

> *Turpe est difficiles habere nugas*
> *Et stultus labor est ineptiarum.*[14]

# 10

# Tragic ends: George Steiner, *The Death of Tragedy* (London: Faber and Faber, 1961)

∾

This is a well-written, well-informed, and (in short space) an opulent book, and even those who reject its main thesis must certainly prize it for the inset estimates of particular dramatists. These appear to be written from an inexhaustible knowledge of European drama, yet at the same time with all the gusto of a young theatre-goer. That on Corneille is perhaps the best; but on Byron's plays the most unexpected. But the author is far too good a critic to make novelty his aim. Where there is nothing both new and true to be said, as on Racine, he is content to say well what most of us already thought.

The discussion of verse in chapter seven is almost equally good. Almost, but not, I think, quite. I welcome Mr Steiner's rejection of the false poetics with which critics and poets have been infected ever since Wordsworth wrote his disastrous passage about diction in the preface to *Lyrical Ballads*.[1] But I think he sees only half the truth. He sees the distancing and exalting power of verse; but he seems to ignore the equal appropriateness of verse – though, to be sure, a very different sort of verse – to the coarsest humour. Some lyrics in Aristophanes, many epigrams of Martial, many lewd limericks of our own day,

Reviewed in *Encounter*, vol. 18 (February 1962), pp. 97–101.

come to mind. The truth seems to be that as verse in tragedy makes splendid what in prose would be sheerly painful, so bawdy verse makes brisk and sportive what, without it, would be sheerly hateful.

Again, in a later passage, where Mr Steiner very justly praises the quality of Yeats's blank verse, I question whether his quotation really illustrates it. The last two lines of it, with their artfully simple syntax and their extremely regular iambic movement, seem to me to show Yeats in one of his unusual Tennysonian moments.[2]

A few details are open to dispute. On p. 11 the letter to Can Grande is attributed to Dante; I believe most scholars now think it spurious. And don't we know something more about the Athenian audience than Mr Steiner allows on p. 114? Surely Aristotle says somewhere that Many are good judges of plays?[3] On p. 320 Milton's refusal to choose between Ptolemy and Copernicus is described as 'a gesture both serene and sorrowful.' I suggest we should rather emphasise the amazing ingenuity whereby Milton exploits the poetic possibilities of both, evoking by his Chaos all the agoraphobia and bewilderment of 'outer space' but also giving us 'hanging in a golden chain'[4] a finite, illuminated universe which, if imperfectly Ptolemaic, is as much a *kosmos*, an artefact, as Ptolemy's.

On the credit side there are felicities enough to fill this review with quotations. Dryden working over Shakespeare is like 'a skillful transcription for piano of a complete orchestral score' . . . 'the stricter a style, the more communicative is any departure from its severity' . . . drama involves 'a miracle of controlled self-destruction.'[5] But it is time to turn to Mr Steiner's real theme. If I express mainly my dissents, that is by way of 'opening the discussion'. I don't doubt that if he had me in the room Mr Steiner could produce satisfactory answers to some of them and interesting answers to all.

He says at the outset that when we say 'tragic drama' we know 'not exactly but well enough'[6] what we mean. What he clearly means is a play with an unhappy ending, arising out of the assertion that 'necessity is blind' in which 'the vengeful spite or injustice of the gods' somehow 'hallows the sufferer.'[7] He has every right to define tragedy thus if he pleases. But he seems also to think that his concept of tragedy covers all the works usually called tragedies, as if it had been reached by induction: 'the word *tragedy* encloses in a single span both the Greek and the Elizabethan example.' But does it, as defined by him? He is well aware that we have a happy ending in the *Eumenides* and something like one in the *Oedipus at Colonus*: but the short paragraph in which he attempts to discount these as special cases did not convince me. If we had more complete trilogies such endings would, I suspect, turn up more often; we know that the Promethean trilogy ended in reconciliation. Even among extant plays we have happy endings in the *Philoctetes* and the *Iphigenia in Tauris*. And what of such French plays as *Le Cid* or *Esther*?[8]

The moral I would draw is that tragedy, taken as a common essence of which all 'tragedies' are instances, is a phantom concept. They share a common name for historical reasons; as the Postlethwaites[9] are all so called not because they all exhibit a common character of Postlethwaiticity, but in virtue of their genetic connections. An Athenian knew whether the play he had seen was or was not a 'tragedy' by far coarser and more objective criteria than ours; more as a modern man knows whether he has been watching rugger or soccer.

And in plays with an unhappy ending do we always find the 'hallowing effect'? Who is hallowed in the *Agamemnon*, the *Medea*, *Macbeth*, or *Phèdre*? Is the hallowing indisputably present anywhere except in *Oedipus at Colonus* and *Lear*?

An even more disquieting question rises in my mind. Is such hallowing a usual, or frequent, result of undeserved and irreparable disaster in the real world? And if it is not, what claim has the art which depicts it to be a specially 'stark insight into human life'? Can we wholly avoid the suspicion that tragedy as Mr Steiner conceives it, is our final attempt 'to see the world as the world's not'?

The purpose of the book is to account for the decay of the tragic drama. The author sees clearly that it has flourished only in a few periods, so that its existence, not its absence, is what really 'calls for particular note.' That being so, to account for its absence from any particular age seems a strange enterprise – like asking why some particular man is not six feet tall, or a champion sprinter. You could answer it only if you knew why anybody was, and then it would answer itself. But this objection is merely technical. If you explain the absence, you will, by implication, have explained the presence. If Mr Steiner can show why tragedy died we shall know why it ever lived.

The best of Mr Steiner's explanations, to my mind, turns on the loss of an accepted, and highly imaginative, *Weltanschauung*[10] once common to the dramatist and his whole audience. This has no doubt raised difficulties for all poetry; but most acutely for the most public forms,

epic and drama. I would even like to add a buttress to Mr
Steiner's view. He wisely admits opera as, in some sort, the
19th-century successor to, or usurper of, the tragic stage.
Is it not then highly significant that we find the nearest
approach to great tragedy in the first three parts of *The
Ring*[11] which do really embody something like a widely
accepted myth – the philosophy of Keats's Oceanus,[12]
the vague evolutionism or developmentalism for which
Darwin was later to supply the scientific super-structure.
By the tragedy I here mean the tragedy of Wotan who
'rises to the height of willing his own downfall.'[13] (In
*Götterdämmerung*, recasting old work, Wagner relapses
both dramatically and musically into his earlier and far
inferior manner.)[14]

I am rather less convinced by the role which Mr Steiner
attributes to the French Revolution, conceived as 'a triumph of the militant *bourgeoisie* – with its lack of literary
background and its taste for pathos and happy endings.'
Courtly romance, no less than popular melodrama, is full
of pathos and happy endings. There is some danger of
making 'the rise of the middle classes' a maid of all work.
I have hardly ever read a historical book which did not
begin by telling me that in the period under consideration this ill-defined class was rising into new importance.
Mysterious body, which appears to have been always rising, and working all evil by its rise, up to the very moment
when I was born into it!

Mr Steiner also suggests that 'the middle-class spectator' in the revolutionary period wanted escapism in the
theatre because the real world was then giving him 'a surfeit and tumult of emotion.' 'After the great levies had
marched and retreated across Europe, the ancient balance

between public and private life had altered.' But does this apply to England? There, surely, no class shared less in these marches and retreats than the *bourgeoisie* or viewed them with greater phlegm? I doubt, furthermore, whether 'surfeit and tumult of emotion' were so absent from the audience at the Globe. In every age the most private life will often be surfeited with emotion; and the Elizabethans lived under the permanent fear of hell-fire, witches, plagues, a second Armada, and a disputed succession with a consequent civil war.

Mr Steiner is good on the ambivalent relations between Romanticism and tragedy. He sees in the Romantics, on the one hand, an 'impulse towards drama.' But he also sees that the essentially lyrical and egocentric character of Romanticism was inevitably fatal to 'the controlled self-destruction' which drama demands ('Falstaff lives because he is not Shakespeare'). I could wish, however, that he had not, without qualification, connected Romanticism with Revolution as a liberation from reason. It was not for nothing that the Revolution made Reason a goddess. It attacked the *ancien régime* not only for iniquities but for 'absurdities' (as the author agrees on p. 125). The 'reason' from which Wordsworth records his liberation in *The Prelude* is not that of Descartes but that of Godwin.

Once, and I think only once, Mr Steiner is misled into blurring a point by the incisiveness of his own style. In distinguishing 'near-tragedy' – drama that ends, like *Faust* or *Peer Gynt* with some sort of redemption – he says 'near-tragedy is, in fact, another word for melodrama.' He may or may not be right. But the trouble is that 'melodrama' is more a pejorative than a descriptive term. And I suggest, as a fundamental canon of exposition, that a distinction of kinds should never be thus combined with a judgment of comparative value. This always weakens it and distracts our attention. If you say, 'This is not port but sherry', you speak to the purpose. If you say, 'This is not port, but the vile drink sherry', you have introduced a red herring. Tell us afterwards how you dislike sherry, but don't mix this up with the distinction.

It would even be argued that when we are discussing the death of tragedy the term melodrama needs to be defined with especial care. I rather suspect that an extreme sensitivity to the charge of melodrama, felt by poet, actor, and spectator alike, may be one symptom of an ethos which renders tragedy impossible. The flamboyant gesture, the uninhibited emotion fully articulated in eloquent speech, are suspect. They were first driven away by the Victorian ideal of the Strong Silent Man and the Stiff Upper Lip, and the collapse of that ideal into mere cynicism has banished them still further. Irony and suspicion have suffered a hypertrophy. Tragedy is certainly a different thing from melodrama; but I doubt whether those who are not prepared to risk the one can ever make, act, or fully enjoy the other. We might perhaps describe melodrama as 'the tragic in exile.' It is what happens to certain elements of tragedy when they are rejected by cultured people and abandoned by the masses.

# 11

# Eros on the loose: David Loth, *The Erotic in Literature* (London: Secker and Warburg, 1962)

~

The busy reader should concentrate on the last three chapters and the appendix of this book. It is there that Mr. Loth has something useful to say. He gives a pretty full and very damaging history of the law's confused and largely futile attempt to control or even to define, pornography. He also casts serious doubts on common assumptions as to what will or will not correct the young reader. Who would have thought that George Eliot or Motley's 'Dutch Republic' would prove inflammatory![1]

But the truth is, as most of us know from experience, that no one can predict what will inflame an adolescent any more than what will frighten a child. Read Lamb on 'Witches and Other Night Fears'.[2] The 'fountains are within'.[3] The ghost story and the erotic book merely provide a channel for what would have made its own channels without them. We have better evidence of this than the answers to questionnaires. For surely most of us, receiving a set of impertinent questions from a stranger, drop it in the wastepaper basket and turn to our own work or pleasure? Those who answer are not, I suspect, a fair cross section. They betray their abnormality by the very act of answering.

Review published in *The Observer* (Weekend Review), no. 8905 (4 March 1962), p. 30.

The Appendix, on the 'Lady Chatterley' affair, was doubtless written before the Warden of All Souls' article appeared in *Encounter*.[4] This reopens a good many questions. It is no answer to accuse the Warden of 'muckraking.' If the 'muck' is there and if the prosecution was too stupid to see it and the defence too prudent to mention it, a little raking was just what was needed. Mr. Loth anyway might welcome the Warden's thesis as fresh evidence for his own main theme – that the law's an ass.

On law he is at his best. But even there he commits himself to strange statements. We are told that 'communications is [*sic*] the only industry catering to [*sic*] the carnal nature of man which is not controlled in practice by those who work in it.'[5] In civilised countries every industry is subject both to civil and criminal law. Again, lawyers are scolded for trying 'to apply their rules outside the courtroom.'[6] But all laws except those against perjury and 'contempt' are designed to regulate what people do out of court. Nor do I understand why the author jeers at an American judge for acquitting 'Ulysses' because it was 'emetic' rather than 'aphrodisiac.'[7] If it is the intention of the law (as it certainly was) to ban what allures it obviously ought to permit what disgusts.

Mr. Loth's literary *dicta* are among the strangest I have ever read. He describes Ford[8] as treating incest 'with a light touch.'[9] He classifies 'Tristram Shandy' among 'worthwhile adventure stories.'[10] Worst of all is the chapter on pornography in the Ancient World. Here he accepts all the confusions which a good book on this subject would have cleared up at the outset. Anything which mentions copulation – for whatever purpose, in whatever tone – is for him 'pornography' – a hymn from a Sumerian fertility rite, the story of Judah and Tamar, Sophocles' 'Electra.'[11]

The nearest we get to a distinction is an unemphatic admission that Aristophanes is a 'more obvious' example. He seems wholly unaware that 'language which later generations call obscene'[12] – the ancient equivalent of 'four-letter' words – is almost exclusively confined to satire and farce. You find it in Catullus' hate poems, not in his love poems: in Horace's satires, not in Ovid's *Art of Love*.

But history of any sort is not Mr. Loth's strong point. 'The Serpent of Shame entered the garden of sex some years after the reign of good Queen Bess'[13] is a statement that leaves one gasping. It would be difficult on this view to explain why the Book of Genesis has an aetiological myth about the birth of shame, why the Greeks spoke of *aidoia* and the Romans of *pudenda* or Dante of 'the member that man hides.'[14] Mr. Loth, I believe, has wholly misunderstood the comic indecencies in earlier writers. He does not see that it was funny to mention these things precisely because they were to some extent – not, of course, to a Victorian extent – unmentionable.

The truth is that most of this book is merely a romp. The author is mainly concerned to pull snooks and score debating points. But he keeps his shafts exclusively for one side. There is room for a book which would chasten the cant and confusion which can be found on both. It ought to be made impossible for the repressive party to include the scatological under the pornographic or to call a book immoral because it offends their taste. It should equally be made impossible for the other party to make remarks like 'sex is innocent.' If *sex* means the biological fact, it is no more innocent or guilty than a turnip. If it is meant that human sexual behaviour is all, and all equally, innocent, we want to be told why. No one claims a similar liberty for all economic or political behaviour.

Such a book would draw far more clearly than Mr. Loth has done the real moral: that when the morality embodied in the law departs too widely, either for better or worse, from that really current in a society, the law must sooner or later either sink or rise into conformity. Till it does, confusion and inconsistence are inevitable.

The author treats *erotica* as a singular and *orgiastic* as the adjective of *orgasm*.

# PART II

# THE INKLINGS: BARFIELD, TOLKIEN, AND WILLIAMS

~

*The membership of the Oxford literary group that came to be known as the Inklings varied over the years of its existence, but always at its centre were C. S. Lewis and J. R. R. Tolkien. Also important were Charles Williams, poet and author of philosophical novels still in print today, and Owen Barfield, whom Lewis called the 'wisest and best' of his 'unofficial teachers' in* The Allegory of Love *(1936), but who could not often attend meetings, since he worked in London as a solicitor. These chapters bring together Lewis's reviews of the works of his friends. Together they give some hint of what discussion, debate and critical argument must have been like, when one or other of the Inklings read parts of a work in progress on a Thursday evening in Lewis's rooms in Magdalen College. When Lewis published* The Problem of Pain *(1942), he dedicated the book to the Inklings.*

# 12

# Who gaf me drink?: Owen Barfield, *Romanticism Comes of Age* (London: Anthroposophical Publishing Co., 1944)

~

*Lewis and Owen Barfield became friends in 1919, and all went well until Barfield became an Anthroposophist in 1923. Anthroposophy is 'a system of theosophy evolved by Rudolf Steiner (1861–1925), based on the premise that the human soul can, of its own power, contact the spiritual world. The concepts of karma and reincarnation are central to it. It acknowledges Christ as a cosmic being, but its understanding of Him is very different from that of orthodox Christianity'.*[1]

*'Barfield's conversion to Anthroposophy', Lewis wrote in* Surprised by Joy *(1954), chapter 13, 'marked the beginning of what I can only describe as the Great War between him and me. It was never, thank God, a quarrel... But it was an almost incessant disputation, sometimes by letter and sometimes face to face, which lasted for years.' While the 'Great War' had ended years before, the problem Lewis faced in reviewing* Romanticism Comes of Age *is that it contains in the Introduction and other places Barfield's 'case' for Anthroposophy.*

\* \* \*

Seventeen years (years chronicled with an admirable stern humour in the preface) separate this book from the same

Review published in *The Spectator*, vol. 184 (9 March 1945), p. 224.

author's *Poetic Diction*. During those years the most important work in the same field has been Professor James's *Scepticism and Poetry*[2] – at least, if you agree with the present reviewer that Professor James in that great book was really writing about scepticism and *romantic* poetry. Like Professor James, Mr Barfield considers the doctrine and discipline of romantic imagination worthy of a serious critique. The difference is that whereas Professor James finds that the ship of (romantic) poetry must 'shipwreck in the harbour', Mr Barfield holds that, though it did so, it need not have done so.

'In the legend of Parsifal', he writes, 'tragic consequences follow the failure of the hero to ask the crucial question at the crucial moment.'[3] This tragedy was repeated in the Romantic Movement when Coleridge, in the *Biographia*,[4] in obedience to the 'very injudicious' letter of his unknown friend, omitted that full account of the Imagination which was the real *raison d'être* of the whole book. The same uncertainty or pusillanimity runs through all Wordsworth's utterances on the subject. The Romantics make huge claims for the Imagination as an organ of truth; but they never have the courage either to withdraw those claims or to support them quite seriously and face their implications. Unless the claims were wholly illusory, it looks as if some real enlargement of human consciousness were, at that moment, offered – and refused; as if the Romantic fell *per null'altro rio che per non aver fé*.[5]

This, according to Mr Barfield, is what happened. The full force of his position cannot be understood except in the context he gives it; a context provided by the 'history of *thinking*', which he distinguishes sharply from the history of *thought*.[6] It is this conception which links the present work to *Poetic Diction*, for while the history of thought is to be found in men's opinions, the history of thinking is embodied in their language. Hence,

The Greek youth of Homer's day, as he approached manhood, did not 'have a beard', he did not even 'grow a beard'; he did not require a substantive at all to express what was happening – he 'foamed'! And again, in order to attribute youth, the Greek language did not require, as we do, the static, logical mode of copula and predicate 'So-and-so-is-young'; it could say 'So and so "blossoms" or "blooms",' using the same word as it used for the flowers of the field. It cannot be too often insisted that this was not a poetical metaphor, but a bedrock element in the Greek language; it is *we*, when we use such expressions to-day, who are trying to get back, *via* poetic metaphor, into the kind of consciousness which the Greek had and could express quite naturally and straightforwardly. (p. 40.)

The point which Mr Barfield is making is not one about the Greeks in particular, but about a phase in the evolution of consciousness in general of which the Greeks are the most convenient example. A later phase began to appear, but has miscarried, in English Romanticism. What might and should have happened is, for the author, hinted in the scientific works of Goethe and fully developed in the thought of Dr Steiner. About the latter he has had the same sort of experience which Chesterton had about the Church of Rome; when he had put the finishing touches to his own private 'doxy' he found that it was almost identical with the orthodoxy of a system that already existed.[7]

And with Dr Steiner we are, of course, landed in a whole world of thought which will be alien, and even disquieting, to most English readers – not least to the reviewer.

But there is one curious fact about it which renders these spontaneous reactions more than usually relevant. One is not asked to believe. 'Think these thoughts', said Steiner, 'without believing them.'[8] This is not a trick. It is a rule which might, with advantage, be at least temporarily applied to all thoughts whatever: for it is easy (and fatal) to be so pre-occupied with proving or disproving a thought that one never actually thinks it at all. The principle is also rooted in Steiner's whole system: for the whole labour is to pass from one *kind* of thinking to another. And in this book the results of this kind of thinking, as applied to Coleridge, *Hamlet*, and above all, to England itself (notice pp. 73–77) are sufficiently tonic and illuminating to justify the procedure.

This is not a perfect book. The author's wit, which is ever present, sometimes borders on petulance. The word *Nature* is never analysed: if it had been we should understand better whether, in the very last resort, the background is theistic, pantheistic, or agnostic. (I do not add 'or idealist' for that is precisely one of the antitheses the 'history of thinking' claims to undercut.) But it is a book which cannot be safely neglected, and which no one will read without feeling that windows have been opened and that strange airs are stirring in the room – perhaps without murmuring like Criseyde 'Who gaf me drink?'[9]

*While Barfield and Lewis were to remain close friends for the rest of their lives it continued to disappoint Barfield that Lewis would not read the works of Rudolf Steiner. When he revised the Introduction to a new impression of* Romanticism Comes of Age *(Middletown, Connecticut: Wesleyan, 1966) he said:*

*It has been the deepest of disappointments to me to find that, when one refers to Steiner, people do not listen. Or rather I have not merely been disappointed, I have been shocked and puzzled to have it borne in on me over and over again that even those who are prepared to lend a very sympathetic ear indeed to my own observations, whether on language and poetry or on the wider issue of the whole evolution of human consciousness, are not in the least interested in the news about Steiner which it has been one of my main objects in life to set before the educated public with all the earnestness and sobriety at my disposal . . . As an example that will serve* a fortiori *for all the rest, even the late C. S. Lewis, who was meticulous, if ever a man was, about passing on hearsay judgments, who would never, for instance, express an opinion even on a minor but all too prolix poet of the sixteenth century without first having read the great bulk of what the man himself had actually written – that even he, on more than one occasion, broke his rule in the case of Steiner? (pp. 16–17).*

# 13

## G. A. L. Burgeon (= Owen Barfield),
### *This Ever Diverse Pair*
### (London: Gollancz, 1950)

≈

It is not easy to review a book of which Mr de la Mare,[1] in a delightful introduction, has said much of what one most wants to say: I pick out what is left.

First let me try to guard against possible mistakes. This is not primarily a book for solicitors. Or rather, it will give a different kind of pleasure-recognition or discovery – according as you have or have not seen for yourself the Lynxies, Glossies and Applejohns at coffee in the cavernous depths of the Law Society or studied the late Lord MacNaughton's judgments (Green Room details interest no one as much as actors; except the public.)

Secondly, this is not a study in schizophrenia. The rift between Mr 'Burgeon' and his 'partner Burden', whom he has created, whose professional smiles he has to manage for him and who threatens one night to kill him, is not pathological. It is the rift in every life between the human person and his public *persona*, between, say, the man and the bus conductor or the man and the king. Schizophrenia occurs when the marriage of these two has ended in divorce or desertion. Mr 'Burgeon' describes the ordinary cat-and-dog rubbing-along-somehow which we all know

Review published in *Time and Tide*, vol. 31 (25 March 1950), p. 286.

so well. But we did not know it nearly so well before we read this book.

That is what shows that the author's separation of 'Burden' and 'Burgeon' is not pathological. It is genuine invention, the *Idea* which organizes and masters all the diverse experiences he is working on. Idea in this sense is not to be confused with the 'ideas' which 'Mr Burgeon' puts forward. Of these there are several; some of his legal 'ideas' seem to me well worth consideration. The *Idea* which I am speaking of is the literary idea, the idea which creates Form; as the 'idea of big and little men' makes Gulliver possible and a darker idea makes possible the *Confessions of a Glorified Sinner*.[2] Books springing from an Idea, in this sense, and especially books in which that Idea does its work exactly and no other Idea would have done it as well, have a good chance of being small scale classics. I am not at all certain that *This Ever Diverse Pair* is not in that category. I suppose (since nearly everyone will mention them) I must say that Jekyll and Hyde are a different idea, and a far older one, as old, indeed, as the *Epistle to the Romans*.

The contrast between Burden and Burgeon is not primarily an ethical contrast. There are, indeed, moments at which they stand to one another as the 'higher' to the 'lower' self or the New to the Old Man.[3] But that is only one aspect of an all-pervasive diversity. In the tragic inner life 'God wot, no villain need be.'[4] Burgeon, the poet and scholar, may chafe at the Burden whom he himself has made so 'like a *real* solicitor'[5] but he is no position to treat him *de haut en bas*.[6] If you do not grasp this, the day of judgment (in more than one sense) which concludes the book will take you, as it took Burgeon, very much by surprise.

In another way, to be sure, it should and will surprise every reader, as the unforeseen, yet inevitable, solution both of a technical and a spiritual problem. Not all Ideas come thus provided with their own *exit*. In this conclusion the gaiety and the gravity of the book reach their height at the same moment. Anguish is inherent in the theme; those who have, with Burgeon, skirted the realm of *Rhematophobia* know that.[7] Yet it is not a sad book with a nagging undertone of melancholy. It is high and sharp philosophic comedy, more fully a work of art and more original than anything I have read for a long time. I wished it longer – which shows, perhaps, that it is the right length.

# 14

## A world for children: J. R. R. Tolkien,
## *The Hobbit: or There and Back Again*
## (London: Allen and Unwin, 1937)

~

The publishers claim that *The Hobbit*, though very unlike *Alice*, resembles it in being the work of a professor at play. A more important truth is that both belong to a very small class of books which have nothing in common save that each admits us to a world of its own – a world that seems to have been going on long before we stumbled into it but which, once found by the right reader, becomes indispensable to him. Its place is with *Alice, Flatland, Phantastes, The Wind in the Willows*.[1]

To define the world of *The Hobbit* is, of course, impossible, because it is new. You cannot anticipate it before you go there, as you cannot forget it once you have gone. The author's admirable illustrations and maps of Mirkwood and Goblingate and Esgaroth give one an inkling – and so do the names of the dwarf and dragon that catch our eyes as we first ruffle the pages. But there are dwarfs and dwarfs, and no common recipe for children's stories will give you creatures so rooted in their own soil and history as those of Professor Tolkien – who obviously knows much more about them than he needs for this tale. Still less will the common recipe prepare us for the curious shift from the

Review published in *The Times Literary Supplement* (2 October 1937), p. 714.

matter-of-fact beginnings of his story ('hobbits are small people, smaller than dwarfs – and they have no beards – but very much larger than Lilliputians')[2] to the saga-like tone of the later chapters ('It is in my mind to ask what share of their inheritance you would have paid to our kindred had you found the hoard unguarded and us slain').[3] You must read for yourself to find out how inevitable the change is and how it keeps pace with the hero's journey. Though all is marvellous, nothing is arbitrary: all the inhabitants of Wilderland seem to have the same unquestionable right to their existence as those of our own world, though the fortunate child who meets them will have no notion – and his unlearned elders not much more – of the deep sources in our blood and tradition from which they spring.

For it must be understood that this is a children's book only in the sense that the first of many readings can be undertaken in the nursery. *Alice* is read gravely by children and with laughter by grown ups; *The Hobbit*, on the other hand, will be funnier to its youngest readers, and only years later, at a tenth or a twentieth reading, will they begin to realise what deft scholarship and profound reflection have gone to make everything in it so ripe, so friendly, and in its own way so true. Prediction is dangerous: but *The Hobbit* may well prove a classic.

# 15

## Professor Tolkien's hobbit: J. R. R. Tolkien, *The Hobbit: or There and Back Again* (London: Allen and Unwin, 1937)

~

All who love that kind of children's book which can be read and be re-read by adults should take note that a new star has appeared in this constellation. If you like the adventures of Ratty and Mole[1] you will like *The Hobbit*, by J. R. R. Tolkien. If, in those adventures, you prized the solidity of the social and geographical context in which your small friends moved, you will like *The Hobbit* even better. The hobbit himself, Mr Bilbo Baggins, is as prosaic as Mole, but fate sets him wandering among dwarfs and elves, over goblin mountains, in search of dragon-guarded gold. Every one he meets can be enjoyed in the nursery; but to the trained eye some characters will seem almost mythopoeic – notably lugubrious Gollum the fish-man, and the ferociously benevolent Beorn, half man, half bear, in his garden buzzing with bees.

The truth is that in this book a number of good things, never before united, have come together; a fund of humour, an understanding of children, and a happy fusion of the scholar's with the poet's grasp of mythology. On the edge of a valley one of Professor Tolkien's characters can

Review published in *The Times* (8 October 1937), p. 20.

pause and say, 'It smells like elves.'[2] It may be years before we produce another author with such a sharp nose for an elf. The Professor has the air of inventing nothing. He has studied trolls and dragons at first hand and describes them with that fidelity which is worth oceans of glib 'originality'. The maps (with runes) are excellent, and will be found thoroughly reliable by young travellers in the same region.

# 16

## The gods return to earth:
## J. R. R. Tolkien, *The Fellowship of the Ring*
## (being the First Part of *The Lord of the Rings*) (London: Allen and Unwin, 1954)

◦

This book is like lightning from a clear sky; as sharply different, as unpredictable in our age as *Songs of Innocence*[1] were in theirs. To say that in it heroic romance, gorgeous, eloquent, and unashamed, has suddenly returned at a period almost pathological in its anti-romanticism is inadequate. To us, who live in that odd period, the return – and the sheer relief of it – is doubtless the important thing. But in the history of Romance itself – a history which stretches back to the *Odyssey* and beyond – it makes not a return but an advance or revolution: the conquest of new territory.

Nothing quite like it was ever done before. 'One takes it', says Naomi Mitchison, 'as seriously as Malory.'[2] But then the ineluctable sense of reality which we feel in the *Morte d'Arthur* comes largely from the great weight of other men's work built up century by century, which has gone into it. The utterly new achievement of Professor Tolkien is that he carries a comparable sense of reality unaided. Probably no book yet written in the world is quite such a radical instance of what its author has elsewhere

Review published in *Time and Tide*, vol. 35 (14 August 1954), pp. 1082–3.

called 'sub-creation.'[3] The direct debt (there are of course subtler kinds of debt) which every author must owe to the actual universe is here deliberately reduced to the minimum. Not content to create his own story, he creates, with an almost insolent prodigality, the whole world in which it is to move, with its own theology, myths, geography, history, paleography, languages, and orders of beings – a world 'full of strange creatures beyond count.'[4] The names alone are a feast, whether redolent of quiet countryside (Michel Delving, South Farthing), tall and kingly (Boromir, Faramir, Elendil), loathsome like Smeagol, who is also Gollum, or frowning in the evil strength of Barad Dur or Gorgoroth, yet best of all (Lothlorien, Gilthoniel, Galadriel) when they embody this piercing, high elvish beauty of which no other prose writer has captured so much.

Such a book has of course its predestined readers, even now more numerous and more critical than is always realised. To them a reviewer need say little, except that here are beauties which pierce like swords or burn like cold iron; here is a book that will break your heart. They will know that this is good news, good beyond hope. To complete their happiness one need only add that it promises to be gloriously long; this volume is only the first of three. But it is too great a book to rule only its natural subjects. Something must be said to 'those without', to the unconverted. At the very least, possible misunderstandings may be got out of the way.

First, we must clearly understand that though *The Fellowship* in one way continues its author's fairy tale, *The Hobbit*, it is in no sense an overgrown 'juvenile.' The truth is the other way round. *The Hobbit* was merely a fragment torn from the author's huge myth and adapted for children; inevitably losing something by the adaptation. *The Fellowship* gives us at last the lineaments of that myth 'in their true dimensions like themselves.' Misunderstandings on this point might easily be encouraged by the first chapter, in which the author (taking a risk) writes almost in the manner of the earlier and far lighter book. With some who will find the main body of the book deeply moving, this chapter may not be a favourite.

Yet there were good reasons for such an opening; still more for the Prologue (wholly admirable, this) which precedes it. It is essential that we should first be well steeped in the 'homeliness', the frivolity, even (in its best sense) the vulgarity of the creatures called Hobbits; these unambitious folk, peaceable yet almost anarchical, with faces 'good natured rather than beautiful' and 'mouths apt to laughter and eating', who treat smoking as an art and like books which tell them what they already know. They are not an allegory of the English, but they are perhaps a myth that only an Englishman (or, should we add, a Dutchman?) could have created. Almost the central theme of the book is the contrast between the Hobbits (or 'the Shire') and the appalling destiny to which some of them are called, the terrifying discovery that the humdrum happiness of the Shire, which they had taken for granted as something normal, is in reality a sort of local and temporary accident, that its existence depends on being protected by powers which Hobbits dare not imagine, that any Hobbit may find himself forced out of the Shire and caught up into that high conflict. More strangely still, the event of that conflict between strongest things may come to depend on him, who is almost the weakest.

What shows we are reading myth, not allegory, is that there are no pointers to a specifically theological, or political, or psychological application. A myth points, for each reader, to the realm he lives in most. It is a master key; use it on what door you like. And there are other themes in *The Fellowship* equally serious.

That is why no catchwords about 'escapism'[5] or 'nostalgia' and no distrust of 'private worlds' are in court. This is no Angria,[6] no dreaming; it is sane and vigilant invention, revealing at point after point the integration of the author's mind. What is the use of calling 'private' a world we can all walk into and test and in which we find such a balance? As for escapism, what we chiefly escape is the illusion of our ordinary life. We certainly do not escape anguish. Despite many a snug fireside and many an hour of good cheer to gratify the Hobbit in each of us, anguish is, for me, almost the prevailing note. But not, as in the literature most typical of our age, the anguish of abnormal or contorted souls: rather that anguish of those who were happy before a certain darkness came up and will be happy if they live to see it gone.

Nostalgia does indeed come in; not ours nor the author's, but that of the characters. It is closely connected with one of Professor Tolkien's greatest achievements. One would have supposed that diuturnity was the quality least likely to be found in an invented world. And one has, in fact, an uneasy feeling that the worlds of the *Furioso* or *The Water of the Wondrous Isles*[7] weren't there at all before the curtain rose. But in the Tolkienian world you can hardly put your foot down anywhere from Esgaroth to Forlindon or between Ered Mithrin and Khand, without stirring the dust of history. Our own world, except at rare moments, hardly seems so heavy with its past. This is one element in the anguish which the characters bear. But with the anguish there comes also a strange exaltation. They are at once stricken and upheld by the memory of vanished civilisations and lost splendour. They have out-lived the second and third Ages; the wine of life was drawn long since. As we read we find ourselves sharing their bur-den; when we have finished, we return to our own life not relaxed but fortified.

But there is more in the book still. Every now and then, risen from sources we can only conjecture and almost alien (one would think) to the author's habitual imagination, figures meet us so brimming with life (not human life) that they make our sort of anguish and our sort of exal-tation seem unimportant. Such is Tom Bombadil, such the unforgettable Ents. This is surely the utmost reach of invention, when an author produces what seems to be not even his own, much less anyone else's. Is mythopoeia, after all, not the most, but the least, subjective of activities?

Even now I have left out almost everything – the sylvan leafiness, the passions, the high virtues, the remote hori-zons. Even if I had space I could hardly convey them. And after all the most obvious appeal of the book is perhaps also its deepest: 'there was sorrow then, too, and gather-ing dark, but great valour, and great deeds that were not wholly vain.'[8] *Not wholly vain* – it is the cool middle point between illusion and disillusionment.

# 17

## The dethronement of power:
## J. R. R. Tolkien, *The Two Towers* (being the Second Part of *The Lord of the Rings*) (London: Allen and Unwin, 1954) and J. R. R. Tolkien, *The Return of the King* (being the Third Part of *The Lord of the Rings*) (London: Allen and Unwin, 1955)

~

When I reviewed the first volume of this work I hardly dared to hope it would have the success which I was sure it deserved. Happily I am proved wrong. There is, however, one piece of false criticism which had better be answered; the complaint that the characters are all either black or white. Since the climax of Volume I was mainly concerned with the struggle between good and evil in the mind of Boromir, it is not easy to see how anyone could have said this. I will hazard a guess. 'How shall a man judge what to do in such times?' asks someone in Volume II. 'As he ever has judged', comes the reply. 'Good and ill have not changed...nor are they one thing among Elves and Dwarfs and another among Men.'[1]

This is the basis of the whole Tolkienian world. I think some readers, seeing (and disliking) demarcations of black and white, imagine they have seen a rigid demarcation

Review published in *Time and Tide*, vol. 36 (22 October 1955), pp. 1373–4.

between black and white people. Looking at the squares, they assume (in defiance of the facts) that all the pieces must be making bishops' moves which confine them to one colour. But even such readers will hardly brazen it out through the two last volumes. Motives, even in the right side, are mixed. Those who are now traitors usually began with comparatively innocent intentions. Heroic Rohan and imperial Gondor are partly diseased. Even the wretched Smeagol, till quite late in the story, has good impulses; and (by a tragic paradox) what finally pushes him over the brink is an unpremeditated speech by the most selfless character of all.

There are two Books in each volume and now that all six are before us the very high architectural quality of the romance is revealed. Book I builds up the main theme. In Book II that theme, enriched with much retrospective material, continues. Then comes the change. In III and V the fate of the company, now divided, becomes entangled with a huge complex of forces which are grouping and re-grouping themselves in relation to Mordor. The main theme, isolated from this, occupies IV and the early part of VI (the latter part of course giving all the resolutions). But we are never allowed to forget the intimate connection between it and the rest. On the one hand, the whole world is going to the war; the story rings with galloping hoofs, trumpets, steel on steel. On the other, very far away, miserable figures creep (like mice on a slag heap) through the twilight of Mordor. And all the time we know the fate of the world depends far more on the small movement than on the great. This is a structural invention of the highest order: it adds immensely to the pathos, irony, and grandeur of the tale.

This main theme is not to be treated in those jocular, whimsical tones now generally used by reviewers of 'juveniles'. It is entirely serious; the growing anguish, the drag of the Ring on the neck, the ineluctable conversion of Hobbit into hero in conditions which exclude all hope of fame or fear of infamy. Without the relief offered by the more crowded and bustling Books it would be hardly tolerable.

Yet those Books are not in the least inferior. Of picking out great moments (such as the cock-crow at the Siege of Gondor) there would be no end; I will mention two general (and totally different) excellences. One, surprisingly, is realisms. This war has the very quality of the war my generation knew. It is all here: the endless, unintelligible movement, the sinister quiet of the front when 'everything is now ready', the flying civilians, the lively, vivid friendships, the background of something like despair and the merry foreground, and such heaven-sent windfalls as a *cache* of choice tobacco 'salvaged' from a ruin. The author has told us elsewhere that his taste for fairy tale was wakened into maturity by active service;[2] that, no doubt, is why we can say of his war scenes (quoting Gimli the Dwarf), 'There is good rock here. This country has tough bones.'[3] The other excellence is that no individual, and no species, seems to exist only for the sake of the plot. All exist in their own right and would have been worth creating for their mere flavour even if they had been irrelevant. Treebeard would have served any other author (if any other could have conceived him) for a whole book. His eyes are 'filled up with ages of memory and long, slow, steady thinking.'[4] Through those ages his name has grown with him, so that he cannot now tell it; it would, by now, take too long to pronounce. When he learns that the thing they are standing on is a hill, he complains that this is but 'a hasty word' for that which has so much history in it.[5]

How far Treebeard can be regarded as a 'portrait of the author' must remain doubtful; but when he hears that some people want to identify the Ring with the hydrogen bomb, and Mordor with Russia, I think he might call it a 'hasty' word. How long do people think a world like his takes to grow? Do they think it can be done as quickly as a modern nation changes its Public Enemy Number One or as modern scientists invent new weapons? When Professor Tolkien began there was probably no nuclear fission and the contemporary incarnation of Mordor was a good deal nearer our shores. But the text itself teaches us that Sauron is eternal; the war of the Ring is only one of a thousand wars against him. Every time we shall be wise to fear his ultimate victory, after which there will be 'no more songs.'[6] Again and again we shall have good evidence that 'the wind is setting East, and the withering of all woods may be drawing near.'[7] Every time we win we shall know that our victory is impermanent. If we insist on asking for the moral of the story, that is the moral: a recall from facile optimism and wailing pessimism alike, to that hard, yet not quite desperate, insight into Man's unchanging predicament by which heroic ages have lived. It is here that the Norse affinity is strongest; hammer-strokes, but with compassion.

'But why', (some ask), 'why, if you must have a serious comment to make on the real life of men, must you do it by talking about a phantasmagoric never-never land of your own?' Because, I take it, one of the main things the author wants to say is that the real life of men is of that mythical and heroic quality. One can see the principle at work in his characterisation. Much that in a realistic work would be done by 'character delineation' is here done simply by making the character an elf, a dwarf, or a hobbit. The imagined beings have their insides on the outside; they are visible souls. And Man as a whole, Man pitted against the universe, have we seen him at all till we see that he is like a hero in a fairy tale? In the book Eomer rashly contrasts 'the green earth' with 'legends.' Aragorn replies that the green earth itself is 'a mighty matter of legend.'[8]

The value of the myth is that it takes all the things we know and restores to them the rich significance which has been hidden by 'the veil of familiarity.'[9] The child enjoys his cold meat (otherwise dull to him) by pretending it is buffalo, just killed with his own bow and arrow. And the child is wise. The real meat comes back to him more savoury for having been dipped in a story; you might say that only then it is the real meat. If you are tired of the real landscape, look at it in a mirror. By putting bread, gold, horse, apple, or the very roads into a myth, we do not retreat from reality, we rediscover it. As long as the story lingers in our mind, the real things are more themselves. This book applies the treatment not only to bread or apple but to good and evil, to our endless perils, our anguish, and our joys. By dipping them in myth we see them more clearly. I do not think he could have done it in any other way.

The book is too original and too opulent for any final judgment on a first reading. But we know at once that it has done things to us. We are not quite the same men. And though we must ration ourselves in our re-readings, I have little doubt that the book will soon take its place among the indispensables.

# 18

## Preface from *Essays Presented to Charles Williams*, ed. C. S. Lewis

~

In this book the reader is offered the work of one professional author, two dons, a solicitor, a friar, and a retired
army officer;[1] if he feels disposed to complain of hotch-
potch (which incidentally is an excellent dish; consult the
*Noctes Ambrosianae*)[2] I must reply that the variety displayed
by this little group is far too small to represent the width
of Charles Williams's friendships. Nor are we claiming to
represent it. Voices from many parts of England – voices
of people often very different from ourselves – would justly
rebuke our presumption if we did. We know that he was
as much theirs as ours: not only, nor even chiefly, because
of his range and versatility, great though these were, but
because, in every circle that he entered, he gave the whole
man. I had almost said that he was at everyone's disposal,
but those words would imply a passivity on his part, and all
who knew him would find the implication ludicrous. You
might as well say that an Atlantic breaker on a Cornish
beach is 'at the disposal' of all whom it sweeps off their
feet. If the authors of this book were to put forward any
claim, it would be, and that shyly, that they were for the
last few years of his life a fairly permanent nucleus among
his *literary* friends. He read us his manuscripts and we read

Published in C. S. Lewis (ed.), *Essays Presented to Charles Williams*
(London: Oxford University Press, 1947), pp. v–xiv.

him ours: we smoked, talked, argued, and drank together (I must confess that with Miss Dorothy Sayers I have seen him drink only tea: but that was neither his fault nor hers).

Of many such talks this collection is not unrepresentative. The first three essays are all on literature, and even on one aspect of literature, the narrative art. That is natural enough. His *All Hallows' Eve* and my own *Perelandra* (as well as Professor Tolkien's unfinished sequel to the *Hobbit*) had all been read aloud, each chapter as it was written. They owe a good deal to the hard-hitting criticism of the circle. The problems of narrative as such – seldom heard of in modern critical writings – were constantly before our minds. The last two essays are historical. Father Mathew's bears on an aspect of the Middle Ages which always seemed to Williams of deep significance and which had, indeed, been the common interest that first brought him and me together. The final essay carries us to seventeenth-century France. My brother's lifelong interest in the reign of Louis XIV was a bond between Williams and him which no one had foreseen when they first met. Those two, and Mr H. V. D. Dyson[3] of Merton, could often be heard in a corner talking about Versailles, *intendants*, and the *maison du roy*, in a fashion with which the rest of us could not compete. Between the literary and the historical essays stands Mr Barfield's work, which is literary and historical at once. We had hoped to offer the whole collection to Williams as what the Germans call a *Festschrift* when peace would recall him from Oxford to London. Death forestalled us; we now offer as a memorial what had been devised as a greeting.

Something must here be said to those who may ask 'Who was Charles Williams?' He had spent most of his life in the service of the Oxford University Press at Amen House, Warwick Square, London. He was a novelist, a poet, a dramatist, a biographer, a critic, and a theologian: a 'romantic theologian' in the technical sense which he himself invented for those words. A romantic theologian does not mean one who is romantic about theology but one who is theological about romance, one who considers the theological implications of those experiences which are called romantic. The belief that the most serious and ecstatic experiences either of human love or of imaginative literature have such theological implications, and that they can be healthy and fruitful only if the implications are diligently thought out and severely lived, is the root principle of all his work. His relation to the modern literary current was thus thoroughly 'ambivalent'. He could be grouped with the counter-romantics in so far as he believed untheologized romanticism (like Plato's 'unexamined life') to be sterile and mythological. On the other hand, he could be treated as the head of the resistance against the moderns in so far as he believed the romanticism which they were rejecting as senile to be really immature, and looked for a coming of age where they were huddling up a hasty and not very generous funeral. He will not fit into a pigeon-hole.

The fullest and most brilliant expression of his outlook is to be found in his mature poetry, and especially in *Taliessin through Logres* and *The Region of the Summer Stars*. As I have in preparation a much longer study of these works, I must here content myself with saying that they seem to me, both for the soaring and gorgeous novelty of their technique and for their profound wisdom, to be among the two or three most valuable books of verse produced in the century. Their outstanding quality is what I would call glory or splendour; a heraldic brightness of colour, a marble firmness of line, and an arduous exaltation. The note struck is very unlike that of the Nineteenth Century, and equally unlike that of most moderns. It is the work of a man who has learned much from Dante (the Dante of the *Paradiso*) and who might be supposed (though in fact he had not) to have learned much from Pindar. If its extreme difficulty does not kill it, this work ought to count for much in the coming years. I am speaking only of his mature work. He found himself late as a poet and in his earlier poems, I, for one, do not see any promise of what he finally became.

He is best known by his criticism. I have learned much from it – particularly from *The Figure of Beatrice* and *Poetry at Present*. But it is distressing that many people, on hearing the name Williams, should think chiefly or only of *The English Poetic Mind*, or even of his criticism at all, for it is probably the least valuable part of his work. Those who find the poetry too difficult would be much better advised to turn to the novels.

*The Greater Trumps*, *War in Heaven*, *Many Dimensions*, *The Place of the Lion*, *Descent into Hell*, and *All Hallows' Eve* present, under the form of exciting fantasy, some of the most important things Williams had to say. They have, I think, been little understood. The frank supernatural-ism and the frankly blood-curdling episodes have deceived readers who were accustomed to seeing such 'machines' used as toys and who supposed that what was serious must be naturalistic – or, worse still, that what was serious could not be gay. And in the earlier stories, it must be allowed, there were technical defects which stand between us and the author's meaning. There was a good deal of over-writing, of excess in the descriptions and, in dialogue, of a false brilliance. But this was overcome in the later work and in this respect the distance between *War in Heaven* and the sobriety and strength of the *Descent* and the *Eve* is a remarkable witness to his continually growing, self-correcting art. But the imagination and the spiritual insight had been there from the beginning; and it is these that always justify both the infernal and the paradisal turns of the story. They are never in excess of what the author most seriously intends. Hence the cathartic value of these fantasies. We are not likely in real life to meet an objective *succubus* as Wentworth does in *Descent into Hell*, nor to be haunted by a pterodactyl as Damaris Tighe is haunted in *The Place of the Lion*. But those who, like Wentworth, are following what seems to be love into the abyss of self-love will know in the end what the *succubus* means; and the frivolously academic who 'do research' into archetypal ideas without suspecting that these were ever anything more than raw material for doctorate theses, may one day awake, like Damaris, to find that they are infinitely mistaken.

I first heard of Charles Williams a great many years ago when a man who was sitting next to me at dinner (Dr. R. W. Chapman[4]) asked me if I had read any of his novels. He described them as 'spiritual shockers'. I was interested and made a mental note that this was an author to be looked into, but did nothing about it. A few years later I spent an evening at Exeter College in the rooms of Mr N. K. Coghill.[5] He was full of a book he had just read called *The Place of the Lion*, by Charles Williams. No man whom I have ever met describes another man's work better than

Mr Coghill (his descriptions of Kafka always seemed to me better even than Kafka himself) and I went home with his copy of *The Place of the Lion*. Twenty-four hours later I found myself, for the first time in my life, writing to an author I had never met to congratulate him on his book. By return of post I had an answer from Williams, who had received my letter when he was on the point of writing a similar letter to me about my *Allegory of Love*. After this, as may be supposed, we soon met and our friendship rapidly grew inward to the bone.

Until 1939 that friendship had to subsist on occasional meetings, though, even thus, he had already become as dear to all my Oxford friends as he was to me. There were many meetings both in my rooms at Magdalen and in Williams's tiny office at Amen House. Neither Mr Dyson nor my brother, Major W. H. Lewis, will forget a certain immortal lunch at Shirreff's in 1938 (he gave me a copy of *He Came Down From Heaven* and we ate kidneys 'enclosed', like the wicked man 'in their own fat')[6] nor the almost Platonic discussion which followed for about two hours in St Paul's churchyard. But in 1939 the Oxford University Press, and he with it, was evacuated to Oxford. From that time until his death we met one another about twice a week, sometimes more: nearly always on Thursday evenings in my rooms and on Tuesday mornings in the best of all public-houses for draught cider, whose name it would be madness to reveal. The removal to Oxford also produced other changes. The English Faculty was depleted by war and Williams was soon making an Oxford reputation both as a lecturer and as a private tutor. He became an honorary MA. It grew continually harder to remember that he had not always been at Oxford. I am afraid that in our pride we half-imagined that we must be the friends whom he had been in search of all his life. Only since his death have we fully realized what a small and late addition we were to the company of those who loved him, and whom he loved.

In appearance he was tall, slim, and straight as a boy, though grey-haired. His face we thought ugly: I am not sure that the word 'monkey' has not been murmured in this context. But the moment he spoke it became, as was also said, like the face of an angel – not a feminine angel in the debased tradition of some religious art, but a masculine angel, a spirit burning with intelligence and charity. He was nervous (not shy) to judge by the trembling of his fingers. One of the most characteristic things about him was his walk. I have often, from the top of a bus, seen him walking below me. The face and hair being then invisible, he might have passed for a boy in the early twenties, and perhaps a boy of some period when swords were worn. There was something of recklessness, something even of *panache*, in his gait. He did not in the least swagger: but if a clumsier man, like myself, had tried to imitate it a swagger would probably have been the result. To complete the picture you must add a little bundle under his left arm which was quite invariable. It usually consisted of a few proofs with a copy of *Time and Tide* folded round them. He always carried his head in the air. When he lectured, wearing his gown, his presence was one of the stateliest I have ever seen.

No man whom I have known was at the same time less affected and more flamboyant in his manners: and also more playful. The thing is very difficult to describe, partly because it is so seldom seen. Perhaps it will be best imagined if I track it to its sources, which were two. Firstly, he was a man fitted by temperament to live in an age of more elaborate courtesy than our own. He was nothing if not a ritualist. Had modern society permitted it he would equally have enjoyed kneeling and being knelt to, kissing hands and extending his hand to be kissed. Burke's 'unbought grace of life' was in him.[7] But secondly, even while enjoying such high pomps, he would have been aware of them as a game: not a silly game, to be laid aside in private, but a glorious game, well worth the playing. This two-edged attitude, banked down under the deliberate casualness of the modern fashion, produced his actual manners, which were liked by most, extremely disliked by a few. The highest compliment I ever heard paid to them was by a nun. She said that Mr Williams's manners implied a complete *offer* of intimacy without the slightest *imposition* of intimacy. He threw down all his own barriers without even implying that you should lower yours.

But here one of my collaborators breaks in upon me to say that this is not, after all, the true picture; that he, for his part, always found Williams a reserved man, one in whom, after years of friendship, there remained something elusive and incalculable. And that also seems to be true, though I doubt whether 'reserved' is the right name for it. I said before that he gave to every circle the whole man: all his attention, knowledge, courtesy, charity, were placed at your disposal. It was a natural result of that that you did not find out much about *him* – certainly not about those parts of him which your own needs or interests did not call into play. A selfless character, perhaps, always has this mysteriousness: and much more so when it is that of a man of genius.

This total offer of himself, but without that tacit claim which so often accompanies such offers, made his friendship the least exacting in the world, and explains the surprising width of his contacts. One kept on discovering that the most unlikely people loved him as well as we did. He was extremely attractive to young women and (what is rare) none of his male friends ever wondered why: nor did it ever do a young woman anything but immense good to be attracted by Charles Williams. Yet, on the other hand, all my memories of him are in bachelor surroundings where he was so at home – and to us speedily so indispensable – that you might have thought them the only surroundings he knew. That face – angel's or monkey's – comes back to me most often seen through clouds of tobacco smoke and above a pint mug, distorted into helpless laughter at some innocently broad buffoonery or eagerly stretched forward in the cut and parry of prolonged, fierce, masculine argument and 'the rigour of the game'.

Such society, unless all its members happen to be of one trade, makes heavy demands on a man's versatility. And we were by no means of one trade. The talk might turn in almost any direction, and certainly skipped 'from grave to gay, from lively to severe'[8]: but wherever it went, Williams was ready for it. He seemed to have no 'pet subject'. Though he talked copiously one never felt that he had dominated the evening. Nor did one easily remember particular 'good things' that he had said: the importance of his presence was, indeed, chiefly made clear by the gap which was left on the rare occasions when he did not turn up. It then became clear that some principle of liveliness and cohesion had been withdrawn from the whole party: lacking him, we did not completely possess one another. He was (in the Coleridgian language) an 'esemplastic' force.[9] He was also, though not a professional scholar, one of the best informed of us all and will always stand in my mind as a cheering proof of how far a man can go with few languages and imperfect schooling. On the ancients and on the early Middle Ages there were one or two present with whom he could not compete, nor had he an exact knowledge of any of the great philosophers: but in history, theology, legend, comparative religion, and (above all) English literature from Shakespeare down, his knowledge was surprising. Malory, Shakespeare, Milton, Johnson, Scott, Wordsworth, Tennyson, Patmore, and Chesterton he seemed to have at his fingers' ends. Before he came I had passed for our best conduit of quotations: but he easily outstripped me. He delighted to repeat favourite passages, and nearly always both his voice and the context got something new out of them. He excelled at showing you the little grain of truth or felicity in some passage generally quoted for ridicule, while at the same time he fully enjoyed the absurdity: or, contrariwise, at detecting the little falsity or dash of silliness in a passage which you, and he, also, admired. He was both a 'debunker' and (if I may coin the word) a 'rebunker'. *Fidelia vulnera amantis.*[10]

This double-sidedness was the most strongly developed character of his mind. He might have appropriated Kipling's thanks

> to Allah who gave me two
> Separate sides to my head,[11]

except that he would have had to omit the word *separate*. The duality was much subtler than Kipling's, who in that poem really (I am afraid) intends little more than a repetition of Montaigne's *Que sçais-je?*[12] In Williams the two sides lived in a perpetual dance or lovers' quarrel of mutual mockery. In most minds, and in his, the lower mocks at the higher; but in his the higher also mocked at the lower.

Thus on the one hand there lived in Williams a sceptic and even a pessimist. No man – and least of all the common run of antitheists – could have written a better attack on Christianity than he. He used to say that if he were rich enough to build a church he would dedicate it to St Thomas Didymus Sceptic.[13] He toyed with the idea that he and I should collaborate in a book of animal stories from the Bible, told by the animals concerned – the story of Jonah told by the whale[14] or that of Elisha told by the two she-bears.[15] The bears were to be convinced that God exists and is good by their sudden meal of children. He maintained that the prayer in which we give thanks 'for our creation' could be joined in only by an act of wholly supernatural faith. 'Thanks!' he would say, and then followed an eloquent pause. He was ready to accept as a revealed doctrine the proposition that existence is good: but added that it would never have occurred to him, unaided, to suspect this. He vehemently denied that he had any natural desire for life after death. In one of his earlier poems the man who is made ruler of three cities says

> I bore the labour, Lord,
> But cannot stomach the reward.

He even said, mocking himself while he said it, that if he were saved, the acceptance of eternal life would be not so much the guerdon as the final act of obedience. He also said that when young people came to us with their troubles and discontents, the worst thing we could do was to tell them that they were not so unhappy as they thought. Our reply ought rather to begin, 'But *of course....*' For young people usually are unhappy, and the plain truth is often the greatest relief we can give them. The world is painful in any case: but it is quite unbearable if everyone gives us the idea that we are meant to be liking it. Half the trouble is over when that monstrous demand is withdrawn. What is unforgivable if judged as an hotel may be very tolerable as a reformatory. It is one of the many paradoxes in Williams that while no man's conversation was less gloomy in *tone* – it was, indeed, a continual flow of gaiety, enthusiasm, and high spirits – no man at times said darker things. He never forgot the infinite menaces of life, the unremitted possibility of torture, maiming, madness, bereavement, and (over all) that economic insecurity which, as he said in *War in Heaven*, poisons our sorrows as well as modifying our joys.

But that was only one side of him. This scepticism and pessimism were the expression of his feelings. High above them, overarching them like a sky, were the things he believed, and they were wholly optimistic. They did not negate the feelings: they mocked them. To the Williams who had accepted the fruition of Deity itself as the true main goal of man, and who deeply believed that the sufferings of this present time were as nothing in comparison, the other Williams, the Williams who wished to be annihilated, who would rather not have been born, was in the last resort a comic figure. He did not struggle to crush it as many religious people would have done. He saw its point of view. All that it said was, on a certain level, so very reasonable. He did not believe that God Himself wanted that frightened, indignant, and voluble creature to be annihilated; or even silenced. If it wanted to carry its hot complaints to the very Throne, even that, he felt, would be a permitted absurdity. For was not that very much what Job had done? It was true, Williams added, that the Divine answer had taken the surprising form of inviting Job to study the hippopotamus and the crocodile. But Job's impatience had been approved. His apparent blasphemies had been accepted. The weight of the divine displeasure had been reserved for the 'comforters', the self-appointed advocates on God's side, the people who tried to show that all was well – 'the sort of people', he said, immeasurably dropping his lower jaw and fixing me with his eyes – 'the sort of people who wrote books on the Problem of Pain'.

I have heard (from a lady) that he himself, before he went into hospital, had some expectation that he was going there to die. We, his male friends at Oxford, had had no notion that he was even ill until we heard that he was in the Radcliffe Infirmary; nor did we then suspect that the trouble was serious. I heard of his death at the Infirmary itself, having walked up there with a book I wanted to lend him, expecting this news that day as little (almost) as I expected to die that day myself. It was a Tuesday morning, one of our times of meeting. I thought he would have given me messages to take on to the others. When I joined them with my actual message – it was only a few minutes' walk from the Infirmary but, I remember, the very streets looked different – I had some difficulty in making them believe or even understand what had happened. The world seemed to us at that moment primarily a *strange* one.

That sense of strangeness continued with a force which sorrow itself has never quite swallowed up. This experience of loss (the greatest I have yet known) was wholly unlike what I should have expected. We now verified for ourselves what so many bereaved people have reported; the ubiquitous presence of a dead man, as if he had ceased to meet us in particular places in order to meet us everywhere. It is not in the least like a haunting. It is not in the least like the bitter-sweet experiences of memory. It is vital and bracing; it is even, however the word may be misunderstood and derided, exciting. A lady, writing to me after his death, used the word *stupor* (in its Latin sense) to describe the feeling which Williams had produced on a certain circle in London; it would almost describe the feeling he produced on us after he had died. There is, I dare say, no empirical proof that such an experience is more than subjective. But for those who accept on other grounds the Christian faith, I suggest that it is best understood in the light of some words that one of his friends said to me as we sat in Addison's Walk just after the funeral. 'Our Lord told the disciples it was expedient for them that He should go away for otherwise the Comforter would not come to them. I do not think it blasphemous to suppose that what was true archetypally, and in eminence, of His death, may, in the appropriate degree, be true of the deaths of all His followers.'

So, at any rate, many of us felt it to be. No event has so corroborated my faith in the next world as Williams did simply by dying. When the idea of death and the idea of

Williams thus met in my mind, it was the idea of death that was changed.

He was buried in St Cross churchyard, where lie also the bodies of Kenneth Grahame and of P. V. M. Benecke.[16]

# 19

## A sacred poem: Charles Williams, *Taliessin Through Logres* (Oxford University Press, 1938)

~

The only reason for reading a difficult poem is some assurance that it contains goodness great enough to outweigh the evil of its difficulty. For Mr Williams' *Taliessin* I have such assurance, partly from his previous works, and partly from what the poem itself discloses even at a first reading.

It makes me see things: snow that 'falls over brick and prickle',[1] a star 'that rode by through the round window in the sky of Camelot',[2] a bucket from a well that as 'a round plane of water rose shining in the sun';[3] or even 'the source of all stone, The rigid tornado, the schism and first strife of primeval rock with itself.'[4] It also delights my ear. The result of its clashing accents is as if we were being continually thrown up or kept off the ground; no verse is, in the Greek sense of the word, more meteorous. I tremble to call Mr Williams Pindaric lest I should rouse associations of Cowley and Dryden.[5] But Pindar is the poet I think of in reading *Taliessin*, with its combination of jagged weight and soaring movement, its ability to narrate while remaining lyric, and (above all) its prevailing quality of glory – its blaze.

Review published in *Theology*, vol. 38 (April 1939), pp. 268–76.

Of the difficulties some are legitimate, some not. When Mr Williams uses 'who fly the porphyry stair'[6] to mean those who fly up, or ascend, not those who shun or avoid, the stair, he is disobeying the language. In the 'background' which his poem assumes he is sometimes guilty of a little 'privatism'; but in the main he demands of us familiarity with books which we certainly ought to know – the Bible, Malory's *Morte d'Arthur*, the *Decline and Fall*. It is also desirable to have read his own essay *He Came Down from Heaven*:[7] indeed, three doctrines from that book are so worked into the texture of the poem that they had better be restated here.

I. The Fall. Genesis means what it says. Man, knowing nothing but good, aspired to know good and evil. This was indeed to know 'as gods',[8] for God knows not only the good He has made but all unrealized possibilities, including those that are evil. Hence in the poem –

> I remembered how the Archbishop in Caeleon at a
>     feast
> preached that before the making of man or beast
> the Emperor knew all carved contingent shapes.[9]

This knowledge man desired, asking himself in Paradise –

> Am I too long meanly retired
> in the poor space of joy's single dimension?
> Does not God vision the principles at war?
> Let us grow to the height of God and the Emperor:
> Let us gaze, son of man, on the Acts in
>     contention.[10]

But man's knowledge is by experience, not by 'pure intelligence.'[11] To know evil means, for him, to experience it. And since all being is good, this means to experience good as evil. Thus for fallen man his heaven-built body becomes an obscenity, and virtue a law fruitful of death, and God Himself 'the headless Emperor'[12] the anti-God. 'The feet of creation walk backward.'[13]

II. 'The Theology of Romantic Love.'[14] Mr Williams combines two positions not often held together. On the one hand, he is with Blake and Lawrence in glorification of the body. Caucasia, which represents its least honourable area, is thus celebrated:

> The Emperor's sun shone on each round mount,
> double fortalices defending dales of fertility.
> The bright blades shone in the craft of the dancing
>    war;
> the stripped maids laughed for joy of the province,
> founded in the base of space,
> in the rounded bottom of the Emperor's glory.[15]

On the other hand, Mr Williams reaffirms the amatory doctrine of the *Vita Nuova* with complete conviction.[16]

III. 'Substitution' or 'exchange.'[17] Anselm was right in holding a substitutional, but not in holding a 'forensic', doctrine of the Atonement. Vicariousness depends on no 'transaction' or 'legal fiction', being the most familiar thing in the world, a fact of daily experience. The taunt 'He saved others; himself he cannot save' is a definition of the Kingdom.[18] What some thought most fantastic in the author's greatest romance (*Descent into Hell*) is serious.[19]

The everlasting house the soul discovers
is always another's; we must lose our own ends;
we must always live in the habitation of our lovers,
my friend's shelter for me, mine for him.[20]

The type of substitution in the poem is Percivale's sister, who in Malory (xvi, xi) 'bled a dish full of blood to heal a lady, wherefore she died.' The parody of substitution is money, the liberated symbol which becomes perilously autonomous: 'small crowns, small dragons', 'the long file of whose snouts crosses the empire.'[21]

The greatest, but also the most legitimate, of *Taliessin*'s difficulties lies in its symbolism. I define the difference between Allegory and Symbolism thus: in Allegory the images stand for concepts (giant Despair, Mr Legality), in Symbolism for something the poet has experienced but which he has not reduced, perhaps cannot reduce, to a concept. Allegory can always be translated back into the concepts: the 'meaning' of a symbolical work cannot be stated in conceptual language because it is too concrete. The thing meant by the poet has probably met him in a variety of situations, and therefore, if we try to treat his work as allegory, we always find that each image has too many 'meanings.' The procedure is not, however, useless, provided that we do not take it for more than a scaffolding to our real reading of the poem. Let us apply it to Mr Williams' central symbol, Byzantium.

(1) The actual Byzantine Empire ruling its 'themes' or provinces by the Acts, the Pandect, and the Code, which issue from the presence chamber at the top of the porphyry stair where 'the lions roar that stand in the Byzantine glory.'[22] These Acts, written in 'Greek minuscula', are

translated into 'all the dialects.'[23] Logothetes run down the stairs,[24] chariots go 'clattering' out of Byzantium to bear missives to the whole empire. Outside the empire we have Broceliande in the west, Islam in the south, to the north mere 'mammoth and bear.' Eastward the world fades away into the utterly unknown, the inverted, the antipodes – P'O-Lu. It is supposed, unhistorically, that Britain was part of the Byzantine Empire.

(2) Man. But the diagram on the endleaf must not be taken too seriously. It works well for 'the breasts of *intellego* and *credo*' in the University of Paris, and for the 'Italian "hands"' – the operative and manipulative organs used in bridge-building, agriculture, and the celebration of the Eucharist ('the heart-breaking manual acts of the Pope').[25] Jerusalem is in the genitals because the author follows the tradition that Jerusalem is on the site of Paradise, a place of generation and regeneration. But the position of Byzantium itself at the navel, though appropriate enough, is not to be stressed. Byzantium, when distinguished from the whole empire, is the total Man or Person as opposed to his members. Thus energy arising from the loins but humanized in the ἡγεμονικόν is 'stuff of Caucasia fashioned in Byzantium.'[26] In fact, Byzantium might as well be the head as the navel: the location of Logres at the head is best disregarded. Logres is mainly the here and now, middle-earth, the scene of the poet's action. It must be remembered that the endleaf is a fanciful comment on the poem, not a 'key.'

(3) Order, discipline, civilization. When we meet a slave in the stocks and another whose back is scarred by 'the hazel's stripes', Mr Williams is not showing us the 'reverse side' of Camelot's glory. For those slaves the stocks and

the rod are a good – the appearance of law proper to their stage of development. When Taliessin awaits the moment to charge at Mount Badon, he sees Virgil 'civilized centuries away' seeking 'for the invention of the City by the phrase.'[27] Identifying that imposition of form upon matter with his own imposition of the King's will upon the barbarians, 'he fetched the pen of his spear from its bearer', and as he advanced, 'the Æneid's beaked lines swooped on Actium.'[28] (A German professor said to me a year ago 'The last war was a war between Homer and Virgil – and Virgil was on your side.')

(4) The Divine Order, 'the army of unalterable law.'[29] Hence –

> In a train of golden cars
> the Emperor went above,
> for over me in my riding
> shot seven golden stars.[30]

The Emperor is God. The Logothetes translating the Acts ('phenomenally abating' them 'to kinds and kindreds')[31] represent what Plato has told us in *Republic* 476 (ἓν ἕκαστον εἶναι, τῇ δὲ τῶν πράξεων κ.τ.λ. κοινωνίᾳ . . . πολλά φαίνεσθαι).[32] The Presence Chamber, approached by the porphyry stair, is the all-explanatory Beatific Vision.

> a tangle of compensations,
> every joint a centre,
> and every centre a jewel.
> Each moment there is the midmost.[33]

Treated as an allegory, Byzantium is all these things and more. If anyone asks, 'Why does he not say what he means?' or 'How am I to know which he means in each place?' we must reply that the poet has not started with concepts like 'Man' or 'Order.' He started with a something in his experience, characterized by glory, but also by a strict or mathematic quality – something that meets him in the life of a great jurist (see *Many Dimensions*),[34] in the gesture of a policeman on point duty (see *The Greater Trumps*),[35] in the orderly conduct of a publishing house (see the Dedication to *Taliessin*),[36] and also in the human body, and in all that he knows and believes in the Divine Order. Byzantium is not a communal fancy-dress for half a dozen concepts: it is an imaginative net to catch that single, utterly concrete constituent of experience which has no name and which we come to know by using the symbol Byzantium. In so far as the poem succeeds we shall find ourselves recognizing 'Byzantium', henceforth in all sorts of hitherto unrelated experiences of our own.

The choice of Byzantium depends principally on the fact that we think of the Byzantiune Empire as something splendid and exotic, but also stiff, formalized, hierarchical; and this union of qualities does justice to the union of glory and severity in Mr Williams' vision. This is essential. His celebration of the human body, for example, has nothing to do with the gulfs of unmediated feeling. He teaches a 'doctrine of Euclidean love':[37] anatomists and drawing-masters are better teachers of the body's importance than psycho-analysts. It is 'the accurate flash'[38] of Iseult's eyes and the perception that, in her, 'curves of golden life define the straightness of a perfect line'[39] by which Palomides is ravished. The hazel wands which make good rods for barbarian backs are also measuring-rods. With them the long roads of the empire are measured out so that in wooded Logres 'the nuts of the uncut hazel fall Down the cut hazel's way.'[40] Virgil is painted on the wall of the presence chamber handing down to Taliessin 'a shoot of hazel – the hexameter, the decasyllabic line.'[41] At the crowning of Arthur this πέρας or *mesur*a is seen riding in peaceful triumph on its opposite:

> The beasts of Broceliande, the fish of Nimue,
> hierarchic, republican, the glory of Logres,
> patterns of the Logos in the depth of the sun.
> Taliessin in the crowd beheld the compélled brutes,
> wildness formalized, images of mathematics.[42]

With this passage I have raised the question of what lies beyond Byzantium, and this reminds me that other symbols have to be considered. Mr Williams' map marks the road to P'O-Lu in the east, but not the road to Broceliande, which as we learn from the text, lies west of Britain. P'O-Lu we know – the antipodes where the 'headless Emperor moves on an inarticulate sea' where 'the Roman hands', 'the substantial instruments of being',[43] are lost. Broceliande is more difficult. It is divided from P'O-Lu by the width of the whole map, but in a round world East and West meet. Out of it comes Merlin and into it he returns. Nimue lives there. Crude beings, unformed energies, 'unthumbed shapes of apes',[44] grow there and stream out of it. It is not evil;

> there too strife
> is except growth from the roots, nor reaction but
>   repose;
> vigours of joy drive up: rich-ringed movements
> thick in their trunks thrive, young-leaved their
>   voices.[45]

Broceliande is rather like 'the mothers' in Faust, the cave of Demogorgon in Shelley, the 'abyss' in Böhme's theosophy.[46] The theologian, tolerating no ultimate dualism, must determine, if he can, the relation of Broceliande to the Emperor; but for the imagination it must generally, I expect, where it is not ignored, be felt as something outside the empire, or meeting the empire only at some *coincidentia oppositorum* which is off the map. At all events the world of the poem would be incomplete without it.

Merlin comes nearest of all Mr Williams' figures to allegory. He is called 'time's metre', and even 'time.'[47] Yet he is more than a mere 'Father Time' with an hour glass. He assists at the birth of Galahad (a type of Christ), and 'the force of the worlds'[48] is in him. He is operative history, the mover, that which brings things to pass. He is the relentless obstacle to the fulfilment of Arthur's fantasies. Conjuring 'at the height of the thin night air of Quinquagesima' when Galahad was born, he sees, in vision, the King 'dreaming of a red grail in an ivory Logres': but –

> magic
> throws no truck with dreams; the rod thrust by.[49]

It will be seen that Arthur is by no means the hero of the poem. Mr Williams' argument is the Fall and the Redemption in Logres. Logres falls partly through the evil and contradiction inherent in every human order as such, partly through the actual sins of its leaders. The first is made clearest in the section entitled 'The King's Coins' – 'What can be saved without order? and how order? ... What without coinage or with coinage can be saved?'[50] For the second the author follows those episodes in Malory which are more significant than Malory saw. He connects the two tragedies of ignorance, Balin's fratricide and Arthur's incest, in a passage of extraordinary power. He makes good use of a heavenly irony in the old story (I think Professor Vinaver first did justice to it)[51] whereby Lancelot, having sinned through love, offends against the code of love to his own shame but by that offence begets Galahad the redeemer. The birth of Galahad is the crisis of the poem. At the moment of his birth the tide turned:

> The Emperor in Byzantium nodded to the
>    exarches;
> it was night still when the army began to move,
> embarking, disembarking, before dawn Asia
> awoke to hear the songs, the shouts, the wheels.[52]

There is only one section in this poem which, in my opinion, sinks below the general level, and that is 'The Coming of Galahad' (not to be confused with the magnificent birth-story, 'The Son of Lancelot'), in which the obscurities are to me impenetrable and the style is dangerously near a mannerism. For the rest, the poem has greatness enough to justify the intensive study it exacts. It shows its greatness, in Pascal's words, not by being 'at an extremity', but by being simultaneously 'at two extremities and filling all the spaces between.'[53] The material may be called, in more senses than one, 'romantic'; the technique is modern both for good and evil – for evil in the obscurities it tolerates, for good in the fresh, harsh energy of its unstaled diction and the headlight sharpness of its vision. Mr Williams does not need by any deprecatory gestures to dissociate his Arthurianism from that of Morris and Tennyson. Some readers who think of the story solely in 'Victorian' terms may prove incurable: but in reality there is a passion in Mr Williams' very rhythms that forbids him to sink to mere 'charm.' But we must also avoid a misunderstanding in the opposite direction, a 'modernist' misunderstanding. Mr Williams can be harsh, he can talk of 'jakes and latrines',[54] and of other things which would once have been thought prosaic. But the precise differentia of his genius lies in offering us something much less usual. He has got all necessary 'disillusionment' over before the poem begins, so that no more need be said on that well-worn theme, and we can proceed at once to something positive. We find throughout an understanding of health, of discipline, and (above all) of courtesy, which are rare at the present time. No poem expresses more clarity or less indulgence.

But perhaps its greatest gift to us is what I have called the quality of Glory. The thing is new, but can only be indicated by reference to those old things which are least unlike it. I have already mentioned Pindar, and I am prepared to maintain, without one moment forgetting Wordsworth and Gray, that the third piece in *Taliessin* (the 'Vision of the Empire') is the first real example in English of 'the greater ode.' If this comparison proves unhelpful to some readers, I would refer them to the Archangels' song from the Prologue in Heaven to *Faust* and tell them that in Mr Williams they will find something of its golden, noonday vitality.

But what finally convinced me that he has written a great poem was a transformation which my judgement under-went in reading it. I liked its 'flavour' from the first, but found it so idiosyncratic that I thought the book might be what Lamb called a 'favourite', a thing not for all days or all palates, like *Tristram Shandy* or the *Arcadia*. But as

I went on I found bit after bit of my 'real world' falling into its place within the poem. I found pair after pair of opposites harmoniously reconciled. I began to see that what had seemed a deliciously private universe was the common universe after all: that this apparently romantic and even wilful poem was really 'classic' and central. I do not think this can happen in a minor work. And I think, to compare great things with small, that in this respect the poem bears a significant resemblance to the Faith it celebrates. The entrance is not very big, not very obvious, but recognizably made for all kinds of men; but, once inside, there is room for everybody, food for most diverse stomachs, medicine for many different diseases.

# 20

# Charles Williams, *Taliessin Through Logres* (London: Oxford University Press, 1945)

~

This is the first of two volumes which contain all that we have of Charles Williams' unfinished cycle on the Matter of Britain.[1] Its appearance marked a turning point in some more senses than one. It was the first major work in the author's mature manner. It was the first application of a radically 'modern' poetic technique to radically romantic material. And it was almost the first reunion since Greek times of a narrative content with an elaborate lyric form; indeed, it reclaimed for the greater ode its long-lost Pindaric provinces.

The basic elements of Williams' technique were two: (1) An irregular disposition of internal rhymes and half rhymes. (2) The use of clashing stresses – by which I mean stressed syllables (which are usually long as well as stresses) coming together with no unstressed syllables between them. Spondees and even *trimakra* abound. It is from these that the peculiar buoyancy of his verse is derived. Thus his music (except once in *Palomides before his Christening*) is at the opposite pole from Mr Eliot's. In reading Mr Eliot one seems to be listening to a voice that is always on the point of dying away – no poetry can more powerfully convey the sense of stillness, hushed expectancy, vacancy, death.

Review published in *The Oxford Magazine*, vol. 64 (14 March 1946), pp. 248–50.

In Williams, on the other hand, we are conscious of soaring energy, as if huge masses were being hurled to great heights, or as if we ourselves were being repeatedly flung up (into sunlight) on the crests of waves. It is the most masculine and arduous verse this century has yet produced. Its severity, when relieved, is relieved not by any of that softness or songfulness which the word 'lyrical' suggests to many modern readers, but by a kind of high playfulness. Like most poets he has unconsciously described, at the moment of illustrating, his own qualities –

> The bright blades shone in the craft of the dancing
> war;
> The stripped maids laughed for joy of the
> province[2] –

where you will spoil the whole effect if you do not give full value to the *trimakra* ('bright blades shone' and 'stripped maids laughed').

At first sight this book will seem as difficult as Blake. But fortunately the difficulty does not result from a purely private mythology; Malory, Gibbon, and the author's own *He Came Down from Heaven* will tell us nearly all we need to know. Before M. Vinaver had written on the Arthurian story, Williams had already read it in a sense very different from that of Tennyson and the Pre-Raphaelites. Arthurian Logres is for him the civilization to which the Grail was offered and which failed (save for the 'remnant' symbolised by Galahad) to rise to the occasion, and so dwindled from being Logres into being merely Britain.[3] In order that the Sender of the Grail may also be represented in the poem, Logres is feigned to be a 'theme' or province of the Byzantine Empire, and the Emperor symbolises God.

But how did the failure arise? Williams finds the answer in the story of the Fall, interpreted *more suo*.[4] The Emperor made nothing but good. Man desires to know evil also. But this can only mean to know good *as* evil (hence 'the lost name, the fool's shame' – man's revulsion from his own body), or else to know things that might have existed but did not; those 'contingent shapes'[5] which the Emperor knew as possibilities but refused to create. Hence a line which by itself would be sheerly meaningless is for those who have mastered the poem charged with immense and sinister significance. 'Did you not see', asks Merlin, 'the contingent knowledge of the Emperor floating into sight?'[6]

The ultimate subject of the poem is, of course, not Arthur, but Man. It is a picture of human life as Williams saw it – not as Hell (like Hardy), not as a Development (like Bridges), nor as a prologue to heaven-on-earth (like the Marxists), but as a place where the highest established good always invites, and yet in the end always rejects, the descent of a higher good still. Thus the 'obedience' of Islam and the 'fallacy of rational virtue'[7] in Logres partly express, but for that very reason also resist, the will of the Emperor.

If it be asked why this should be expressed through the medieval legend of Arthur and an unhistorical image of Byzantium, there are answers in plenty. Medieval chivalry and mysticism are themselves the most striking example of the process Williams is concerned with. That great and elaborate attempt at a spiritual civilization seemed, up to a point, to be preparing all the conditions in which the higher good could have descended: but something went wrong. A medieval legend is, therefore, an appropriate, 'objective correlative'[8] (as Mr Eliot would say) for the poet's theme. And in this particular legend that theme is already almost expressed – waiting, demanding to be disengaged – in the subtle and tragically intertwined conflict between Carbonek and Camelot, Launcelot and Galahad.

The choice of Byzantium to represent the unmoved centre, the Noumenon beyond all these phenomena, is dictated by a deep necessity in the poet's imagination. Byzantium is associated in everyone's mind with hierarchical rigidity, with ritual and straight lines. It thus responds to a passion for the orderly, the disciplined, and even the geometrical, which led Williams constantly to envisage the good in a 'Byzantine' form. If he had been bred (as he was not) on Greek thought from his earliest years he could not have felt more clearly or continuously the hunger of the ἄπειρον for πέρας. This is why Logres and, beyond it, the sea-wood of Broceliande come together with the 'Byzantine glory' in his poem.[9]

And that also is why the human body has for him such significance; for there he thought one can see geometry in the very moment of turning into life, warmth and fertility in the very act of submitting to measure and definition – can see, in his own words,

> How curves of golden life define
> The straightness of a perfect line.[10]

Things that are said about a work of this sort – a work which must be either great or an almost total failure – while it is still new are apt to sound very ridiculous even twenty years later. I will confine myself to giving a few of my reasons for anticipating that it will finally take its place among our great poems.

(1) The world into which this poem carries me is emphatically not mine. My admiration is not based on that secret affinity which makes even the first reading of some books feel like a home-coming. It is therefore, in my opinion, more likely to be a just admiration. Taliessin takes me where I never intended to go and where I remain a foreigner: but it takes me. *Ecce deus fortior me.*[11]

(2) Closely connected with the preceding point is the fact that the poem, once read, lays its images permanently on the mind. The 'light of flooding seas'[12] pouring after Taliessin in the wood, 'Thule, the skull-stone',[13] the snow falling 'over brick and prickle',[14] the heraldic massing of painted metal in 'The Crowning', the unicorn's head hanging above two lovers in a forest, the terrible flint shapes of the islands and the more terrible flint face of Morgause – these lie on the memory with the uncompromising solidity of something we have dreamed for ourselves.

(3) The total effect of the poetry is something more and better than any enumeration of its qualities would lead one to predict. You have a severe and hard melody, a philosophical content deep, dark, and searching, and a predominance of images that are either gorgeous or frankly disquieting. And there is very little use made of Nature in her softer and sunnier aspects to relieve all this – always excepting the recurrent image of the human body. How comes it, then, that our actual experience of the poem is full of something I must almost call gaiety, some kind of shy, elusive laughter; angelic rather than elfin laughter, suggesting that neither the tragedy nor the

Byzantine splendour (though indispensable) have quite the last word? How, indeed – unless we have here a work which in the long run says *exactly* what the poet meant and what cannot otherwise be described?

(4) If this poem is good at all it is entirely irreplaceable in the sense that no other book whatever comes anywhere near reminding you of it or being even a momentary substitute for it. If you can't get an orange, then a lemon or a grapefruit will give you a taste that has something in common with it. But if you can't get a pineapple, then nothing else will even faintly put you in mind of it. Taliessin is like the pineapple. You may like or dislike that taste; but once you have tasted it, you know you can get it from no other book in the whole world. It is as unique as *Tristram Shandy* or the *Pervigilium Veneris.*[15]

To me, I confess, it seems unlikely that a poem which passes these four tests can be other than good; and if this is at all good, it must be very great indeed. But I must not attempt prophecy. The question will be decided not by us and our kind, but by the unknown young poets who are at the moment finding their feet; *maneat nostros ea cura nepotes.*[16]

\* \* \*

*In between reviewing Charles Williams's two volumes of Arthurian poems mentioned above, Lewis completed the third of his cosmic trilogy,* That Hideous Strength *(1945) which made use of many Arthurian elements. Perhaps the one that meant most to Lewis was his explanation of 'Logres'. In Chapter 17, part 4, Dr Dimble, the Arthurian expert, explains:*

*There was a moment in the sixth century when something that is always trying break through into this country nearly succeeded. Logres was our name for it – it will do as well as another. And then, gradually we began to see all English history in a new way. We discovered the haunting. . . How something we may call Britain is always haunted by something we may call Logres. Haven't you noticed that we are two countries? After every Arthur, a Mordred; behind every Milton, a Cromwell. . . What they mistake for hypocrisy is really the struggle between Logres and Britain.*

That Hideous Strength *was followed by an invitation to take part in a symposium entitled 'What France Means to You' in* La France Libre, *a magazine published in London with the intention of helping the allies in France. As is seen below in Lewis's contribution to the symposium, Lewis had come to see that each country is haunted by its better self:*

### What France Means to Me[a]

On m'a demandé d'écrire quelques mots sur la France, et plus particulièrement sur son avenir. Des circonstances futures, nous ne savons rien; et nous ne pouvons imaginer l'avenir d'un être vivant que d'après son passé et son présent. Ce qui me conduit à me demander ce que la France a été pour l'homme. Inévitablement, je pense d'abord à la France médiévale: car c'est au moyen âge que votre nation a exercé sur l'Europe une hégémonie spirituelle que ni elle, ni aucune autre nation, n'a égalée depuis lors. Avant tout, la France représente les Croisades,

[a] Published in *La France Libre*, no. 7.42 (15 April 1944). Translated by G. E. M. Lippiatt.

la Chanson de Roland, la cathédrale de Chartres, le Cycle d'Arthur, l'Université de Paris. Dans tout cela, ce qui frappe, c'est l'éclat: éclat des épées, de la courtoisie, de la logique. En second lieu, je pense à la France « éclairée », celle de Voltaire et des Encyclopédistes. L'éclat en a pâli, mais la clarté demeure. Cette France-là, je la considère un peu comme mon ennemie, mais c'est une noble ennemie; à défaut d'amour, elle m'inspire du respect. Enfin, pour être tout à fait franc avec vous, je pense à une troisième France, celle où les pires cancers du monde moderne ont trouvé leur climat d'élection, celle où adorent flâner les Américains décadents, celle où Edgar Poë passe pour un grand poète, celle des petits « mouvements » vermiculaires, du Dadaïsme, du Surréalisme et des Messes Noires – celle qui au pays même de la Raison a dressé l'idole de la Bêtise.

Il semble que votre être soit double. Sans doute en est-il de même de toutes les nations; je vois qu'il en est de même de mon pays. Derrière l'Angleterre de Sidney, je distingue (hélas!) celle de Cecil Rhodes. Si l'une affranchit les esclaves, l'autre s'engraisse à faire la traite. Nous qui avons failli inventer la Liberté avons aussi péché contre elle plus que presque toute autre nation. Pour vous comme pour nous, le Démon est véritablement l'envers de l'être authentique; il incite les concitoyens de Shelley à la Tyrannie, comme ceux d'Abélard à la Bêtise. L'avenir dépend, pour chacun de nos deux pays, du choix que nous ferons entre notre bon et notre mauvais génie. Est-il trop tard pour retrouver cette autre France, cette autre Angleterre?

Pour les retrouver, il ne suffit pas d'y penser. Ce n'est pas d'«idéal» ni d'«inspiration » que nous avons besoin, mais

144

de simple probité, de charité, de diligence, pour faire face successivement à toutes les tâches qui s'imposeront. Je ne sais si les Français ou les Anglais, ou les Allemands (qui, eux non plus, n'ont pas toujours connu le seul Démon) parviendront à redevenir eux-mêmes. Le salut d'un peuple, comme celui d'un individu, est toujours possible, mais aussi impossible à prédire; car nous avons des volontés libres, et l'avenir reste à faire.

*

I have been asked to write a few words on France, and more specifically on her future. Concerning future circumstances, we know nothing; and we cannot imagine the future of a living being except according to its past and present. This leads me to ask what France has been for humanity. Inevitably, I think first of medieval France; for it is in the Middle Ages that your nation exerted over Europe a spiritual hegemony that neither she, nor any other nation, has equalled since. Above all, France means the Crusades, the *Chanson de Roland*, the cathedral of Chartres, the Arthurian cycle, the University of Paris. In all these, what strikes one is brilliance: the brilliance of swords, of courtliness, of logic. Secondly, I think of 'enlightened' France, that of Voltaire and the Encyclopédistes. The brilliance has paled, but the clarity remains. This France to some degree I consider my enemy, but she is a noble enemy; in default of love, she earns my respect. Finally, to be entirely frank with you, I think of a third France; here the worst cancers of the modern world have found their chosen climate, here decadent Americans love to loiter, here Edgar Poe passes for a great poet, here are the little vermicular 'movements' of Dadaism, Surrealism, and Black Masses – here the very country of Reason has built an idol of Stupidity.

It seems that your essence may be double. Without a doubt it is the same in all nations; I see it even in my own country. Behind the England of Sidney, I perceive (alas!) that of Cecil Rhodes. If the one frees the slaves, the other fattens herself on trafficking them. We who failed to invent Liberty have also sinned against her more than almost any other nation. For you as for us, the Demon is truly the opposite of our authentic essence; he incites Shelley's countrymen to Tyranny, as those of Abelard to Stupidity. The future depends, for each of our two countries, on the choice that we make between our good and evil geniuses. Is it too late to recover this other France, this other England?

To recover them, it is not enough to think of them. It is not an 'ideal' or 'inspiration' that we need, but simple probity, charity, and diligence to face successively all the tasks which will confront us. I do not know if the French or the English or the Germans (who have not always known only the Demon, either) will manage to become themselves again. The salvation of a people, like that of an individual, is always possible, but also impossible to predict; for we have free wills, and the future remains to be made.

# Charles Walter Stansby Williams
# (1886–1945): an obituary

∼

With the death of Mr Charles Williams, Oxford loses one of those extraordinary gifts which the upheaval of war sometimes bestows. Evacuation brought him to Oxford, and he hardly survived the victory. To that part of Oxford which is concerned with English poetry, and to that part which is concerned with the Christian religion, the war years will always be associated with this remarkable figure. There were, of course two reactions to him. Those who did not greatly love were, quite frankly, bewildered. He suffered fools gladly, but fools, specially of the solemn kind, did not return the compliment and some who were not fools distrusted an outlook so widely different from their own. In this I think they were mistaken.

His critical views, however idiosyncratic, were all derived from the texts before him. His fundamental postulate was that great poets meant exactly what they said; the plain sense of the words was the only key. The incantatory richness of his recitation was not in the least an irrelevance; it was an exposition. The excitement which he aroused in his audience was one which sent them back to the poets, not one which focused their attention on him.

It is indeed possible, and it is to be hoped, that his death will for the first time, turn the attention of many from his

Published in *The Oxford Magazine*, vol. 63 (24 March 1945), p. 265.

critical to his original work. As a novelist and, above all, as a poet, Mr Williams represents an unexpected transformation of the romantic impulse – a transformation conveniently symbolized by the 'Byzantine' and 'Arthurian' elements in his poetry, or again by the fact that, being of Welsh descent, he yet gloried in being a 'cockney.'

In all his best work we find the storminess, the richness, and the suggestive qualities of romantic art, but all directed towards and composed by a love for order, discipline, ritual, dogma, even for the geometric. In him the tradition which had begun in being pantheistic, revolutionary, and antinomian becomes Nicene, hierarchical, severe. It is not a Celtic Twilight, but a Celtic Noon ('patterns of the Logos in the depth of the sun').[1]

It is, of course, too early to predict his final literary position; but it would not be absurd to guess that he will in the end stand as the great English poet of this age. At least, if the difficulty of his work prevents this, we shall have lost the only poetic experience in English which can, in any profound sense, be called Pindaric. Of the man himself – no one in Oxford who would care to hear needs to be told.

# PART III
# REFLECTIONS ON
# CHRISTIANITY AND
# LITERATURE

~

*In these essays, Lewis balances his vocations as a Christian apologist and a professor of English literature. He approaches religious topics obliquely and looks at aspects of Christianity through a literary lens. Within the compass of a review or the foreword to a friend's book, he serves – like Virgil in Dante's* Divine Comedy *or George MacDonald in* The Great Divorce *(1945) – as a guide to those looking for a deeper understanding of faith. The voice is unmistakable. In his review of a book of readings for Christians, he writes, 'I am a little uneasy lest the absence of Plato and the presence of Carlyle may encourage some readers in the false notion that the difference between Pagan and Christian is somehow less important in modern than in ancient times – that no one who wore a collar and tie and trousers could really be a pagan teacher in the same way as a man in sandals and a robe.' And in his foreword to* Smoke in the Mountain *by Joy Davidman, whom he married in 1956, he comments on 'religion' as a word: 'How odious ... how seldom used in Scripture, how hard to imagine on the lips of Our Lord!'*

# 22

# A Lectionary of Christian Prose from the Second Century to the Twentieth Century, ed. A. C. Bouquet (London: Longmans, 1939)

~

Dr Bouquet expresses a hope – already justified as regards one reader – that his book may 'prove a useful anthology for private reading', but he makes it quite clear that this is not his main concern.[1] His real aim is to find non-scriptural 'lessons' suitable for reading aloud at 'school and college prayers...special Lenten services...guild instructions', and, indeed, at all services where scriptural lessons are not laid down by the use of our Church. He naturally disclaims any intention 'to challenge or supersede the canon of the Christian Scriptures'.[2] He distinguishes rather sharply between the doctrinal and the edificatory functions of the Canon. Lessons are read to a congregation in order to edify it; not everything in the Bible edifies, and much that is not in the Bible does; hence, Dr Bouquet argues, the Church in the past has omitted parts of scripture from the Lectionary and included non-scriptural lessons from saints' lives, the Fathers, and the like.

His own book offers a preliminary selection of extracts for such a use, which he desires to see revived. I say a 'preliminary' selection, partly because the editor himself modestly claims only to have 'made a beginning',[3] and partly

Published in *Theology*, vol. 39 (December 1939), pp. 467–8.

because the actual survival of any extract under liturgical conditions may depend – as, in some sort, the formation of the Canon itself doubtless depended – on a kind of 'natural selection'. I very much doubt whether the rhapsodical passage from Professor Holland given on p. 43 could be endured twice by most English congregations.[4] I also doubt whether the piece of Berkeley (p. 4) will be of much use to those who know nothing of Berkeley's system:[5] but Dr Bouquet may reply that the Church still sees fit to tear from their context and read as epistles scraps of Pauline argument at least equally difficult. What I feel more certain of is that those who do not know the medieval meaning of 'sensuality' will not be edified by Chaucer's statement (p. 134) that it ought to 'have lordship over the body of man'.

These, however, are points of minor importance, for the collection as a whole is rich and varied, and it was not to be hoped that 100 per cent of successes could be attained. A more serious criticism might take the form of a question: Why, in a Christian lectionary, do we find Carlyle, Emerson, R. L. Stevenson, and G. B. Shaw? Dr Bouquet's answer, I suppose, would turn once more on his distinction between doctrine and edification and on the obvious truth that many unbelievers have written what can edify Christians. As Justin Martyr says on p. 61: 'Whatever all men have uttered aright belongs to us'.[6] But if this principle is accepted, it at once raises the question whether such great pagan doctors as Plato (whom Dr Bouquet's chronological limit excludes) would not have been much more edifying than any of the unbelievers whom he has admitted. To say this is, of course, to demand that Dr Bouquet should have made a different plan, and this may be bad criticism:

but I am a little uneasy lest the absence of Plato and the presence of Carlyle may encourage some readers in the false notion that the difference between Pagan and Christian is somehow less important in modern than in ancient times – that no one who wore a collar and tie and trousers could really be a pagan teacher in the same way as a man in sandals and a robe. In this connection it is, perhaps, unfortunate that the nineteenth century should be represented by more than forty authors, while the seventeenth, which comes nearest, shows only fifteen; but anyone who has tried to collect good extracts on any subject will know that this is not Dr Bouquet's fault – do what you will, that maligned and golden period is bound to top the list. Of the pagan witnesses in this book, Stevenson seems to me to bear the test of Christian surroundings better than any other.

The fate of this book as a lectionary will be decided by experience: in the meantime the reader in solitude cannot help judging it as an anthology, and as such I have found it a valuable work. No man ever agrees with another man's choice, and to disagree is one of the pleasures of using an anthology. I myself should have liked more Chesterton and von Hügel and less Robertson and Jowett, and am longing to ask Dr Bouquet, 'Where is Boethius? Where (since you admit dissenters) is George Macdonald?'[7] But this is only to say that Dr Bouquet and I are two men and not one man. I have found in his collection much edifying and pleasing work that I did not know before, and much of what I already know and hoped to find there. The book will be useful to hundreds of readers.

If a second edition is called for I hope the editor will tell us where, in the works of its authors, each passage is to be found; otherwise one of the chief uses of an anthology – that of directing us to the originals – is frustrated. I hope, too, that he will be persuaded to follow a different reading (that of the C text) in the third line of his extract from *Piers Plowman*, and, indeed, to give us the whole passage in plain prose rather than in a half-hearted attempt at the metre of the original. There are also some misprints to be corrected.

# 23

# *The Oxford Book of Christian Verse*, ed. Lord David Cecil (Oxford: Clarendon Press, 1940)

~

With the exception of textual criticism there is perhaps no scholarly activity in which the work is so disproportionate to the reward as in the compiling of an anthology. The labour of reading through all, or nearly all, our sacred poets from Rolle to Ruth Pitter;[1] of flogging into activity a critical faculty which must, before the end of the task, become as jaded as that of an examiner; of seeking – what is never attained – perfect accuracy in transcription and proof-reading, is very great; the reward is usually to have one's final choice criticized by reviewers who have not given a hundredth part of the editor's thought to the subject and who, perhaps, take for granted considerations which he has had to abandon after serious reflection. I find myself just such a reviewer. I have a strong inclination to pull Lord David Cecil's book about – to shove a poem in here and remove a poem there. I would have selected differently than he from Chesterton; I would have had Mr Charles Williams represented by one of the great odes from *Taliessin*. I would have read *worlds* for *words* on p. 398. But all this is so little to the purpose that I think it better to

Review published in *The Review of English Studies*, vol. 17 (January 1941), pp. 95–102.

leave all detailed criticisms unwritten and discuss instead certain questions arising out of his preface.

Lord David Cecil explains the rarity of good Christian poetry (which here means poetry about Christianity from within) by a tendency to insincerity on the part of the poet who 'feels it profane to show himself in all his earthly imperfections' (p. xii), and 'will allow himself to express only unexceptionable sentiments' (p. xiii). I am neither convinced of the fact nor satisfied by the explanation. I do not know whether good Christian poetry is rare. Is the percentage of rubbish in the whole corpus of such poetry higher than in the whole corpus of heroic, or erotic, or 'nature' poetry? It is a question of statistics, and I do not know where those statistics can be found.

But on the supposed tendency to insincerity or a borrowed attitude, I have something to say. This seems to me precisely the reverse of the truth. Let us see the Christian poets actually at work. 'But yet, alas, for all this, I Have little mind that I must die', confesses Southwell.[2] 'If, what my soul doth feel sometimes, My soul might ever feel!' sighs Herbert.[3] 'If ought is felt, 'tis only pain To find I cannot feel', says Cowper with almost scientific accuracy.[4] 'I cannot will', says Christina Rossetti, 'I cannot wish' – 'can neither choose nor wish to choose'.[5]

The important thing to notice is that the poets are not merely making general confessions of sinfulness; that might be part of a borrowed attitude. They are recording, with the most clearsighted fidelity, the failure of their feelings to respond to the object with which their poetry is concerned. Now we do not find other poets doing this nearly so often. The nature poets do it now and then, doubtless because the romantic love of nature is, in some degree, a religion. But the great mass of poets almost ignore that phenomenon which stands to their subject-matter as 'dryness' stands to the Christian life. This is not in the least because it does not occur. There are plenty of days when the lover cannot love (and even, if truth were told, the lecher cannot lust!), the warrior cannot feel martial, the patriot cannot feel patriotic, and the satirist cannot feel indignant. But hardly a word of this comes out in the poetry.

A visitor from another world who judged humanity simply by its poetry would get the impression from profane poetry that we were creatures who lived habitually on a high, level plateau of consistent passion; from our sacred poetry, and from it almost alone, would he get any notion of human experience as it really is, with all its lee-shores and doldrums and rudderless hithering and thithering. If any such contrast as Lord David Cecil draws between sacred and profane verse is to be drawn at all, we must draw it the other way round. It is the profane poetry which assumes attitudes of greater clarity and consistency than inner experience will really support; it is the sacred poetry which gives us life in the raw. For whatever else the religious life may be, it is apparently the fountain of self-knowledge and disillusion, the safest form of psycho-analysis. I had almost said 'and the least expensive', but that's as may be. Most Christians, I suspect, would say that while the cost is merely nominal if we regard the value of the goods, it is seldom less than the total wealth of the purchaser.

'The average hymn', writes Lord David Cecil, 'is a by-word for forced feeble sentiment, flat conventional expression' (p. xi). Now it is certainly true that all hymnbooks are full of very bad poems. But before we explain this by the hypothesis that the sentiments are forced (which is an inference from the felt badness of the poems and not, as we too easily suppose, a *datum*) it would be well to remind ourselves of two facts. In the first place, many very bad English hymns are translations of very good Latin hymns. The uninspiring jingle of

> O what their joy and their glory must be,
> Those endless Sabbaths the blessed ones see!

Derives from the very delicate and sophisticated dance of

> O quanta qualia sunt illa Sabbata,
> O quanta gaudia Sabbatizantium![6]

The badness of the English certainly does not tell us that Abelard's sentiments were 'forced'. And what it tells us about the translator (Neale) is that he was misled by an error of judgement.[7] Abelard was dealing with Latin in the light of his own vernacular, which had little or no stress-accent, so that the *dum-de-de-dum* of bad English verse was not in his ear at all. Neale, using a vernacular in which stress-accent is positively tyrannical, selected a metre whose similarity to Abelard's is wholly superficial, and was too insensitive to notice how he had vulgarized his original. And that, if not the whole story, is surely as much of the story as we shall ever know. Speculations as to whether Neale's own desire for heavenly bliss was or was not 'forced' are, in my opinion, wholly futile. Christians will feel sure that it was in some degree 'forced' (as all ordinate desires have been ever since the Fall), but they will know this on grounds external to the poem. Purely literary criticism, if it tries to answer such a question, will find nothing but mares' nests.

And secondly, we must replace the badness of the hymns in its proper context, side-by-side with the badness of most modern attempts at what may be called 'public' poetry – the badness of most modern laureate poems, installation odes, epithalamiums, and other such occasional pieces. This is a purely modern phenomenon. Once, if you wanted an ode to celebrate your victory at the games, you went to the poet (Pindar or another) and ordered it, just as you ordered your banquet from the cook; and you had the same assurance of getting a good poem, if you chose a good poet, as of getting a good dinner, if you chose a good cook. If you wanted a diversion in your own house winding up with a compliment to the chief guest, you gave your order to Peele or Shakespeare or Milton; and got an *Arraignment of Paris*, a *Dream*, or a *Comus*. A poet who could not practice his art to order would then have been no less ridiculous than a surgeon who could not operate or a compositor who could not print except when 'inspired'.

But in the last few centuries we have unquestionably lost the power of fitting art into the processes of life – of producing a great work to fill up a given space of wall in a room or a given space of time in an evening's festivity. The decay of the hymn (for there was no difficulty about it in the Middle Ages) is only one instance of this general phenomenon. I do not doubt that this escape of poetry from the harness is a very great evil, and a very bad omen for the future of the culture in which it has occurred. But to trace it to some peculiarity in the subject-matter of the hymn is unscientific. For all phenomena of a class a single cause should be given. In the meantime, the bad modern hymns have still the use of preserving, however feebly, in the minds of churchgoers the idea (elsewhere almost lost) that poetry has the possible function of being controlled and used by human life as a whole. If ever a revival of 'used' or 'public' poetry occurs, it may be because even this thin and muddy trickle in our churches has preserved the old watercourse.

A subtler question is raised when Lord David Cecil says of the 'devout' poem, 'as for using any but the most decorous language to express his feelings, the very idea horrifies him' (p. xiii). The number of devout poets who have overcome this 'horror' seems rather remarkable – indeed, a student accustomed to the propriety and reverence of profane literature might well be shocked on first encountering the familiarity, or even the incivility, with which the sacred poets sometimes treat the Almighty. 'Wert thou my enemy, O thou my friend, How wouldn't thou worse, I wonder, than thou dost?' enquires Hopkins;[8] a shrewd question. Hardy used to scold God a good deal – whether for existing or for not existing, it is sometimes difficult to make out – but he never touched the quick of the nerve as do those terrible words in Herbert,

> Oh that Thou shouldst give dust a tongue
> To cry to thee
> And then not hear it crying...[9]

After this, it is little that he should accuse God of first 'enticing' but afterwards 'betraying' him. But such direct railing is only one way in which the sacred poets abandon 'the most decorous language'. Indecorum of one sort or another is broadcast over the whole book. The Absolute and Ubiquitous is offered a pipe, a skirt, a tarbox, and a scrip by a shepherd who 'swet; he had gon faster than a pace'.[10] Sexless spirit is represented explaining to the mortal beloved that 'hyr bed is made, hyr bolster is in blysse'.[11] A miracle is performed in order that the Virgin Mary, after some plain speaking from Joseph, may have cherries. The Creator, making man, has 'a glass of blessings standing by',[12] or comes near like an innkeeper to ask if the newly arrived guest lacks anything, or is warned that 'in vain He struggles to get free'. 'How narrow is He', exclaims Patmore.[13] 'Is thy love indeed A weed?' asks Thompson.[14]

In explanation of all this it is not sufficient (though it is true) to say that a religion which enthrones at its very centre the monstrous indecorum of the Incarnation cannot be expected to be very decorous about anything else. For the poets do not merely accept, they often seem anxious to exaggerate, the paradox of their faith – to wed the very great with the very little and to present the transcendent under symbols almost impudently mundane. And I think I see the reason of this. Lord David is right in thinking that the sacred subject, considered in itself, demands an almost stifling degree of decorum from the poet; if he is to 'rise' to his subject, he must rise very high indeed, and will be tempted to borrow stilts. But sacred poets have, in varying degrees, been aware of this difficulty, and the history of the fashions in religious poetry is partly the history of the various ways in which they met it.

The obvious way of meeting it is the frontal attack – simply to be as 'high' as you know how. This is the method of Pseudo-Caedmon, of Dante, of the great Latin hymns, of Dunbar's *Rorate Coeli*, of Smart.[15] It has produced some of the best poetry in the world. The pieces from Young in this collection show what it is like when it fails;

and so does Toplady's address to the soul ('Deathless principle', 'celestial tenant').[16] This is, in one obvious sense, the most *naïf* or ingenuous solution, though of course, in technical detail, the work it produces may be highly sophisticated. It is employed either by very great poets who have a right to such audacity, or by fools who do not know they are being audacious.

The second method may be called that of transferred classicism. It aims, like the first, at splendour, but at splendour with a difference. It arises from two impulses which were often present in the same mind but which are distinct and complementary. One is the impulse which leads the poet to say, 'We too ought to have our classics, our great epics, tragedies, and odes in the ancient manner. But if so, they must deal with Christianity, for that is our Great Subject, just as the *Fata Jovis*[17] and the founding of Rome were Virgil's Great Subject'.

The complementary impulse says, 'We want a great Christian work. But that means doing for Christianity what the ancients did for Paganism; we must therefore produce epics, tragedies, and odes in the ancient manner'. The urge to classicized Christian, or Christianized classical, work was further reinforced by the conception that 'machines' were necessary to epic, but that Pagan and 'Gothic' machines were childish, exploded, and profane. (These critical problems are largely discussed in Tasso, Davenant, and Cowley.)[18] The method was almost wholly successful in Milton, and wholly successful in Tasso. What pitch of blasphemy and absurdity it can reach at its worst is known only to those who have read Vida's *Christiad*.[19] But there is one thing to be noticed about this whole school.

Bold and massive as its ornaments are, it is in a sense declining the frontal attack. Its God is, in some degree, disguised as a mere god, its Angels as inferior gods. There is an element of solemn masquerade in it: the poets and reader almost know they are treating one thing in terms of another.[a] I believe that part of the pleasure was the pleasure of *idem in alio*. Just as in reading Johnson's *London* you enjoyed the skill with which modern parallels were found for detail after detail in the Juvenal, so in the *Davideis*, the *Christiad*, or the *Paradise Lost*, you enjoyed seeing how well Christianity could produce the councils, catalogues, Mercuries, and battlepieces of ancient epic. And indeed the pleasure of seeing that A is to B as C is to D is entwined with the pleasures of poetry throughout.

The third method is that of humble sobriety. The subject of our poetry is high beyond all height; we shall not try pitifully to scale that height with the carnal beauties of poetic diction. Nor shall we evade it by the classical and Pagan disguise. As cleanliness and convenience are the only beauties, other than those of the spirit, to which our Protestant churches aspire, so strong sense, rigid sincerity, genuine English, and the firmness of the metre shall be the only beauties of our sacred poetry – unless, indeed, a new uncovenanted beauty creeps in from the very

---

[a] But we must not decide *a priori* which elements are part of the masquerade and which are a more direct expression of the poet's belief. The corporeality of Milton's angels, which looks to a modern so like mere machinery, must be judged in the light of what we read in the Platonic Theologians such as Ficino or Henry More. It is up-to-date pneumatology of Milton's day and may well have been seriously believed by him.

contrast between the horrors or ecstasies described and the stern, unshaken lucidity of the form. We may, as in Cowper's *Castaway*,[20] be standing on the brink of hell: that is no reason why our grammar, our scansion, or the shape of our lyric should be modified. The heart may be broken but the head is clear. It is the method of Watts and the Wesleys at their best, of Cowper nearly always.[21] It is divided by a hair's breadth from flatness; but when it comes off it can no more be ignored than the blow of a hammer. It can, on occasion, lift such dull poets as Tate and Brady to the perfection of

> Fear Him, ye saints, and you will then
> Have nothing else to fear.[22]

Those three methods are all more or less what Dr Tillyard would call 'direct';[23] those that follow are 'oblique'. They decline the whole problem of the 'high' subject, and become at ease in Sion[24] by disguising Sion as their native hamlet. The first and more obvious way of doing this is to fasten on the Incarnation, while leaving the thought of what is incarnate in the background. Hence all those songs, both medieval and modern, in which the infant Christ is given toys and fruit and generally treated like any other baby. It would, of course, be a naivety on our own part to suppose that this kind of poetry is *naïf*. The whole piquancy comes from the consciousness, never absent from the poet's mind, that this baby is also the Absolute, the Unconditioned, the *Ens Entium*.[25] 'By, by, lully, lulley'[26] derives its whole point from this consciousness, and the age of 'lully, lulley' is also the age of *Pange lingua*.[27] The medieval poets, in their own different way, are practicing the same deliberate *litotes* which we see in Mr Eliot's 'it was (you may say) satisfactory'.[28] And this can be done even without reference to the Incarnation. The monosyllable *Sir*, used by Hopkins to God, does it to perfection;[29] and so does Fredegond Shove's 'for the greatness of their love neither of them could speak'.[30]

The mention of love brings us naturally to the commonest of all the forms of 'oblique' religious verse. Working on a hint from *Canticles*[31] – not to say another hint furnished by the very nature of things and agreed upon, in very different senses, by Christians and Freudians – the poets present the relations of God and the soul in terms of the relations between two human lovers. The Middle Ages do this, once more, with a deceptive appearance of naivety, borrowing the forms and phrases of popular songs which are very 'profane' indeed: at the other end of the scale, Patmore does it in the lofty and abstruse manner, taking the symbol more seriously than the old poets, and always on the verge (some would say, beyond it) of the greatest obscenity that can be imagined. Herbert, writing with the sonneteers and the erotic poetry of Donne behind him, writes much of the *Temple* as if it were the poetical history of all the ups and downs (meetings, partings, quarrels, and reconciliations) of an earthly love. But he has other symbols as well; and with these we are embarked on the wide sea of symbolic sacred verse – the innkeeper of Herbert's *Love*, the hound in Francis Thompson, the shepherd in Ruth Pitter's *Turn not aside*.[32]

The ways of making sacred poems are innumerable. The 'devout poets' of Lord David's preface who are stifled by the difficulties he mentioned, are stifled not because they are devout but because they are no poets.

This seems to me in one way an encouraging book; the harvest of the nineteenth and twentieth centuries is, in my opinion, more vivid, more varied, and more excellent than that of any preceding age.

# 24

# Dorothy L. Sayers, *The Mind of the Maker* (London: Methuen, 1941)

~

The purpose of this book is to throw light both on the doctrine of the Blessed Trinity and on the process whereby a work of art (specially of literature) is produced, by drawing an analogy between the two. It has often been a cause of wonder to me that the image of author and book for the relation between God and the world, though popular among the Stoics, has been so little used by the Christians; and, since this image is one that I have often found helpful myself, I have followed Miss Sayers' use of it with intense interest. I know from experience that if one ventures to use analogy a number of very tedious reviewers will rise up and point out that there are differences, as well as similarities, between the things compared – to which the only reply seems to be 'Quite!'

I hope it will not be thought that I am suffering from this confusion when I mention the one serious dissatisfaction I feel with Miss Sayers' book. It is dissatisfaction on the practical, or pastoral, side rather than on the theoretical. I think that in an age when idolatry of human genius is one of our most insidious dangers Miss Sayers would have been prudent to stress more continuously than she does the fact that the analogy *is* merely an analogy. I am afraid

Review published in *Theology*, vol. 43 (October 1941), pp. 248–9.

that some vainglorious writers may be encouraged to forget that they are called 'creative' only by a metaphor – that an unbridgeable gulf yawns between the human activity of recombining elements from a pre-existing world and the Divine activity of first inventing, and then endowing with substantial existence, the elements themselves. All the 'creative' artists of the human race cannot so much as summon up the phantasm of a single new primary colour or a single new dimension. It is one thing, having known many men, to 'think of' one more man, Mr Pickwick; to 'think of' man himself, of time and matter themselves, *de novo*, is an activity simply heterogeneous to any that we can conceive. Nor do artists give their so-called creatures substantial existence. Miss Sayers quotes from N. Berdyaev that 'the image of an artist and poet is imprinted more clearly on his works than on his children'.[1] More clearly, perhaps, but less substantially. For his son, like himself, has biological life, thought, freedom, and the hope of everlasting glory, while his work has only a *mimesis* of all these and is, in that deeper sense, wholly *unlike* a man.

I must therefore disagree with Miss Sayers very profoundly when she says that 'between the mind of the maker and the Mind of the Maker' there is 'a difference, not of category, but only of quality and degree' (p. 147). On my view there is a greater, far greater, difference between the two than between playing with a doll and suckling a child. But with this, serious disagreement ends.

In general I find Miss Sayers' development of her analogy full of illumination both on the theological and on the literary side. I recommend specially to anyone's attention the following passages. (1) The chapter on Free Will and Miracles. Miss Sayers distinguishes 'a tale about marvels' from 'a tale abruptly modified by marvels'.[2] If our Lord had descended from the cross when challenged to do so, this would have been an 'irrelevant miracle', not 'an integral part of the story';[3] the Resurrection, on the other hand, is part of the plot – it is one of the things the story is *about*. This is very well done; and it will be noticed that it comes directly out of the analogy Miss Sayers is using and could hardly have come in any other way. (2) Chapter VI, on the Incarnation. A writer can put himself as a character into his own book (I think Miss Sayers spoils the parallel by making the book an autobiography – the *Divine Comedy* is a much better example) and say – 'This is what my eternal idea looks like in terms of my own creation . . . this is my characterhood in a volume of created characters'.[4] (3) The very badly needed Note A (pp. 116, 117), which states something well known to anyone who has written the humblest story himself but maddeningly misunderstood by nearly all modern criticism. (4) The chapter on Scalene Trinities. This cannot be explained to those who have not read the book, but I believe it to be a really illuminating contribution to literary classification. It may be that the 'ghost' in Miss Sayers' human trinity is the least easily classified of the three persons, but the same is true of his Divine Archetype in the real Trinity.

This is the first 'little book on religion' I have read for a long time in which every sentence is intelligible and every page advances the argument. I recommend it heartily to theologians and critics. To novelists and poets, if they are already inclined in any degree to idolatry of their own vocation, I recommend it with much more caution. They had better read it fasting.

# 25

## Selected sermons: *A Selection from the Occasional Sermons of Ronald Arbuthnott Knox*, ed. Evelyn Waugh (London: Dropmore Press, 1949)

~

Monsignor Knox's literary career has been one that we can contemplate with unusual satisfaction. So often the wit of his year, the delight of the common rooms, fades out in middle life or (worse still) continues in his grey hairs to let off the same sort of squibs that made his reputation as a freshman. Monsignor Knox's work, on the other hand, has shown continual enrichment; from topical lampooner to translator of the Bible, the ascent has been marked at every step by increasingly valuable productions. He would have some right, if he were that sort of man to complain of insufficient recognition. The important introduction to *Essays in Satire* (without reading which no man should presume to write on Falstaff) has been strangely neglected by literary specialists, and his New Testament received rather less attention than a mere curiosity like the 'Basic' version.[1] Yet its handling of the Pauline epistles could hardly be bettered. If it is complained that Monsignor Knox lacks the colour and melody of the Authorised Version, he can reply '*Salva reverentia*, so did St Paul'.[2]

Review published in the *Times Literary Supplement* (20 May 1949), p. 332 (unsigned).

The present volume shows its author in a less familiar light, in his pastoral capacity. By Mr Waugh's calculation Monsignor Knox must in his time have preached about fifteen hundred sermons: we are offered eleven, and cannot help feeling that a larger selection in a humbler and cheaper form would have been more welcome. Monsignor Knox is not an author who requires the fine printing and wide margins.[3]

Yet he can bear them. He is not indeed, and no one expected him to be, one of the floral preachers, like Fisher or Taylor, but neither is he (in his own words) 'a conscientious Philistine' like Faber or Latimer.[4] These little homilies are works of art. He has not ventured to recall the medieval liberty of joking in the pulpit, though no man could more happily have made the venture, and his wit, ever present as a controlling force, comes to the surface only at rare moments. Sometimes it does so in an epigram that might be by Chesterton: 'a hundred years ago our enemies blamed us for thinking wrong, to-day they blame us for thinking'.[5] More often it finds a disguised outlet in oxymoron, or what the Elizabethans would call conceits. ('In a Jesuit school martyrdom is on the syllabus' – 'That creative afterthought, *It is not good for man to be alone*'.)[6]

But we must not number among the conceits what will appear to some the audacity of the prayer: 'May the face of Jesus Christ show gay and gentle to him'.[7] That is only the great tradition of Lady Julian's 'homely and courteous' revived; a welcome revival.[8] But all such passages are the plums, not the cake. The texture of the work is very plain, the masculine style of one who can use language at his ease because he has long been a scholar and who can be grave without being portentous because he has often been merry. Only once does it suffer by the transition from the spoken to the printed word; the fourth sentence from the end of the last sermon does not run easily.[9]

Monsignor Knox's matter cannot, in the nature of the case, demand the same universal response as his style. He is addressing his co-religionists and there are (naturally) no concessions to *nous autres*. He is indeed adroit in the art of implying unmeasured condemnation without exactly saying anything uncharitable or uncivil; thus the parallel and contrast between Lord Northcliffe and Edward the Confessor in the first sermon becomes a thing to make the blood run cold. But in almost every piece there is much that will find a welcome outside the author's Church as well as within.

A Coronation sermon is in our days an unpromising thing: we yawn (loyally, but still we yawn) at the thought. Monsignor Knox starts with the naked fact that we 'are putting a gold crown on the head of a man like ourselves and telling him that he is a more important person than we are', and from this goes on to develop a profound defence of monarchy.[10] Marriage sermons often warn the young couple of the 'sacrifices' necessary in married life, but the word 'sacrifice', as it has now been degraded, may mean anything or nothing. Monsignor Knox warns them of 'a curtailment, a diminishing, of the individual life'; after that we listen.[11]

Elsewhere the interest is more personal and historical. The preacher's own experience has given him a peculiar and poignant insight into the spiritual history of Newman. There is an unforgettable sentence here about the 'grace

of conversion' as it 'first comes to a man, still very far off
like the sound of a gnat singing in his ears'.[12] But the best
of all is 'Individuality'. Our Lord did not speak only of
lilies, but of this lily, held in His hand. The occasion of
that sermon was a meeting of the British Association.

# 26

# Foreword to Joy Davidman, *Smoke on the Mountain: An Interpretation of the Ten Commandments*

*∼*

Joy Davidman, who began her career, appropriately enough, as nursery governess to a lion-cub,[1] first came before the public as the poetess of *Letter to a Comrade*, which won the Yale Series of Younger Poets award for 1938.[2] The volume showed, side by side with a delicate precision of imagery (one remembers the crabs 'jointed, Japanese, and frail') an occasional orotundity, a deep bell-like note, not very typical of its period; in 'The Empress Changes Lovers' and 'Absolution' it successfully answered the question we must put to all young poets: 'Can you go beyond the pageant of your bleeding heart and the general state of the world, and present a *situation*?' They all date from her Communist period.

How she got into the Party and how she got out again she has described in a beautifully balanced little essay, 'The Longest Way Round', contributed to Dr Soper's *These Found the Way* (1950). The adult convert to Christianity is of course a characteristic figure of our age. Joy Davidman is one who comes to us from the second generation of unbelief; her parents, Jewish in blood; 'rationalists' by

Published in Joy Davidman, *Smoke on the Mountain: An Interpretation of the Ten Commandments* (London: Hodder and Stoughton, 1953), pp. 7–11.

conviction. This makes her approach extremely interesting to the reclaimed apostates of my own generation; the daring paradoxes of our youth were the stale platitudes of hers. 'Life is only an electrochemical reaction. Love, art and altruism are only sex. The universe is only matter. Matter is only energy. I forget what I said energy is only'; thus she describes the philosophy with which she started life.[3] How, from the very first, it failed to accommodate her actual experience, how, as a result of this discrepancy, she was for some years almost 'two people', how Communism, too, broke up under the impact of realities more formidable even than itself, must be read in her own words.[4] Re-reading the poems in the light of the essay one is struck by a recurring image; that of the brain within the skull as with a fortress which may, or may not, be held against 'the universe'. The essay describes exactly how 'the universe' – indeed, something much more important than it – broke in. For of course every story of conversion is the story of a blessed defeat.

Another point of interest in Joy Davidman's work comes from her race. In a sense the converted Jew is the only normal human being in the world. To him, in the first instance, the promises were made, and he has availed himself of them. He calls Abraham his father by hereditary right as well as by divine courtesy. He has taken the whole syllabus in order, as it was set; eaten the dinner according to the menu. Everyone else is, from one point of view, a special case, dealt with under emergency regulations. To us Christians the unconverted Jew (I mean no offence) must appear as a Christian *manqué*; someone very carefully prepared for a certain destiny and then missing it. And we ourselves, we christened gentiles, are after all the graft, the wild vine, possessing 'joys not promised to our birth';[5] though perhaps we do not think of this so often as we might. And when the Jew does come in, he brings with him into the fold dispositions different from, and complimentary of, ours; as St Paul envisages in Ephesians ii.14–19.

Before she became a Christian, even before she had (temporarily) considered the possibility of Judaism as a religion, Joy Davidman was keenly aware of this difference in the blood. In one poem, there is a suggestion that the whole 'Aryan' *ethos* could be regarded as a 'clinging fog'.[6] I suppose when Elijah on Carmel cried out 'How long halt ye between two opinions?'[7] he was dissipating a fog. I suppose we Northerners, pagan, romantic, and polytheistic in grain, are a kind of people of the mist when seen from the dreadfully unambiguous standpoint of Israel. If 'fog' is too severe a word, at least it is no severer than what she says of her own people: 'My root / Who evolve viciously in the east'.[8] Not perhaps viciously, but without doubt fiercely – I cannot help here remembering the lion's governess. The finer spirit of that fierceness, if one must describe it in an abstract noun, is presumably what our father's called *zeal* (a word disquietingly absent from the Christian vocabulary these last hundred years or so). But it is best grasped not in any abstraction but in an image, in that glorious, sustained image from the XIXth Psalm where the Sun and the Law became fused in the poet's mind, both rejoicing, both like a giant, like a bridegroom, both 'undefiled', 'clean', 'right', and 'there is nothing hid from the heat thereof'.[9] One sees the whole desert landscape – no rock nor hillock large enough to throw a shadow in which one could hide from that tyrannous, disinfectant blaze.[10]

Something of that old Hebraic quality has gone into the book to which I am writing this preface. First there is the style. I do not of course mean that Joy Davidman's style is derived from her blood. It comes, like all good writing, from an individual talent, from reading, and from discipline. But how well it fits the theme! Many writers on 'religion' (how odious a word, by the way, how seldom used in Scripture, how hard to imagine on the lips of Our Lord!) have a positive love for the smudgy and the polysyllabic. They write as though they believed (in the words of the late George Gordon) 'that thought should be clothed in pure wool'. There is no wool here. The author, to be sure, is an American and uses her own language, not always lexically or idiomatically the same as ours; but it is none the worse for that. A test comes in chapter nine where she quotes a great rocky piece of sheer sense from Johnson which would have instantly shown up any vagueness or fustian in its neighborhood if such had existed, and comes off unscathed.[11] She even dares to lay a stone on top of that grim cairn and it is worthy of its place. ('The pay is bigger nowadays – but then, so are the lies'.)[12] For the Jewish fierceness, being here also modern and feminine, can be very quiet; the paw looked as if it were velveted, till we felt the scratch. At the opening of chapter nine, where we English may perhaps feel that some withers are more wrung than our own, the apparent innocence which puts us off with Titus Oates is an example. So, in another passage, is that much needed coinage 'others-denial'.[13]

Secondly, there is the very theme of the book. What should a Jewish Christian write on if not the Law? But notice that the choice of a subject means no relapse into mere Judaism, nothing that need alarm the most Pauline of us. The author knows quite as well as any of us that Mr Legality will never bring us to the Celestial City[14] and has got over the fallacies of Moralism fairly early in life. She had good opportunities for studying it at close quarters. She knows that only love can fulfil the Law. That, I think, is the answer to a criticism which someone is sure to make of this book; that in most of its chapters we have much more about diagnosis than about cure. In reality, of course, a 'cure' in the sense of some recipe added at the end of each chapter – some 'law to be a fence about the Law' and inevitably breeding more Law – is not really being offered at all. The author is not a quack with a nostrum. She can only point, as in her concluding chapter she does point, to the true Cure; a Person, not a set of instructions. Pending that, she is no more inhibited than her ancestors about diagnosis; one might frankly say, about denunciation. A Jeremiad? But should we not read Jeremiads? If it comes to that, should we never read Jeremiah himself? The Canon judges otherwise.

The sins of the Americans (for whom, in the first instance, the book was written) are doubtless not exactly the same as our own. Many of their sins, indeed, we are now hardly in a position to commit. Hence, inevitably, there are passages in this book which English readers may make a bad use of, reading them with complacent self-congratulation. But in the main it is a true bill against all Western civilisation. The flaw in us which Joy Davidman seems to me to expose with most certainty will be to some perhaps an unexpected one: the sin of fear, not in Donne's sense but, quite simply, cowardice. Hence she can speak of one minority as being 'protected by a fortunate illiteracy from the bombardment of fear propaganda'.[15] I am doubtful whether many readers, after reflection, will be prepared to give her the lie. It may be true that great nations have never before faced a greater danger: but have great nations ever met danger with such an appearance of poltroonery? Perhaps it is only appearance. Perhaps, if the moment comes, our bite will prove better than our howls. If not, we shall have to confess that two millennia of Christianity have not yet brought us up to the level of the Stoics and Vikings. For the worst (according to the flesh) that a Christian need face is to die in Christ and rise in Christ; some were content to die, and not to rise, with Father Odin.

I have ventured to use the word 'denunciations'. This must not be taken to mean anything wild or indiscriminate. On the contrary the quality in this book which, I anticipate, will stand out more clearly the better it is known, is precisely the union of passionate heat with an intelligence which, in that passion, still modifies and distinguishes and tempers. Notice (what I especially value, because it supplies a corrective which I especially needed) how after exposing what is banal, meretricious, and greedy in the popular idea of 'Progress', our author unexpectedly, and truly, points out what pure and noble elements originally contributed to that idea. Notice, again, how while admitting the sins worse than murder she shows how disastrously the concept 'worse than murder' can be used to confuse and etiolate the reality of murder itself.[16]

I do not of course agree with Miss Davidman at every point. In such a book every reader will have his own crow to pluck with the author. For my own part, what I would most gladly see altered are certain passages where she quotes myself for thoughts which she needed no sense save her own to reach and no pen save her own to express. But every old tutor (and I was not even that to Miss Davidman) knows that those pupils who needed assistance least are generally also those who acknowledge it most largely.

# 27

# Preface to Austin Farrer, *A Faith of Our Own*

∾

To say that this book set me wondering why there are so few like it may seem a left-handed compliment, but it is far from being one. Nearly everything that is very well done looks easy to do, especially if you have never tried it yourself. And if it is also very well worth doing, we naturally ask why more people do not at any rate attempt it. Actually, books like this are rare. We have plenty of religious literature: books of devotion, controversies, apologetics, Christian reflections on 'the present situation', Drives, Recalls, Appeals, and New Approaches. But except on a far lower level, both literary and theological, than Dr. Farrer's, the unabashedly homiletic – undisguised instruction and exhortation – is not common. Dr. Farrer offers it. He comes before us in this book not as a missioner, nor a journalist, nor a philosopher, but simply as a priest.

This priestly quality is almost the opposite of the parsonical. No author is so free from labored *bonhomie*, emotional rhetoric, or conventional pietisms of phrase. He writes everywhere as one who both has authority and is under authority. This is what constitutes his priestliness, and this dictates everything else in the book.

Published in Austin Farrer, *A Faith of Our Own* (Cleveland and New York: World Publishing, 1960), pp. 7–10.

It dictates, first of all, the style. This, in its impeccable sobriety, will seem to every critical reader a model of good taste; but no one who was consciously bothering about taste would ever have achieved it. Its source is elsewhere. Because he writes with authority, he has no need to shout. The truth and importance of what he says are already vouched for. It is assumed that we acknowledge both. He is there to expound, to explain, to remind; to draw again any lines in the bright diagram that have been smudged. But equally, because he speaks under authority, he must practise many abstinences: no exaggerations, however effective, no half-truths, however stimulating. He must not go beyond his commission. And all this, far from producing any flatness, turns out to be what, unconsciously, we were longing for. We have been bullied, flattered, wheedled, and generally 'got at' enough. It is a blessed relief to be simply *told*, to sit quietly listening to this firm, level, unaffected voice.

Again, Dr. Farrer is far too wise and workmanlike in his pastoral office to waste any time on being topical. You will find nothing here about the Bombs or Sputniks. What is usually called 'the contemporary' is in fact a composite picture of the recent past, based on secondary sources (chiefly newspapers) and touched up with guesses about the future. Dr. Farrer, at any rate in working hours, has no leisure to spare for such a phantom. He deals with what is really and knowably contemporary – with the august and terrible coincidence of the present moment and the eternal, in which each one of us lives. He is never speaking to the abstraction 'modern man'; always to you and me, whom he seems to know sufficiently well. That is how – unobtrusively, and with all respect for the individual mysteries we are – he gets under our skin. We close the book aware of tasks we never thought of attempting, and of those others which we repeatedly resolved to attempt and instantly forgot.

His severe self-discipline is nowhere more apparent than in the simplicity with which he writes. Sometimes – in 'The Fish out of Water' or 'Chastity' – he is reminding us of truths that are not in themselves difficult to grasp. But there are other essays of a very different character: 'Christ's Atoning Death', 'Christ is God', and 'This is My Body'. In each of them there is matter out of which some theologians would have made a whole book. Even as they stand, they lead us through a structure of thoughts so delicately balanced that a false word, even a false tone, might land us in disaster. Opposite errors threaten from both sides, so that the author has to tread a path as narrow as a hair. Yet I believe the simple reader will be perfectly capable of following them and will remain quite unaware of all the shoals and rocks that have been avoided. When the author was really dancing among eggs, he will seem to have been strolling across a lawn. It would indeed be possible – if you didn't know – to read the whole book without ever suspecting that it is written, not only by one of the most learned theologians alive but by the theologian whose critics most often accuse him of excessive subtlety. This does not mean that the simplicity of these essays is spurious. It means that it is a final product. None of them began in simplicity. It is a costly distillation. The work is all done and out of sight by the time they reach us.

Perhaps, after all, it is not so difficult to explain why books like this are rare. For one thing, the work involved is very severe; not the work on this or that essay but the

lifelong work without which they could not even have
been begun. For another, they demand something like a
total conquest of those egoisms which – however we try
to mince the matter – play so large a part in most impulses
to authorship. To talk to us thus Dr. Farrer makes himself
almost nothing, almost nobody. To be sure, in the event,
his personality stands out from the pages so clearly as that
of any author; but this is one of heaven's jokes – nothing
makes a man so noticeable as vanishing.

# PART IV
# CLASSICAL LITERATURE

~

*In 1922, Lewis gained First-Class Honours in Literae Human-*
*iores, as Classics was then called at Oxford, and in the following*
*year, he gained First-Class Honours in English Language and*
*Literature. Though he taught English, rather than Greek and*
*Latin, at Magdalen College, his interests in Classical Liter-*
*ature continued throughout his life, and the articles in this*
*chapter show the breadth of his reading. Subjects range from*
*Homer's* Odyssey, *with roots in the Greek Late Bronze Age,*
*to Boethius'* Consolation of Philosophy, *written in the sixth*
*century* AD.

# 28

# Odysseus sails again: *The Odyssey*, trans. Robert Fitzgerald (London: Heinemann, 1962)

~

Robert Fitzgerald follows the traditions of the great translators. The rule in that tradition, first formulated by Dryden, is to make your author speak as he would have spoken if he had been your fellow countryman and your contemporary.

I myself think that ideal certainly wrong and probably meaningless. I want a translation, say, of Hafiz,[1] to give me as nearly as possible the experience of a modern Englishman who can read Persian with ease.

I am not at all interested in what Hafiz would have written if he had been a modern Englishman. I know already how modern Englishmen write.

But we must judge Mr Fitzgerald by the rules he accepts. He is trying to do for our age what Chapman, Pope and Morris did for their ages.[2] His version, like theirs, becomes an unconscious critique of the period that begot it. The prevailing taste acts like a stencil: it lets through some Homeric qualities and excludes others.

Chapman made Homer cryptic, Machiavellian, and fantastical. Pope made him elegant and epigrammatic; Morris, romantically Nordic. Mr Fitzgerald makes him

Review published in *The Sunday Telegraph*, no. 84 (9 September 1962), p. 6.

tough, stark, colloquial and rather like Stephen Vincent Benét.[3]

Translations are often subjected to very unfair criticism. Nothing is easier than to pick out, even from the best of them, places that conspicuously fail to catch the force of the original.

But the unfortunate translator has to choose, from among the styles his age will accept, one style and keep within it. He knows, no one better, that it will not be the ideal style for every single passage; it may none the less be, in his period, the best on the whole.

I will try to avoid this unfairness. I have also a special reason to be cautious. I know some Greek, but I know very little American.

Some of Mr Fitzgerald's renderings seem to me, by English usage, unpardonable. With us 'her ladyship Kalypso' would imply a silly sneer.[4] The statement that Zeus 'made conversation' would, with us, imply that the god really had nothing to say but wanted to tide over an awkward pause at the dinner table.[5]

'Papa',[6] (from Nausikaa to Alkinoos) would have been right for us 50 years ago: it is now archaic – colloquially archaic, which is the worst sort of archaism. But perhaps the overtones of all these expressions are different on the far side of the Atlantic.

Having once decided to use an essentially modern, hard-hitting, intimate style, free from all poetic diction, Mr Fitzgerald has to give up, once for all, any attempt to represent the ritual, bardic quality of *The Odyssey* – all its splendid formalities.

I think he made the right choice, and if the price is heavy we must blame the age, not Mr Fitzgerald: if he had done something more like Homer in its texture he would have had few readers.

The price is heaviest in dialogue, and here perhaps the author goes further than he need. Menelaos, describing his ambush for Proteus under the seal-skins says:

> a strong disguise; oh, yes terribly strong
> as I recall the stench of those damned seals.[7]

It is certainly what a man might say. But a man like Menelaos? No one wants Homer's characters to have the Augustan polish that Pope gave them, but though they may act like savages, they all talk like great aristocrats, descendants of the gods. Mr Fitzgerald makes them too like the next guy you meet in a saloon. But this fault decreases as he goes on.

There remains much on the credit side. This version has a strong, salty flavour of its own. And it makes you see things. Here is Alkinoos's house:

> High rooms he saw ahead, airy and luminous
> as though with lustres of the sun and moon,
> bronze-panelled walls, at several distances,
> making a vista, with an azure moulding
> of lapis lazuli. The doors were golden
> guardians of the great room. Shining bronze
> plated the wide door-sill; the posts and lintel
> were silver upon silver . . . [8]

And here is the great moment at the end of Book XXI:

> . . . so effortlessly
> Odysseus in one motion strung the bow.
> Then slid his right hand down the cord and
>     plucked it,

so the taut gut vibrating hummed and sang
a swallow's note.
    In the hushed hall it smote the suitors
and all their faces changed. Then Zeus thundered
overhead, one loud crack for a sign.
And Odysseus laughed within him . . . [9]

It is hard to explain why a long poem where, as in this, the verse, though not technically *libre*, is very free, produces in the end a greater danger of monotony than one in a regular metre. I think it is because, where an imaginary metronome is ticking away, every departure from it tells: curves show best when there is a straight line near them.

Mr Fitzgerald has much rhythmical vigour: perhaps if he had worn a tighter metrical *corsage* – a little tighter – we should have felt the vigour more. But then I am a confessed square.

On the whole this version has much to commend it. As a substitute for Homer, tolerable – and what substitute was ever more than that? As a book to send the old back to Homer and goad the young on to Homer, it is very well worth while.

I wish Odysseus were not called 'the strategist'[10] at the very moment when he is telling Kalypso that he prefers Penelope. Why not give this immortal liar credit for the least strategical speech he makes in the whole poem?

# 29

# Ajax and others: John Jones, *On Aristotle and Greek Tragedy* (London: Chatto and Windus, 1962)

~

One's attitude to other individuals and other cultures tends to swing like a pendulum between 'How like me after all', and 'How inconceivably unlike'. John Jones's *On Aristotle and Greek Tragedy* embodies the second reaction at the extreme end of the swing. After you have read it the Greeks will seem far further off than you dreamed.

The book falls into two parts: the first and shorter on the *Poetics* and the second on the tragedies. They are mutually relevant, but they do not necessarily stand or fall together. You may – and I do – agree with the first part and be much more doubtful about the second.

On Aristotle, Mr Jones appears to me simply right. We are familiar with the idea that the Renaissance critics misrepresented his theory of poetry. Mr Jones maintains that the moderns, seeing him through the coloured glasses of Shakespeare and Romanticism, have fared no better.

He holds that there is in Aristotle no doctrine of the tragic hero, the great flawed character. All that comes from mistranslating *hamartia*[1] and substituting singulars for plurals in certain passages.

Review published in *The Sunday Telegraph*, no. 98 (16 September 1962), p. 6.

We have also misunderstood the function of character in Aristotle. To us, doubly introverted, first by Christianity and then by liberal individualism, behaviour is primarily a symptom: something from which to infer the 'haunting latencies' of the psyche.[2]

For Aristotle, it is the actual: what we regard as the inner reality is mere potentiality. Hence, as he ought to be, Mr Jones is very good on Masks.

Very fine points are here involved. It makes all the difference whether we translate *mellein* as 'to intend' or as 'to be about to'. The former rendering throws us into a quite un-Aristotelian subjectivism.[3]

All this I fully accept, and with gratitude. It clears away many cobwebs. It might even help to banish from many a critical work, and from many a syllabus, the phantom subject called 'Tragedy'. There is one omission. Mr Jones distinguishes well between *praxis* and *muthos*: but I wish he had explained *praxis* itself. To render it by 'action' invites misunderstanding.[4]

I also wonder whether he would, as I would, go a step further and say that Aristotle, that very great man, was never less great than in the Poetics. It is difficult to think well of a book which, however diversely interpreted, has always had a bad influence on criticism and dramaturgy.

When we turn to the tragedies, I find Mr Jones harder to agree with and certainly harder to understand. His polemic against the picture of Aeschylus either as a monotheist or as a 'primitive' seems to me sound: so is his comment on Clytemnestra's identification of herself with the 'thrice-gorged bitter avenger'.[5]

But when he refers to the predicament of Agamemnon, ordered to sacrifice Iphigenia, as 'the beautiful, wisdom-yielding dilemma', and says that in such deadlocks Aeschylus sees 'the world making sense', and a sense whose cruelty is 'unqualified but not absolute' because they are not divorced from 'the rich concrete objectivity of life', I don't think he is giving his readers as much help as they need.[6]

He is trying to make the words 'unqualified', 'absolute', and 'life' (a very dangerous monosyllable nowadays) do more than they can.

He attributes to Sophocles a vision of 'mutability' and is at pains to distinguish this (to its advantage) from the medieval commonplace about Fortune's wheel. But not, I submit, at pains enough. Nothing that he says seems to me to establish so wide a difference as he desires.

And even this second part is full of interest. The analysis of the 'Ajax' is especially good, and Euripides, though severely, and justly, criticised as an artist, emerges from Mr Jones's treatment as a really gigantic figure in the history of the European mind.

No one who cares for the subject should neglect this book: though works equally profound have been more lucid.

# 30

# Lucretius

~

Although his poem contains no direct revelations concerning himself, there are few writers whose character is
more open to the reader than that of Lucretius. More than
a philosophical system, more than a picture of the world
conceived by Epicurus, the *Rerum Natura* is a poignant
and often painful psychological document. The facts that
are definitely known of the poet may be very briefly stated:
born, as it would seem, in 95 and dying about 54, he had
lived through a period of terror and bloodshed into one
of comparative security. He was acquainted with Cicero: a
tradition relates that he died by his own hand in madness.[1]

Though it would be foolish to accept Jerome's statement as literal truth, yet here the mythopoetic faculty of
ancient criticism has fabled not without discretion. The
poem is the work of an unbalanced mind. No reader can
have failed to mark the atmosphere of weirdness and terror which, while it does not prevent him from joining
hands in one direction with Wordsworth and Milton,
allies Lucretius in another with Edgar Allan Poe or
Apuleius. The gods are down: dreams, magic, and portents
have had their fangs drawn. But the old evil is not banished

This essay on Lucretius (*c.* 94–*c.* 54 BC), is published here for the first
time. The draft of it is written on blank pages interleaved and bound into
Lewis's copy of *De Rerum Natura*, now in the Rare Book Collection of the
Wilson Library of the University of North Carolina at Chapel Hill.

so far that it cannot continually disturb the peace of the saints. Lucretius must watch and pray lest he enter again into religion. Reason must fight a ceaseless hardly triumphant battle against the old terrors. And even inside the garden of Epicurus we are not safe. How significant is his sudden parenthesis when in the midst of explaining the world's mortality he suddenly turns aside with a hysterical prayer that the awful proof may not even then descend upon them. His account of love, again, is not that of a whole or happy mind: alternating between passages of rich sensuality and brutal satire and intolerable revulsion he reveals a mind torn with overwhelming passions and equally overwhelming disgust. One feels the presence of some great tragedy, some terrible disillusion. Here as elsewhere the *Rerum Natura* is a photograph of Hell.

It has always been difficult to account for the extraordinary violence of Lucretius's attack on the degrading terrors of religion. If his work had been lost we should have scarcely thought it possible that educated men in the Ciceronian age could entertain such feelings. Probably they did not. We may suppose that Plutarch's reply to the Epicureans[2] gives a truer account of the universal feeling of paganism. With Lucretius, however, to exaggerate the horrors of supernatural dogma and the relief of atheism was partly a tradition inherited from his master, partly a polemical device. But when we have made full allowance for both these reasons, there remains a passionate sincerity in his indictment which can be accounted for only by the sensitive melancholy of an abnormal mind to whom the cold safety of Epicureanism represented a very real and necessary salvation.

Yet Lucretius was not mad: the lucid disposition and sustained power of his work is sufficient proof to the contrary. His moments of noble calm and even of holy ecstasy are not less but more admirable because he has come through fire to find them. Yet even here the old spectres survive, transformed in the light of attainment

> *His ibi me rebus quaedam divina voluptas*
> *Percipit atque horror*[3]

His highest joy is an emotional thrill of awe that recalls the nightmare horror of an earlier state. He is still swayed by the majestic force of nature and prostrates himself before the 'élan vital', the '*rerum natura creatrix*', the '*hominum divumque voluptas*', rising to his highest poetry while he sings of a life for which his mechanism really found no place.[4] One sees that he was ill fitted to be an Epicurean: but the intensity of feeling which drove him for very safety into the garden, preserved his poet's heart even within. As a man he represents a tortured and troubled spirit rising by sheer strength of will above persistent melancholia and fear: as a poet he is an artist who surmounts with all the success possible the difficulties of an abstract subject, a newly-tamed language, and a scarcely naturalized metre. His character excites the strongest feelings of sympathy and admiration. None felt more keenly the burden of mortality, the old 'weltschmerz',[5] yet he will seek no solace elsewhere. Annihilation is the cold Nirvana of his system. Hopelessly inadequate as the Epicurean doctrine was to his great tho' sombre genius, it was a defence against worse evils: his first step out of the garden must be into terror, perhaps into madness. Clinging desperately to the one teacher who seemed to offer peace, he went no further and produced a poem where the earnest devotion of the poet almost ennobles the paltry creed upon which it was lavished.[6]

# 31

# T. R. Henn, *Longinus and English Criticism* (Cambridge University Press, 1934)

≈

This book is something much more exciting, and less utilitarian, than a history of the influence of Longinus on modern criticism.[1] It is rather an attempt to relate his teaching to the 'advanced' criticism of the Cambridge Left Wing – the diagrammatic, psychological and 'practical' school. Mr Henn's task is to find parallels and equivalents by which the main conceptions of the *De Sublimitate* can be restated in terms acceptable to his skeptical and anti-romantic colleagues – a task, in some ways, analogous to that undertaken by the eighteenth century 'imitators' when they fitted passage after passage of Horace or Juvenal into the context of contemporary London. The work of transplanting is carried out by Mr Henn with much skill and judgement – witness his heroic and learned struggle with the ὥσπερ νέφος[2] passage on pp. 76 *et seq*. – and can always be followed with pleasure.

That we should always agree is not to be expected. I would disagree strongly with Mr Henn's view that the modern English sense of the word 'sublime' is a mere error. Surely it is rather a semantic development; the healthy linguistic tendency to differentiation taking over a word which, in Longinus, came dangerously near to

Review published in *The Oxford Magazine*, vol. 53 (6 December 1934), p. 264.

meaning good writing of any sort whatever, and enriching our vocabulary by narrowing and deepening it till it means one only of the many kinds of excellence. I would even disagree with Mr Henn's statement that the modern meaning has necessarily theistic associations. Doubtless the fear of such associations explains the distaste of some contemporaries for the word – such distaste being a symptom of theophobia.

But I submit that their alarm is needless. Theism is 'sublime'; but if anyone thinks 'sublimity' theistic, let him read Lucretius. Nor could I lean so heavily as Mr Henn does on the amorality of Longinus' aesthetic theory. If Longinus does not put great art among the causes of virtue, he certainly puts virtue among the causes of great art. Μεγαλοφροσύνη[3] is an ethical term, and his theory is 'moral', not after the fashion of the Elizabethans but after that of Ruskin. Such disagreements, however, go far to prove that this is a living and provocative book. I could wish that it had been longer. An almost parenthetic (and so to me quite revolutionary) suggestion on page 24 about Lucretius' debt to Plato, tempts one to murmur *tantamne rem tam negligenter*![4] The doctrine (p. 148) that there is 'so much that we can justify, not in relation to ultimates ... but on the pragmatic basis of the art of living', clamours for further development: in its present form it lies open to the nonsensical interpretation, 'there are so many things one can approve as means without knowing the end'. But these, and all other difficulties, will perhaps be solved when Mr Henn gives us another book; and I, for one, hope that he will do so soon.

An unusually happy printers' error on p. 122 commits Burke to the theory that 'excessive litters' are sublime.

# 32

## Helen M. Barrett, *Boethius: Some Aspects of his Times and Work* (Cambridge University Press, 1940)

~

This is a welcome book, and no one but a fool will dispute Miss Barrett's view that Boethius is 'a man who ought not to be forgotten'.[1] Fortunately, as the present writer knows by experience, a respectable minority of modern undergraduates in every year can be awakened to a more than historical interest in him, and it may be hoped that Miss Barrett's book, which translates all its Latin, and is within the grasp of the ordinary student, will increase the number. It includes a short sketch of Theodoric, a life of Boethius, a chapter on the obscure subject of his fall, and three chapters on the *De Consolatione* which, very wisely, pass beyond the merely historical estimate and treat its thought as something of living concern. Miss Barrett upholds tradition, rejecting Usener's theory that it is based on an abridgment of the lost Aristotelian *Protrepticus*, and believing that it is an original work and that it was really composed in prison.[2] She accepts the theological tracts, largely on the evidence of the *Anedoton Holderi*, with the exception of the *De Fide Catholica*, about which she is doubtful.[3]

Review published in *Medium Aevum*, vol. 10 (February 1941), pp. 29–34.

In the historical sections, Miss Barrett's favourable view of Theodoric may, of course, be questioned.[4] That he could show himself, on occasion, a bloody and treacherous scoundrel, no one denies. The success in establishing a *modus vivendi* between the Romans and barbarians with which Miss Barrett credits him (p. 26), receives grim comment from Boethius himself: '*impunita barbarorum semper avaritia*' (*De Cons.* I. Pr. iv) he writes of the invaders, and of their king, '*avidus exitii communis*' (*ibid.*) I could wish, too, that Miss Barrett had been more consistent in her sceptical attitude towards evidence drawn from Cassiodorus.[5] Thus on p. 72 she rejects Dr Hodgkin's naïf view that the informers Cyprian and Opilio are to be estimated in the light of the 'high praise' which Cassiodorus gives them; and rightly.[6] In what age, and under what government, has a newly appointed functionary ever appeared in the official announcements as less than a blend of Solomon and Aristides?[7] Yet on p. 25 Miss Barrett seems to accept the authority of Cassiodorus for a statement whereof the intrinsic improbability appears to me overwhelming.

In the philosophical part of her work I think Miss Barrett does very well. She is lucid and represents the argument of the original, on the whole, accurately. Some disagreements are only to be expected. On p. 96 I think that the words 'a double method', used of Providence and Fate, will prove puzzling to some readers. They might suggest that Providence and Fate were two distinct and concurrent divine instruments. But the real distinction (as Miss Barrett well understands) is more like that between the static score of a symphony and the actual playing out of it, in time, by the orchestra. That very same pattern which, in itself (*'ipsa illa divina ratio'*) is Providence, becomes, or appears as, or is called, Fate, when executed in the temporal series (*'inhaerens rebus mobilibus'*).[8] On p. 120, I question whether Miss Barrett has given the doctrine that 'evil is nothing' a fair run for its money. Boethius certainly tells us in so many words *'malum igitur nihil est'* (III, Pr. xii).[9] But he does not mean that *malum* = zero, that it is a word with no meaning.

One clue has been given a few lines above: *'nihil est quod naturam servans deo contraire conetur'* (where the operative words are *naturam servans*), and another follows a few lines below, *'Nec ullam mali esse naturam'*.[10] He means that no *nature* is evil, using *natura* in the Augustinian sense and in the last of the four senses enumerated in his own *contra Eutychen et Nestorium*, where *natura* is defined as *unamquamque rem informans specifica differentia*.[11] In other words, the statement *'malum nihil est'*, means that evil is not a *thing*, like grass or virtue, has no nature of its own, was not created, but consists always in the depravation of some *thing*, which, in being so depraved, departs from its true nature (from 'what it is') and therefore, in a sense, tends towards nothingness.

Evil consists not in being, but in failing to be; it is privative, defective, parasitic. In this form the doctrine is not only not ridiculous but, as some of us think, the only sound basis for any metaphysic of value. Indeed, the opposite theology that evil is as substantial as good and has a *natura* of its own, invites a desperate dualism and makes the choice between good and evil, in the long run, something like an arbitrary allegiance to one of two parties.

My third philosophical disagreement with Miss Barrett arises out of her statement that 'strictly speaking the word *present* can only be employed where there has been a *past* and will be a *future*' (p. 137). But most fortunately *present* is the opposite, not only of *past* and *future*, but also of *absent*; nor is it a mere pun to remind ourselves that we also call a gift a 'present'. To come between the past and the future is not the sole characteristic of the present, as to come between 7 and 9 is the sole characteristic of 8. The present has another – a qualitative and not a merely serial – differentia; in it alone reality is *present* or *presented* to us, in it alone we perceive, will, enjoy, and suffer. From this point of view the Boethian doctrine of God's eternal present becomes more intelligible; it means 'having to all reality that direct access which we have to *some* realities, to those, namely, which we meet in the temporary present'.[12]

But these questions must be left to the philosopher; for the medievalist the great problems raised by Boethius are two. (1) Why does a man waiting in a dungeon for death and torture treat loss of fame, wealth, and office, as the typical misfortunes for which Philosophy is needed to console the human spirit? Is it not rather as if a man who has just seen his wife and children blown to pieces by a bomb, sat down to compose a *consolatio* for losing the golf championship? (2) Why should a Christian in such circumstances confine himself so rigidly to those consolations which he shares with any kind of civilized theist whatever?

As regards the first problem, we must note that there is no trace in the *De Consolatione* of the dungeon where it was traditionally composed. The *catenis* of I. M. ii seems to be metaphorical, and the *ipsa loci facies* of I. Pr. iv is answered not, as we might expect, with some philosophical proof that all mortal habitations are in the long run prisons, but with the statement that the place which Boethius regards as *exilium* is to others *patria* (II. Pr. iv).[13] It is true that a conceit is based on the idea of exile – for Boethius means exile from Rome and Philosophia means exile from his spiritual country; but then an almost identical play upon material and spiritual 'prison' would have done just as well. There is also very little in the book to suggest the imminence of More's *Dialogue of Comfort*;[14] indeed if we take *contum gladiumque*[15] (II. Pr. v) to be merely general and typical (as the quotation from Juvenal suggests), I believe we are reduced to a single reference '*morti proscriptionique damnamur*'.[16] (I. Pr. iv.)

If, in the face of all this, we wish to retain the tradition, we must make a distinction. What is written in prison while awaiting death need not be written *about* prison and *about* death. In other words, either the *De Consolatione* was composed (as Fortescue maintained) before the author was imprisoned and before he knew that his case was hopeless, or else it does not directly bear on his own situation (except for the self-defence in Book I) so closely as we have imagined. This would not mean that it was any the less sincere. The author meant every word he wrote, but he was not writing directly about himself. The problem of Fortune was offered him by his own experience, but he generalized it and wrote a *Consolation* for all her victims in all ages, not an autobiography. Even in the condemned cell so great a man would be more interested in making a good book than in self-expression. If this view were accepted, the second Metre of Book I would gain a new pathos; he had not meant to write about his own imprisonment but when he seeks metaphors for spiritual desolation his longings for free air and sky, and the burden of the fetters, all find their way in.

As to the second problem – that of the absence from the *De Consolatione* of all specifically Christian elements – I think the drastic solution of saying that Boethius had never really held or had lost the Faith, is now pretty generally abandoned. There is, in my opinion, a curious indication of Christianity within the book itself. In Pr. xii of Book III the author tells Philosophia that her last remark pleased him not only by its content but also, and much more, by the very words in which it was expressed. Now those words were '*regit cuncta fortiter suaviterque disponit*', an obvious reminiscence of *Wisdom* viii I, and if the author's reply does not mean 'How pleasant in this merely philosophical discussion to catch an echo of Holy Scripture', I can find no meaning for them.[17]

Yet it remains true that the *Consolation* is as empty of theology as the *Tractates* are full of it. I cannot accept the remark of Dr H. F. Stewart and Professor E. K. Rand (Loeb *Boethius*, p. xi) that 'the answer is simple. In the *Consolation* he is writing philosophy; in the *Tractates* he is writing theology'. Of course. But surely what we wanted to know was *why* he chose, at such a time, to devote himself to pure philosophy. Granted the scope of the *Consolation*, the exclusion of theology follows: but why that limitation of scope? I find much more help in Miss Barrett's conclusion that Boethius had, after all, devoted his life to pre-Christian philosophy and turned to it at the end because 'this was the work nearest his heart, the work in which he was happiest, most himself' (p. 160).

I would not accept this in any sense which involves Dr Stewart's earlier view that the composition of the *Consolation* was a mere distraction for unquiet thoughts; nor again in any sense that threw doubt on the author's

Christianity. Its philosophy is a profoundly religious philosophy. It might be described as 'prolegomena to any of the great religions'; it teaches the insufficiency of the world and points on to the Eternal – after that the various religions can have their say as to the nature of the Eternal and the means of approaching it. We need not doubt that Boethius had passed through this philosophical preliminary and reached that particular religion described in his *De Fide*.

If, in the *Consolation* he returned to write about the preliminary and not about the Faith, I suggest that there were two reasons. Firstly, as Miss Barrett says, this was what he did best – his job, his vocation – and no man wants to make a book simply, but a good book. Nor would it surprise or shock us to find that his intellect was obstinately inclined to dwell on that preliminary. There are many pious Christians whose minds always dwell on apologetics and protreptics, who are always describing the foundation and never proceed to describe the building. Secondly, those who have tried to live the Christian life will tell us (I suspect) that though these spiritual preliminaries are logically the mere presupposition of Christianity, yet in real life the point never comes at which we can say they have been got over once and for all. If I remember aright, Thomas More in prison made a resolution to woo his mind 'little by little' from the world.[18] In logic each step of argument is finished before the next is taken; but in life everything is always beginning over again. There is nothing really irrelevant in discussing things preparatory to conversion twenty years after you have been converted; for continual re-conversion is, perhaps, the nearest most mortals come to stability.

I suggest, as a hypothesis which covers all the facts, the following account of the composition of the *De Consolatione*. Boethius' mind had long been occupied on the general philosophical case for the religious life, which he may have designed either for a work on its own, or as the introduction to a larger work on Christian theology. He began to execute it after his disgrace, and perhaps in prison. His motive was neither to distract his mind nor primarily to console himself, but to edify and instruct the human race – to deliver his message. Under the pressure of strong emotion he allowed himself to include a section on his own particular wrongs and even to avail himself of an imaginative version of his own plight for the sake of the dramatic emphasis it lent to the argument. In the main, however, the calamities referred to are general, typical instances of 'fortune' and the personal element is properly subordinated. The fact that it decreases as we proceed may mean that only the earlier parts were conceived after his disgrace and that in the later he is simply reproducing what had been already composed or giving final literary form to what already existed in rough draught or in notes.

I have included the *De Fide*, above, among the genuine works. Its peculiarities – including the peculiarity which, I confess, I notice most readily, of being in unusually easy Latin – can all be explained on the assumption that it is written for school use. It is not easy to see for what other purpose such an author would compose such a jejune summary of such very elementary matters.

# PART V
# MEDIEVAL AND RENAISSANCE LITERATURE

~

*In 1954, Lewis was appointed to the Chair of Medieval and Renaissance Literature at the University of Cambridge. Since he was a specialist in that subject, it is not surprising that the majority of reviews published in this book are about the literature of those periods. Here Lewis addresses problems within different medieval and Renaissance genres, the literary criticism of those times, and the enigmatic figure of Arthur. He also considers such poets and writers as Andreas Capellanus, Dante, the authors of the* Romance of the Rose, *Malory, Wyatt, Spenser and Shakespeare. A long essay on Malory, 'The English prose* Morte', *published in 1960, is reprinted for the first time.*

# 33

## Ruth Mohl, *The Three Estates in Medieval and Renaissance Literature* (New York: Columbia University Press, 1933)

≈

'We are familiar', says Miss Mohl on her first page, 'with such forms as the love allegory, the metrical romance, the pastoral or the beast epic. A pattern no less character-istic...has hitherto escaped thorough treatment'.[1] This pattern is later (p. 5) defined as 'the verse or prose cat-alogues of the classes of society and their "defections"', and these, we are told, 'were regarded in their own day as a distinct literary form'.[2] This is a promising enterprise. No department of literary history is more fruitful than the study of extinct forms, in so far as such study enables us to understand what our ancestors liked and why, and silences that kind of criticism which concentrates on those features of the old texts which were, to their writers, quite unessential.

At the same time no study is more difficult. It is not easy to get inside the skin of men long dead, and I find indica-tions in Miss Mohl's work of a frame of mind especially unpropitious to the operation. When we read that '*even in his own day*, Athens was more democratic than Aristo-tle's philosophy of government, and he was *already* con-siderably *behind the times*' (p. 11, italics mine), we become

Review published in *Medium Aevum*, vol. 3 (February 1934), pp. 69–70.

uneasy.[3] And our fears are confirmed on p. 339, where the author speaks of 'a medieval conception that is now wholly lost: namely that every individual soul is of equal value in the eyes of the Deity and that all inequalities and injustices and sufferings in this world are blotted out in the next'.[4]

As Miss Mohl is not writing modern history, it does not perhaps greatly matter than she has been misinformed as to the total loss of this conception: what is serious, as arguing historical error, is the use of the word 'medieval' as a synonym for 'Christian', or (even if we regard the first part of her 'conception') for 'Stoical' as well.

It must be admitted, then, that Miss Mohl lacks certain qualifications for a sympathetic reconstruction of the past. To this she may well reply that her aim was less ambitious. She describes more than she explains and explains more than she criticizes: hers is the modest, though laudably laborious, task of mere observation and record; and on this level she has done a great deal of work. I have learned from her much that I am glad to know. The value of the book is to be sought less in its main theme than in the facts that arise by the way: for Miss Mohl interprets the 'form' she set out to study, so very liberally that it almost disappears, and we are left in some doubt as to its very existence.

At the outset it has to be admitted that the definition 'catalogues of classes' is too narrow; for women are one of the items of most of the catalogues. On p. 43 the *Roman de Miserere* is introduced not because it *is*, but because it *contains*, a catalogue of estates. As we proceed we find more and more space devoted to texts whose only relevance is that they somewhere or other contain a list of, or even a reference to, the classes of society.

A section headed 'Lydgate's *use of the Form*' (pp. 110 *et seq.*, italics mine) opens with a list of purely incidental references to 'statis' from the Troy Book.[5] Passages on Death and Fortune are quoted because the authors mention all 'estates' as being equally their prey. Lyndsay's description of Hell is quoted, and Henryson's is not, because Lyndsay, in his list of the damned, adds 'commoun pepill' to the Kings and Prelates whom he found in Henryson.[6] More and Elyot are discussed at length.[7] *The Book of Precedence*, John Russell's *Boke of Nurture*, and the like are liberally quoted:[8] but the author does not show that they have more claim to illustrate her 'form' than the *Guide to Whipsnade* has to illustrate the Beast Epic.

It is easy to be too severe on such catholicity. The utility of research books is, to speak frankly, a matter of chance. The man who seeks them out in libraries is always following some trail of his own: and who knows what may, or may not, be useful to him? But Miss Mohl's procedure, if it does not destroy her book, at least raises the question whether what she is pursuing is really a Form at all. Is she contributing to the history of literary kinds or to the history of political thought? If to the latter, we can justify many of her quotations, which do illustrate a common *matter*, though they fail to illustrate a common *form*. We can justify the space devoted to More and Elyot. But if More and Elyot deserve seven pages, why is Aquinas dismissed in as many lines?

If, on the other hand, Miss Mohl is writing the literary history of a Form, it cannot be denied that we hear surprisingly little of that form in her pages, and surprisingly much of a certain body of ideas, occurring now in verse, now in prose, now in *débat* and now in allegory, sometimes in satire and sometimes in serious political propaganda, and illustrating more often than not no literary phenomenon except the medieval love of catalogue.

Some points of detail are open to criticism. '*Works*, ed. Henry Davis, London, 1861, II, 49' is an unusual and inconvenient way of directing us to a passage in Plato. Gower's *Confessio Amantis* is not, as Miss Mohl states on p. 106, 'a series of love stories'. In a passage quoted by Miss Mohl on p. 124, with no sign of disapproval, we read that 'they' (*sc.* Cessoles and his translators) 'had no more doubt as to the divine right of the monarch, than the Thibetan has of the divine right of the grand lama'.[9] If so, Cessoles and his translators stood almost alone in the Middle Ages. On p. 28 Miss Mohl tells us with admirable caution that 'it has been assumed' that Gower was a merchant: it is the more disappointing that by p. 63 he has become, with no tinge of doubt, 'Gower the self-made man', to explain – what needs no explanation – his use of the *locus communis* on our common descent from Adam.

On p. 329, after referring to Gower's doctrine that 'constellacion' is not to blame for the state of the world (*Conf. Am. Prol.* 529 *et seq*),[10] Miss Mohl proceeds, 'Though Gower thinks so little of the stars as an excuse . . . Spenser, in the late sixteenth century, reasserts their influence in much the same way that the Middle Ages did'. I very much doubt the suggested antithesis.

In the first place Astrology neither began nor ended with the Middle Ages. In the second place, within the Middle Ages themselves, Gower does not stand alone in rejecting rigid astrological determinism (cf. *Roman de la Rose* 17070 *et seq.*).[11] Finally, Spenser is not speaking, like Gower, of *influencia planetarum*, but of the general secular movement of the Heaven as a whole, which he had read about in the *Somnium Scipionis*.[12]

Miss Mohl writes throughout in an easy and agreeable manner and is quite free from the pseudo-scientific jargon which literary research work seems to encourage. In the difficult art of writing abstracts of diffuse medieval texts without extreme dullness she is unusually successful.

# 34

## J. W. H. Atkins, *English Literary Criticism: The Medieval Phase* (Cambridge University Press, 1943)

≈

Literary criticism in medieval England is a subject which would seem at first sight to admit the same terse treatment as the snakes of Iceland.[1] Professor Atkins deserves our gratitude for having undertaken the long and unrewarding labour of extracting from many copious authors their rare (and often unilluminating) *obiter dicta* on literature. He has resisted the temptation to disguise the fact that most of what he finds is very small beer. He makes it abundantly plain that the history of criticism is at first merely the history of rhetoric – in particular that form of rhetoric which descends from the New Sophistic. In this context Boccaccio's *De Genealogia Deorum* occupies a more important position than I had suspected, and its allegorical and inspirational theory of poetry appears as a positively liberating influence.[2] The most interesting part of Professor Atkins' material is provided by the vernacular writers. Among these I think Barbour deserved mention,[3] and I do not always agree with Professor Atkins' interpretations of Chaucer. But perhaps after a few years I should not agree with my own.

Published in *The Oxford Magazine*, vol. 62 (10 February 1944), p. 158.

# 35

## Arthuriana: *Arthurian Literature in the Middle Ages: A Collaborative Study*, ed. R. S. Loomis (Oxford: Clarendon Press, 1959)

~

Few of the contributions to this Arthurian encyclopedia (for it is little less) would feel competent to give an opinion on all the articles it contains. It was therefore difficult to find an adequate critic, and I am well aware that the *Review* has not done so: I am not master even of all the languages involved. I am reduced to picking about here and there for what I can tackle, like a dyspeptic at a richly-spread banquet.

The chapters are not only diverse in subject but different in kind. At one end of the scale in Professor Frappier's 'Chrétien de Troyes' we have full-blown literary criticism designed to 'set in relief the creative work of the poet' (p. 163).[1] This is perhaps the masterpiece of the book. We have here the high French academic tradition at its best, learned as Dryasdust but urbane as Sainte-Beuve.[2] We could do with more such Arthuriana. At the other end there are chapters (far more numerous) which are entirely taken up with close reasoning to conclusions about matter of fact.

These latter are often of great interest and value. No discipline is to be blamed for not answering questions outside

Review published in *The Cambridge Review*, vol. 81 (13 February 1960), pp. 355, 357.

its own scope. The danger is lest it should, unconsciously and by implication, prejudge them. In his 'Origin of the Grail Legends' Professor Loomis sets out 'to account for' the 'absurdities' (p. 277) and 'irrationality' (p. 276) of the story as told by Chrétien. That is, he wants to know why the Host appears in a *graal* instead of in a chalice or ciborium, carried by a damsel instead of by a priest. This itself, we may remark, is simply the particularization of a question which might be asked about nearly every scene in every Grail romance in the general form: 'Why does the sacred appear in a romantic, chivalric, and to that extent secularized, guise? Why does the Grail haunt a castle, not a cathedral or abbey? Why does its pursuit take the form of knightly adventures, not of the 'religious' life? Why does its presence provide carnal good cheer on the table rather than grace?'

His general answer is, as we all know, that in these works we see a Pagan myth – or a whole muddle of myths – partially Christianized. But press him as to why any myths, or why just these myths, were Christianized, and you get the answer: 'No procedure could be more reasonable than to seek the cause of the sanctification of the Grail legends in a series of misunderstandings' (p. 287). The Body of Christ comes into the Grail romances because somebody mistook *cors* (a horn) for *cors* (body) (p. 288).

With this, you see, all the poets and romancers as such – all the concrete, talented human individuals, producing works of art for the delight and edification of other individuals – vanish from the picture. Authors are, in fact, being treated like scribes, and literary history conducted by the methods – Lachmann's methods of textual criticism.[3] When a scribe departs from his original we assume he

does so in error: because a scribe *ex officio* is behaving as
like a machine as he can. To treat authors like scribes is to
reproduce the absurdity of Bédier when he said that a certain variation from the supposed archetype of the Tristan
story would not have been made independently by Eilhart
and Béroul (pp. 136–7).[4]

In reality it could be predicted that any number of
authors, faced with that supposed archetype, would independently think of just this variation as one possible way
out of its main difficulty. Supposing people did mistake
*cors* (horn) for *cors* (body), what induced them to write
just these poems about the Body? Poets are not passive
pipelines through which *motifs* pass by their own energy.
Of the things that come into his head (even if some come
by error) the poet selects what he chooses.

I submit that Professor Loomis has here, like Percevale
himself, failed to ask a question.[5] He has failed to ask what
*why* ('Why is the Grail borne by a damsel?') means. *Why*
demands either an efficient cause (why did the dam burst?)
or a final cause (why are you going to London?). But the
Celtic myths and their possible misunderstanding are not
the efficient cause of any episode in Chrétien. Their mere
existence did not force him to put anything into his poem.
They are at most a *conditio sine qua non*. He could not have
put them in if he had not had them; but, having them, he
put them in because (for some reason) he chose.

Nor could they be the final cause. The final cause is the
effect that Chrétien intended them to have on his readers. And might not that effect be the very one which they
have actually had? Might not the quasi-secularization of
his sacred theme have been intended to produce just that
liberation from reverential inhibitions, that fresh wonder,

which the Christian matter elicits by catching us off our guard? Might not the cryptic quality be designed to exercise just that fascination which has kept Professor Loomis's attention fixed on these stories (to our delight) for so many years? When we are dealing with a genius we must not exclude the hypothesis that he meant to do just what he has in fact done.

On the other hand, we get real literary criticism from Dr Loomis on *Gawain and the Green Knight*.[6] He ignores the anthropological approach which, for some years, so darkened counsel. That was an attempt to explain the knowable by the unknowable; the poem, which we can enter into, by the prehistoric rite which, if it existed, no man alive has experienced from within.[7] It ignored the profound ambivalence of Bercilak,[8] to which Professor Loomis does justice. Personally, I would go further than he. The final Bercilak who solemnly pronounces Gawain 'the fautlest freke' is not merely the madcap Bercilak whom we have seen in his own castle, still less the ogreish Bercilak of Arthur's hall. He rises high, grows more numinous.

On Laȝamon also Professor Loomis is good, but I suggest that he follows too readily Tatlock's strictures on his ferocity.[9] We must indeed admit that the English *Brut* foists upon Arthur, without disapproval, one atrocity not found in Wace.[10] But this is not typical. In general his rough-hewn heroes have kinder hearts than Wace's more elegant knights. His Brennus repairs war-damage and repatriates enemy refugees (5938 *sq.*). His Caesar – alas that ever such a soul had to go to Hell! (7223) – treats the captured Cassibelaun with courtesy (8942 *sq.*) Vertimer plans the liberation of all slaves (18852). Arthur vows that if he wins France every poor man shall fare the better for it (23741); he provides lovingly for his discharged veterans and sends them home with pious advice (24115 *sq*.). The difference between the two poets is epitomized in their descriptions of Arthur: for Wace, one of love's lovers and the founder of country manner, but, for Laȝamon, one who was a father to the young and a comforter to the old (19936). Laȝamon constantly – Wace, I believe, never – remembers the sufferings of common people. He was almost one of them. We may conjecture that he expends on the Saxons of his imaginary past a hatred aroused by the actual Normans and 'their nith craefte' (7116). He makes this happen at Badon which ought to have happened at Hastings. He is at once fiercer and tenderer than Wace.

Professor Loomis has well divined that Laȝamon's sea is always seen from the shore. We feel this in the gradual appearance of Ursula's scattered fleet (12036 *sq*.) We feel it still more in the waves that foamed 'as if villages burned there' (4528). These are breakers coming in against an off-shore wind, not deep-sea billows. But are such passages 'landlubber's commonplaces' (p. 110)? Landsman's, if you like; but for 'commonplaces' read 'strokes of genius'.

As was expected, Professor Vinaver contributes one of the richest articles. Though he has, necessarily, much to say about sources, he never slips into the sort of scholarship that tends 'away from the masterpiece' (p. 546). Though he has done work enough on Malory to weary ten men, there is no hint of *crambe repetita*:[11] one gets the impression that the author is still growing in his mind. Much that he has to say is controversial, but the temper is not. For him, obviously, the important thing about dissentients is not that they should be silenced but that their discussion should throw new light on Malory for us all.

This brings me to a final subject for congratulation. This is a civilized book. There is in it none of the veiled calling [of] names and unveiled resentment which, in so much modern criticism and scholarship, are rapidly restoring *la brutalité des journaux anglais.*[12] The rising tide of neo-barbarism has not yet submerged medieval studies. Long may their immunity last!

# 36

## Introduction from *Selections from Laȝamon's* Brut, ed. G. L. Brook

~

The English *Brut*, like Malory's *Morte Darthur* or Chaucer's *Troilus* and *Knight's Tale*, is a work for which we can thank no single author. Touching up something that was already there is almost the characteristically medieval method of composition.

In 1147 Geoffrey of Monmouth produced his prose *Historia Regum Britanniae*. It gives the British story from the birth of Brutus to the death of Cadwallader and claims to have got it out of an ancient book in the British tongue (i. 1). We know no such book, but much genuine legend and some true history may survive in Geoffrey's narrative. To the Arthurian section (vii. 20–xi. 2) it was probably his own rather vulgar invention that added the tasteless fiction of Arthur's foreign conquests.

Wace (ob. 1175?) turned Geoffrey's matter into Norman French octosyllabics as the *Geste des Bretons* or *Roman de Brut*. He approached his work neither like a modern historian nor like a modern novelist. On the one hand, he thinks his story mainly true, though not completely reliable, and is anxious to avoid errors; from a different poem, the *Roman de Rou*, it appears that he sometimes took pains to test a tradition by personal investigation. On the other

Published in *Selections from Laȝamon's* Brut, ed. by G. L. Brook (Oxford: Clarendon Press, 1963), pp. vii–xv.

hand, he feels himself quite free to touch up Geoffrey's narrative, describing scenes as if he had been an eyewitness and adding details from his own imagination. His poem is bright and clear, not without gaiety, and slightly touched with scepticism. In it the courtesy and pageantry and some of the love-lore of the High Middle Ages appear.

Then came Laȝamon, who probably wrote before 1207. He tells us he was a priest of Ernleȝe (King's Areley) on the Severn, and had travelled much. Whether only in England, is not clear; but an amusing passage about 'muglinges' suggests that he had visited the Continent and there been twitted with coming from an island where men have tails (M<sup>a</sup> 29593–8). He tells us – speaking here like a true book-lover – that he used three sources: an English book by Bede (no doubt the Old English translation of the *Ecclesiastical History*), a book by *Seinte Albin and þe feire Austin*, and Wace (M 30–40). The second item is a puzzle, and we are not satisfied with the explanation that it is simply Bede over again, but this time in Latin. It is, however, only the last source, Wace, that really throws much light on Laȝamon's work.

The English *Brut* differs importantly from Wace's *Roman*. Before asking why, it is best to make clear how.

I. Its very language – still more its metre and phraseology, which both descend from Anglo-Saxon verse – make it inevitably sterner, more epic, more serious. Nothing in Norman octosyllabics ever had the hammer-like impact of *Godes wiðersaka* (M 1808), *mid orde and mid egge* (M 5202), *sæwerie* (M 6205), *weorld-scome* (M 8323), or *feollen þa fæie* (M 14038).

<hr>

<sup>a</sup> M = Madden's edition.

II. It is more archaic and less sophisticated than the *Roman*. Wace's characters are knights and courtiers; those of the *Brut*, heroes and thanes. Wace's battles often have some real strategy; the *Brut* blurs or ignores it and shows us only what primary epic would show – the war-hedge like a grey wood (M 16372), old warriors hewn with swords (M 4166–7), shields cloven (M 5186), heathen souls packed off to hell (M 18321). Wace writes like one who knows contemporary courts; the *Brut*'s picture of a court is something like Hrothgar's hall. In Wace the Roman ambassadors are real diplomats, grave old men carrying olive branches; in the *Brut*, 'valiant thanes, high battle-warriors, high men with weapons' (M 24741). In the passage which immediately follows, the differences are even more interesting. Arthur summons his council in a room at the top of a tower. As Wace's knights go up the spiral stair Cador calls out merrily to Arthur that this threat from Rome is welcome; there's been too much peace and love-making. Gawain replies in defence of love ' . . . thus the lords joked'. In the *Brut* there is no joking and no chatting on the stairs. First the tower itself is characterized – 'an ancient stonework, stout men wrought it' (M 24885) – and this Beowulfian glance at a remoter past alters, as it were, the whole lighting of the passage. There is nothing about love. Cador seriously denounces idleness; Gawain utters weighty praise of peace. There is a real strife or *flit* between them, and Arthur, who knows the swords might be out any minute, quells it sternly (M 24966–72). Not a trace of the Norman gaiety remains.

III. The *Brut*, though fiercer, is usually kinder than the *Roman*. Once, indeed, it introduces an atrocity (M 22841 ff.) of its own. But it was done in hot blood, and far more often its rough-hewn heroes have tender hearts. Its Brennus saves Rome from pillage and massacre and brings home the refugees (M 5944 ff.). Its Vortimer has a project for emancipating all slaves (M 14852). Its Arthur swears that if he wins France every poor man's life shall be the easier for it (M 23741). He dismisses his veteran knights to pass their last days in prayer (M 2411f ff.). He is a father to the young and a comforter to the old; Wace's Arthur had been one of Love's lovers and the founder of all the courtesies that kings have used since. Its charity extends even to pagans (provided, of course, that they are not Saxons); alas that ever such a man as Julius Caesar should have gone to hell! (M 7223).

IV. It is rather more interested in marvels than Wace had been. It tells us that elves took and enchanted Arthur as soon as he was born (M 19253 ff.; 1894 below), and that an elvish smith had made his byrnie (M 21131; 2830 below). In addition to the prophetic eagles mentioned by Geoffrey and the *Roman*, nikers people its Loch Lomond till it becomes very like Grendel's mere (M 21739 ff.; 3134 ff. below).

V. It has touched up Wace as Wace touched up Geoffrey. In it all becomes one degree more actual, closer to the reader. It has far more dialogue than Wace, much of it excellent. Where he had said merely that people gave certain news or made certain arrangements, the *Brut* sets them talking, soliloquizing, too, or praying. It might have been written by one who had learned from Aristotle that the narrative poet should speak as little as possible in his own person. It realizes visually and emotionally much that Wace merely stated or ignored. It shows us the pirates watching the arrival of Ursula's storm-tossed fleet, 'ships...one...and one...sometimes more...sometimes none...then four...then five' (M 12034 ff.); Merlin in his trance twisting like a snake 'as those said who had seen it' (M 17906 ff.; 1221 ff. below); Arthur turning alternately red and white, when they told him he was king (M 19887 ff.; 2210 ff. below). It adds to the account of Merlin's begetting all that renders the story worth telling – the virgin bower, the beautiful ladies-in-waiting, the glimmering golden shape of the aerial ravisher (M 15700 ff.). Chaucer himself is hardly more vivid and immediate than scores of passages in the *Brut*.

VI. It has a wealth of simile that Wace lacks. Troops muster thick as hail (M 14517). Ridwathlan rushes on his enemies as a whirlwind, with its cloud of dust, rushes on a field (M 27645). An army advances 'as if the earth would catch fire' (M 4577, 11978). More surprisingly, we find those long-tailed or Homeric similes which were not a characteristic of Anglo-Saxon epic: the wolf (M 20120–7), the hunted crane (M 20163–75), and the goat (M 21301–15). That of the 'steel fishes' (M 21323–30) is in a class by itself. Its complex imaginative structure illustrates the 'esemplastic faculty' better than anything in Wordsworth.

The *Brut* has many faults, but they are those of its source; it is tied to Geoffrey's amorphous, and sometimes uninteresting, matter. Its (often astonishing) merits are its own. Can we say 'Laȝamon's own'? This, for several reasons, would be rash.

I. Many scholars think that he did not work from the text of Wace, as we now have it, but from a recension already incorporating other materials.

II. Laȝamon never mentions Geoffrey, and, since medieval 'historical' poets are far readier to boast of learning than of invention, we may probably infer that he never saw the *Historia*. Hence passages where he agrees with Geoffrey but not with Wace may well indicate an independent recourse to the same – presumably Celtic – tradition on which Geoffrey depended. Such are his 'thirty days' (M 1275, Wace, *trois jors*), his specification of the fief given to Hengist as Lindesey (M 14050), *Pridwen* as the name of Arthur's shield (M 21152), and others. But even if we assumed that he had read Geoffrey, we should still have evidence that he knew more of Geoffrey's sources than Geoffrey transmitted. At vii. 3, Geoffrey makes Merlin prophesy that Arthur's acts will be food to those who tell them (*actus eius cibus erit narrantibus*). Laȝamon gives us six lines (M 18856–61) in the same strain. The manner is quite unlike his usual style and quite un-English. He must be giving us more of the same Welsh poem that under-lies Geoffrey. Again, in a passage peculiar to the *Brut* (M 13563–90), the name Gille Callaet for Constance's mur-derer suggests Celtic tradition.

III. The *Brut* alone relates (M 12253 ff.) the revolt of Ethelbald and Ælfwald. The thoroughly English names given to these supposed Britons, and the firm localiza-tion of their revolt in East Anglia – no regional patrio-tism would lead Laȝamon there – strongly suggest that he is here in touch with an English, not British, tradi-tion of some later revolt, perhaps against Danes, or even Normans.

IV. Mr H. S. Davies[b] has acutely observed that many of the *Brut*'s best similes, and all its long-tailed similes, are bunched in one section (M 20000–22000). He also finds

[b] In the *Review of English Studies*, May 1960.

that Arthur's character is a little different in this section, and that the course of events – we are dealing with Arthur's defeat of the Saxons – departs considerably from that in Wace. It is difficult to explain how a poet who had once achieved the long-tailed simile should then abandon it completely in his subsequent work. Mr Davies therefore suggests that Laȝamon may here be following closely a lost poem in Old, or early Middle, English. This seems not improbable.

An acceptance of this hypothesis would make a differ- ence to our estimate of Laȝamon's individual genius. But what most interests the historian of poetry would not be changed. Either way – in Laȝamon or in the lost poem – we see the vigorous survival of our native poetic style. Either way, we see it enriched by the long-tailed simile, and must still wonder whether this is due to the sheer leap of some remarkable genius or to the influence (possibly at many removes) of Virgil.

Mr Davies modestly raises a needless difficulty against himself by stressing the paradox of a work so very English as his hypothetical poem must have been which neverthe- less celebrated the defeat of the English by the Britons. But it would not have differed in this respect from the *Brut* itself, which professes to tell the story of the 'Engle' (M 13) and actually tells that of the Britons, making of the real 'Engle' a comparatively brief and wholly hate- ful interruption. It would not have differed in this from later treatments of Arthur. They all take the British side. Ignorance of racial fact and indifference to strictly racial sentiment are the norm. In poets so early as Laȝamon there might be a special reason. The Normans with their *nið cræfte* (M 7116) were still fairly new. The Saxons, like

them, had been foreign invaders. Arthur, like Harold, had
been fighting for our homes. It was perhaps some compen-
sation to show Colgrim actually faring at Bath as William
the Bastard ought to have fared at Hastings. Perhaps after
all we need no lost poem to explain (if that were all) why
Arthur should be fiercer and far more alive in this part of
the *Brut* than in his foreign wars.

The metre of the *Brut* descends from Anglo-Saxon verse.
Its direct ancestor was probably not the 'classical' verse of
Beowulf but a looser and more popular form. It is, however, by starting from the classical type that the metre
is most easily analysed. Its units were selected blocks of
speech rhythm, known as Half-lines. The elements of each
Half-line were Lifts and Dips. A Lift is either one long and
accented syllable or two short syllables with accent on the
first. A Dip is any reasonable number of unaccented syllables. There were five types of Half-line, all of which can be
traced in the *Brut*. We add modern equivalents in brack-
ets, and all the Anglo-Saxon examples are from *Beowulf*.

A. Lift–Dip–Lift–Dip. *prým gefrúnon* (2), or *mónegum
mǽgþum* (5). ('Wells and Winches or Merry-eyed maid-
ens'.) *Brut: mónnen fróure* (M 25570) or *cómon to an kinge*
(M 17089). Anacrusis (a prelusive unaccented syllable or
syllables) may occur. *Ne frín þu æfter sǽlum* (1322). ('At
Wells and Winches'.) *Brut: and lúden bilæfden* (M 20584).

B. Dip–Lift–Dip–Lift. *Siþþan ærest wearþ* (6). ('For a
pint of beer'.) *Brut: na his clápes na his hórs* (M 17053).

C. Dip–Lift–Lift–Dip. *Ofer hrónráde* (9). ('Or of rough
cider'.) *Brut: þat he fléon wólde* (M 17058).

D. Lift–Lift–Dip. There is here only one Dip, and
it must contain an element nearly, but not quite, as

strong as a Lift. *Ýmbsíttènde* (8). ('Hood's housekeeper'.) *Brut*: *wíltídènde* (M 17090). Or expanded: *mǣre méarcstàþa* (102). ('Hunter's housekeeper'.) *Brut*: *hǽȝe hérekèmpen* (M 24743).

E. Lift–Dip–Lift. Here also the single Dip must contain a strengthening element. *Wéorþmýndum þáh* (8). ('Bed-makers' binge'.) *Brut*: *Séilien òuer sæ* (M 20889) or *Jàphèth and Chám* (M 12).

The first (and only the first) Lift of the second Half-line was linked by alliteration with one or both of the Lifts in the first Half-line; if with only one, then normally with the first. The *Brut* ignores these rules, alliterating any Lifts, or none.

Some of its Half-lines reproduce the Anglo-Saxon types perfectly, some approximately, and others not at all. In the latter class we find (1) four-beat types: *Láuerd hu háuest þu ifáren toníht?* (M 28011). (2) More often, three-beat: *Séléste álre ræden* (M 16986), *þe nes nánes mónnes súne* (M 17107). The two Half-lines are often linked by rhyme (*umbe lutle stunde hi wurþeþ al isunde*, M 17191–2), assonance (*and ferden swa longe þat hi comon to Irlonde*, M 17262–3), or consonance (*wiþuten and wiþinne mon toȝenes monne*, M 22917–18).

The *Brut* thus varies between passages that an Anglo-Saxon poet's ear would have wholly approved – such as

<blockquote>

*æðela iwurðen,*
*Wihte wal-kempen, on heora wiðer-winnan*
(M 776–8) –

</blockquote>

and the nursery-rhyme jingle of *He makede swulc grið, he makede swulc frið* (M 4254–6). But the result is not intolerable as a mixture of different syllabic metres would be,

because Laȝamon's irregular Half-lines are, no less than
the classical types, blocks of genuine speech rhythm. In
pathetic, derisive, or gnomic comment they have great
pungency. The total effect of the poem is really closer than
the rumble of much fourteenth-century alliterative verse
to the crusty, emphatic quality of Anglo-Saxon poetry.

Dr. J. Hall in his *Laȝamon's* Brut (1924) selected passages from all over the poem. We have preferred to disengage and to give as continuously as possible Laȝamon's
Arthuriad, which we think on the whole the best part of
the *Brut*. Even from this the limits of our space forced
us to omit something, and we jettisoned without reluctance the Icelandic, and the Roman wars. The record of
monotonous victories, even when true, is not the stuff of
epic; when it has no roots in history, legend, or myth, it is
hardly endurable.

# 37

## Andreas Capellanus, *The Art of Courtly Love*, with introduction, translation, and notes by John Jay Parry (New York: Columbia University Press, 1941)

∼

Mr Parry quotes from M. Bossuat the opinion that the *De Arte Honeste Amandi* is 'one of those capital works which reflect the thought of a great epoch, which explain the secret of a civilization'.[1] This, I submit, is to put its claims too high. Courtly Love itself does not suffice to explain the secret of medieval civilization and the treatise of Andreas does not, in all senses, 'explain' Courtly Love. The formal, and perhaps whimsical, systematization of his book makes it an extremely useful text for the modern scholar who wishes to illustrate the sentiment in its most distinctive and paradoxical form; but when we want to understand this sentiment from within, to think ourselves back into the attitude of the medieval lover, we may find better guidance from the poets, and not always from those poets who carry the feeling to its furthest extremity.

An English version of Andreas is, none the less, a very desirable thing, and especially for the audience Mr Parry has in view. The existence of this audience marks a stage worth noting in the history of culture. There is

Review published in *The Review of English Studies*, vol. 19 (January 1943), pp. 77–9.

now, apparently, a public sufficiently advanced in medieval studies to wish to read Latin 'source-books' about Courtly Love, and at the same time so innocent of Latin that when Mr Parry (p. 4) mentions Ovid he finds it advisable to slip in tactfully the information that Ovid was a poet and 'lived in Rome in the time of the Emperor Augustus'. What, after all, could be more medieval than this?

Mr Parry's Introduction brings readably together a good deal of information about the circumstances in which medieval love poetry arose and the suggestions offered by scholars as to its origin. He himself is a moderate upholder of the Arabian theory which he supports by liberal quotation from Arabic sources, especially from the *Dove's Neck-Ring* of Ibn Hazm.[2] The evidential value of these quotations varies. I do not myself think that Ibn Hazm's references to sighs and tears, pallor, jealousy, secrecy, and loss of appetite are very conclusive. On the other hand the Arabic convention whereby 'for decency's sake' the mistress is given masculine pronouns and adjectives, and the fact that she can be addressed as 'lord' and 'master' (*sayyidi* and *mawlaya*) are a very striking parallel to the Provençal use of *midons* and *senhor*.

But the most difficult bit of evidence to interpret is the Platonic element in Ibn Hazm. He seems to know the Myth of the *Symposium* and represents lovers as divided parts of a single pre-natal soul striving to recover its lost unity; and he says that the soul, being herself beautiful, desires Beauty, and therefore 'inclines to perfect images'.[3] Now this idea, unless I am mistaken, is not found in the poetry of Courtly Love. On the other hand, when Plato's erotic mysticism became known to Western Europe a few centuries later, the courtly tradition immediately embraced it, as we see in Ficino, Castiglione, and Spenser. Courtly Love and Platonism are, then, things eminently congenial to each other. One might say indeed that they had long been waiting for each other: that Platonism which found in Athens no better soil than Greek pederasty had to wait for the Renaissance to find its true embodiment, and that Courtly Love, which in the Middle Ages had to make shift with the mock theology of Cupid, had to wait for the same period to find its true metaphysic. It therefore becomes a nice question whether the Platonic element in the Moslem poets supports the theory that the Troubadours are indebted to them, or whether it is, in fact, the strongest argument against that theory. For it might well be argued, 'This thing, as later history proves, is so congenial to Courtly Love, that if the Provençals had encountered it they must have reproduced it. If they did not, the most natural explanation is that they knew nothing of Arabic literature'. I leave the question to those now working on a subject with which I have somewhat lost touch.

One point which Mr Parry does not make quite clear is the extent to which such sentiment as Ibn Hazm expresses was a novelty in Arabic literature. Ibn Hazm himself, however, is quoted as saying that the ways of 'the Bedouins and the ancients' in love were 'different from ours' (p. 9). If this means that the Moslem love poetry of his own age is as great an innovation in the Moslem tradition as that of the Troubadours is in the Christian, then the question of Spanish or Provençal precedence sinks into secondary importance compared with the massive originality – and mystery – of the sentiment that arose about this time at the Western end of the Mediterranean. When a phenomenon

AB is new as a whole, we must be careful not to whittle this fact away or to imagine that we have 'explained' it by tracing the relations of A to B and of B to A.

In his Preface Mr Parry says that he has tried to keep his translation close to the original even at the cost of 'somewhat awkward English'.[4] 'Awkward' is much too harsh a word for the lucid version he has actually made. There is, indeed, a sort of unleavened taste about nearly all translations from Latin prose, and Mr Parry has not avoided it. (The verb *seem* is one of the traps. It is seldom a good rendering of *videri* on stylistic grounds, and not always on lexical grounds either.) He has certainly not succeeded in reproducing the 'colloquial' character which he attributes (p. vii) to the original: but I am not quite clear wherein the colloquialism of Andreas' Latin consists.

This is a useful book and ought to be in College libraries.

# 38

## Rhyme and reason: Dorothy L. Sayers, *The Poetry of Search and the Poetry of Statement* (London: Gollancz, 1963)

~

This collection offers us 12 papers read by Dorothy Sayers to various academic and literary societies between 1946 and 1957: some reprinted from the Proceedings of the societies, and some here printed for the first time.

*The Poetry of Search and the Poetry of Statement* makes good, I think, the distinction it proposes, but does not convince me that this distinction is very fruitful. Thus it leads us to an unexpected re-interpretation of the *Idylls of the King*. I tried it out by re-reading some of the best of them, and I thought it worked.

But the trouble is that it made no difference to the qualities I already liked and disliked in them. I continued to like and dislike them just as much as before and in just the same way – which leads me to doubt whether this distinction has really much to do with the reality of a poem as a poem.

Four of the essays are concerned in varying degrees with Dante, and of these the richest is that 'On Translating the *Divina Comedia*'. I suppose we are not all agreed as to the two characteristics of Dorothy Sayers's own Dante.[1] One,

Review published in *The Sunday Telegraph*, no. 148 (1 December 1963), p. 18.

eminently laudable, is the apparatus. No doubt there are some errors: but as a whole it is a model of judicious popularisation which has already proved useful to thousands. Such work was never more needed than now and is in very short supply.

The other characteristic is more controversial. As a translator Dorothy Sayers is the arch-rebel against the Cary tradition.[2] It had represented Dante as an earlier Milton. She discovered for herself Dante as the exciting story-teller, the writer of high comedy, even the writer of low farce.

Nor is there the least doubt that the very un-Miltonic qualities she saw in Dante are really there. The question is whether her reading of Dante did not exaggerate them or whether the colloquialism and comically violent rhythms by which she tried to represent them did not carry the exaggeration further.

A passage in the essay shows, I think, how she arrived at her practice and suggests a possible error. She is undoubtedly right in thinking that the passage on military music in *Inferno* xxii must be read as burlesque: its attachment to the Rabelaisian slapstick of *avea del cul fatto trombetta* makes this certain.[3]

But can she be right when she finds in *quando con trombe, e quando con campane* the lilt of 'Diddle-didle-dumpling, my son John'?[4] The resemblance seems to me extremely faint. In so far as it exists at all it depends upon the fact that the English line is really two lines and that the Italian similarly breaks in two after *trombe*. But don't all Dante's lines so break when read by an Italian?

His verse has a caesura in the proper sense, as English has not – for to use that word of the syntactical pause which may come anywhere in our line and need not come at all is a confusion. We English tend to read Dante to the rune of our own decasyllable. It looks as if Dorothy Sayers did. As a result, lines which do not submit to that treatment (most will) stuck out for her as they do not for the Italian reader, and the effect she tries to reproduce by her metrical extravagance does not exist.

This does not of course dispose of her version. It goes to one extreme in trying to correct another. It will presently be corrected by some of its successors. Such is the history of translation.

Two of the most cogent essays are 'The Work Tools of Learning' and 'The Teaching of Latin', and it would be too much to hope that they will influence educational practice. The book everywhere exhibits the style and temper for which the author was both loved and hated. The essays are full of cheerful energy. The young people would call them 'bonhomous'.

By a bonhomous writer they mean one who seems to like writing and what he writes of, and to assume that his readers will mostly be people he would like. I think that this last assumption is what infuriates them.

# 39

## Alan M. F. Gunn, *The Mirror of Love: A Reinterpretation of* The Romance of the Rose (Lubbock: Texas Technological College, 1952)

≈

This long, but never tedious, book has the charm of being written by an enthusiast. Professor Gunn loves the *Roman de la Rose*. The highest praises given to it by previous critics are for him wholly inadequate: we are all mere enemies and traducers of Jean de Meun.[1] For in Professor Gunn's view the second part of the *Roman* has not only incidental merit but true poetic unity.

His first proof of this thesis, from medieval and Renaissance testimony, is by far the weakest. Professor Gunn has no difficulty in showing that the *Roman* was regarded, in the centuries that immediately followed its appearance, as a work on a single subject, Love. But in some sense or other no one would deny this: of course it is about Love, as the *Metamorphoses* are about shape-changing or Burton's *Anatomy* is about melancholy. The question is whether it has true organic unity. Again, Professor Gunn shows that in early times it was not accused of lacking unity. But surely it is very possible that a medieval book might in fact commit that fault though no medieval critic complained of it.

Review published in *Medium Aevum*, vol. 32 (1953), pp. 27–31.

The second argument is much stronger. Professor Gunn maintains (in my opinion successfully) that all the apparent ramblings of Jean de Meun conform to the rules of *amplificatio*. His various topics sprout out of his main theme in such manner and such profusion as the rhetoricians commended. Critics who have complained of them as irrelevancies were not reading his work 'with the same spirit that its author writ'.[2] As one of those critics I plead guilty. For certainly, as Professor Gunn says, 'Every artist deserves to be judged first by the standards of his own time' (p. 141). There is a profound difference between Dante's work and Jean de Meun's when both are obeying the rhetoricians. We hardly need to notice – we certainly do not need to plead in extenuation – Dante's obedience to local and temporary rules, because his work is, in addition, obedient to rules of a far subtler and more permanent kind. Two women, the one beautiful and the other absurdly dressed, may be in the fashion. We think of fashion when we look at the second because it is her only excuse. When we are looking at the first her conformity to fashion hardly seems to matter.

Of this distinction Professor Gunn is, of course, perfectly well aware. That is why, having shown Jean de Meun's construction to be satisfactory by the standard of medieval rhetoric, he proceeds to argue that it is also satisfactory by a far higher standard; that it has a unity which is 'fundamental and not simply rhetorical' (p. 141).

We are now at the heart of the book and Professor Gunn writes with a fervour and exaltation which will arouse suspicion in some but which I myself have found curiously impressive. In these glowing pages, seeing the

*Roman* through Professor Gunn's eyes, I certainly feel the presence of an 'esemplastic' imagination imposing unity on a great wealth of attractive material. What is hard to decide is whose imagination it is. Are we being shown at last the poetic whole which Jean de Meun made out of chaotic experience, or are we being shown the poetic whole which Professor Gunn has made out of the chaotic *Roman*? Either way, it is excellent reading: but as scholars we should like the question to be settled. At the same time it is not easy to see how the methods of scholarship can settle it.

At first sight the solution may seem easy. On p. 151 Professor Gunn says that in certain passages of the *Roman* hitherto suspected of irrelevance, 'there is no part which is not related in some way to the theme of love'. The words 'in some way' are ominous. Surely it is not enough that the parts of a poem should be in some way related to the main theme. The question is, in what way? We may then turn back to our text and find that the various topics are actually related like this. At 18488 we are reading about *Dame Abonde*. This subject arose out of illusions in general, which arose out of optical illusions in particular, which arose out of optics, which arose out of rainbows, which arose out of meteorology in general, which resumed (after a discussion on Free Will, 17101–874) an account of planets, which arose out of a general account of Nature, which was part of Nature's confession, which is relevant to the main theme because Nature is concerned with procreation, and an instance of procreation might occur if the Amant won the Rose.

Thus, if we go back a very long way, we shall find ourselves on the main road, without anywhere proceeding *per saltum*.[3] To which one is naturally tempted to reply that, if we are satisfied with a unity dependent on such connexions, then Jane Austen's Miss Bates has long been shamefully misrepresented as a type of irrelevant garrulity. In her speech (*Emma* cap. xix) beginning 'Thank you. You are so kind' everything is related to the main theme – Jane Fairfax's letter – far more closely than most of Nature's topics seem to be related to the theme of Love.

But Professor Gunn's withers would be quite unwrung by such criticism. From his point of view our abstract has left out all the real links in the passage under consideration. First of all (and here I agree with him) we have left out the grand connexion between the whole figure of Nature and Jean de Meun's theme of fertility, the 'Philosophy of Plentitude', which is dealt with in a fine chapter. But Professor Gunn wants to go much further than that. He sees the poem as a unity because he sees all sorts of implicit links which Jean de Meun has not put into words at all. The rainbows (18021–44) may be superficially and verbally linked as my abstract shows; to Professor Gunn they recall 'the familiar bow and arrows of Amors' (p. 266). The passage on optics reveals its true (implicit) relevance when it includes an account of mirrors (18045–208) and so becomes 'expressive of what is most central and profound in the poet's thought' (p. 267); for of course the whole *Roman* is *le mirouer aus Amoreus* (10651) and the original Amant had first seen the rosebed in a mirror (1615). In the same way a passage on alchemy (16083–148) is highly relevant because the Philosopher's Stone is gold, which begets gold and is thus (like the lover) concerned with begetting, perpetuation, and 'the perfecting of Nature's work' (p. 263).

It is needless to multiply examples. Professor Gunn's case depends mainly on connexions which Jean de Meun has never mentioned. It is idle to ask Professor Gunn to prove his case 'from the text' in the ordinary sense. He is not pretending that the *words* of the text prove it: he is claiming, if I understand him rightly, that the text as a whole will show this sort of implicit or occult unity if read by a sufficiently alert and suggestive mind. For he believes that Jean de Meun 'makes use of suggestion and indirection, of symbolic rather than logical reference, of foreshadowing and repetition and variation and contrast of significant images and apologies': in fact, of a method rather like that of the symphony (pp. 299–300).

It is easy to foresee how a book like this may be rejected with contempt by a certain kind of scholar, or swallowed whole (and turned into a public nuisance for a year or two) by some literary man writing in an unscholarly but 'high-brow' weekly. It would be better that judgment should be suspended till we have all had time to re-read the *Roman* in its entirety (nothing less would be fair) and to consider how far Professor Gunn's conception of Jean de Meun is consistent with all we know about medieval habits of composition and even of the medieval mind in general. Could Jean really have been quite so like a modern *symboliste* as Professor Gunn's theory demands? Could that theory be propounded in Old French or medieval Latin and made intelligible to Jean de Meun himself? Perhaps Professor Gunn would think such a test worthless: for he very honestly admits (p. 312) that the poet 'can hardly, indeed, be proved' to have used this symphonic method consciously.

Of Jean de Meun's ideas, as distinct from his technique, Professor Gunn is aware that his view will seem 'strangely

un-medieval – according to the usual modern view'
(p. 255). Historically considered, the protests against vir-
ginity and praises of generation uttered by Nature and
Genius might be regarded as a magnificent hypertrophe of
similar speeches given to Cupid in Latin epithalamiums.
Most of us would go further and say that Jean, excus-
ing such sentiments by their obvious dramatic propriety,
pours into them his real delight in the spectacle of Nature's
fecundity. Many of us would go a stage further still and
say that, through dramatic hyperboles not perfectly serious, he is seriously pleading (against extreme ascetics) the
view of Bernardus Silvester that the use of our procreative
powers is *commodus* if it is *quando, qualis, quantus oportet*
(*De Mundi Universitate*. Metr. xiv.155).[4]

But when we have done all that, we shall still be very
far from Professor Gunn. Unless I misunderstand him, he
attributes to Jean de Meun as wholly serious the doctrine
that copulation is (1) 'the chief duty of every human being'
(p. 488); (2) 'the chief concern of God' (p. 487); obligatory
on pain of damnation (p. 258); and (4) 'the chief manifestation of the goodness, the love, the overflowing bounty
of God' (p. 495). (This last, if taken seriously, would mean
that it was a greater manifestation of divine bounty than
the Passion.)

That any man of European stock could have thought
thus before the twentieth century is to me incredible. Such
ideas seem to me to belong wholly to a modern monistic
outlook in which biological values are primary. But Jean
de Meun is not monistic: his Nature herself tells us that
there is a part in every man which is not of her making
(19055 *et seq.*). I think he would have been very startled
to hear Professor Gunn calling Nature (p. 498) and even

Genius (p. 501) 'emanations' of God, and puzzled at a phrase like 'the decision of life itself, insisting upon its own perpetuation' (p. 494). I am not arguing that Professor Gunn is wrong; I am trying to make clear what very drastic revolutions in the history of ideas will be necessary if he should be right.

There is, however, one point on which I think him almost certainly wrong. Quoting (on page 221) Bernardus (II *Metrum* xiv) he treats as unacceptable the view that the genitals come last in the order of exposition because Bernardus placed them lowest in a hierarchical order. But surely this becomes quite clear if we glance back at *Prosa* xiii, where the parallel between the macrocosmic and microcosmic hierarchies is fully drawn out and *regerentur partes infimae* answers to *terrena gubernantur*?[5]

Some of Professor Gunn's best work is done in answer to the charge that Jean de Meun has no final and coherent view of love, sketching the 'period of ferment' (p. 476) in which he lived and exhibiting his 'plural-mindedness' (p. 479) or 'systematic pluralism' (p. 480). I am not certain how far the author means to carry this view. In chapter xxiv it would seem that the pluralism extends to an unresolved tension between the assertions of Raison on the one hand and those of Nature and Genius on the other: in the preceding chapter Professor Gunn comes near to saying (p. 495) that on one subject, 'the value of human love' (as understood by Nature and Genius) Jean de Meun had really made up his mind.

No one who is interested in the subject can afford to neglect this book; its quality can hardly be represented in a review. If Professor Gunn has hold of a truth at all, it is a very novel truth: we run the risk of losing it if we do not listen to him with sympathy and even with a certain (temporary) readiness to meet him halfway. Then, of course, we must go back to the text, and the whole text. He has offered us a new interpretation of an old score; the only test is to try playing it that way.

# 40

## The English prose *Morte*

~

I begin by considering certain paradoxes which have been thrown up by the remarkable discoveries made in the last fifty years about Malory and the book (or books) which he translated, with modifications, from the French and which Caxton printed in 1485. They are five in number.

I. The work has long passed for a mirror of honour and virtue; the author appears to have been little better than a criminal.

II. The work strikes every reader as a rich feast of marvels, a tale 'of faerie damsels met in forest wide'; but a comparison of it with its sources seems to show Malory almost everywhere labouring to eliminate the marvellous and introduce the humdrum.

III. The work seems to many of us the typical specimen (because it is the first specimen we met) of Interwoven or Polyphonic narrative. But once again, comparison with the sources shows everything proceeding as if Malory detested this technique and did his best to pluck the threads apart.

IV. Its handling of the Grail story sounds deeply religious, and we have the sense that it is somehow profoundly connected with the final tragedy. But a case can be made out for the view that Malory evaded the religious significance and ignored or severed the connexion.

Published in *Essays on Malory* (Oxford: Clarendon Press, 1963), pp. 7–28.

V. Malory seemed to Saintsbury (and doubtless to many) the man who alone 'makes of this vast assemblage of stories one story and one book'. The evidence of the Winchester MS. convinces Professor Vinaver that he really wrote several works which were never intended to form a whole.

If all these Paradoxes stand, they build up into a single grand Paradox. It is not of course paradoxical that a man's work should be other than he intended. What is paradoxical is that a man's work should succeed by its failure to realize every single intention he had when he made it. For it is as a mirror of honour, as a feast of marvels, as a Polyphonic narrative, as a romance of chivalry haunted by the higher mystery of the Grail, and as (in some sort) a unity, that the *Morte Darthur* has pleased. And not only pleased, but so far outstripped its rivals that it alone of all medieval prose romances has survived as a living book into our own century. In Malory's case, apparently, nothing succeeds like failure.

The reader should be warned at once that I am not attempting a *reductio ad absurdum*. I am not sure whether all the Paradoxes, in their sharpest form, will stand; but neither am I sure that all of them will completely fall. It therefore may be true that something like this paradoxical 'success by failure' has actually happened. If it has, then I want to draw a conclusion from it. But that will come later; in the meantime I will proceed to examine the five Paradoxes one by one.

I. The apparent discrepancy between the man and the work has seemed to some so formidable that they seek refuge in the possibility that the wicked Malory of the records is not our author but another man of the same name. But this is rather a desperate expedient. By all sound methodological principles a Malory whose Christian name was Thomas, who was a knight, who lived at the right time, and who was sometimes (like our Malory) in prison, must be assumed to be the author until any evidence to the contrary turns up. A far more respectable alternative is Professor Vinaver's view that the discrepancy is an illusion because the book (or books) are not in fact noble; the common belief in their 'morality' is based mainly on Caxton's preface.[a]

Yet I cannot quite accept this. It must of course be admitted that there are in the text untransmuted lumps of barbarism, like Arthur's massacre of the children (*C* 1.27). And even when we discount these, no one can claim (or should demand) that the general tone conforms to the standards either of the New Testament or of modern, peace-time respectability. But I find in it, sometimes implicit, sometimes explicit, an unforced reverence not only for courage (that of course) but for mercy, humility, graciousness, and good faith. The best way to see it is to compare Malory's heroes, the characters he obviously admired, with those of Homer, Virgil, Renaissance drama, or even our earlier novelists. I cannot conceive that even the best of them – even Hector, Pallas, Othello, or Tom Jones – could ever have been made to understand why Lancelot wept like a beaten child after he had healed Sir Urry (*C* XIX. 12). A character from Corneille

---

[a] *The Works of Thomas Malory*, ed. E. Vinaver (Oxford 1947), p. xxi. [In references to Malory in this volume *W* denotes this edition and *C* that of Caxton. Numbers refer to Book and chapter of *C* and to page, or page and line, of *W*.]

might understand the scene when Gawain, unhorsed, bids Marhaus to dismount, 'or else I will slay thy horse', and Marhaus, instantly obeying, replies, 'Grammercy, of your gentleness ye teach me courtesy' (*C* IV. 18); I doubt if he could equally have understood Lancelot's unresponsive endurance of Gawain's challenges (*C* XX. 20). I cannot deny either 'morality' (it is not a word I love) or something better to the imagination that shows us Lancelot refusing to take Gareth's victory from him at the tournament (*C* VII. 28), or Pelleas laying his sword across the throats of Gawain and Ettard (*C* IV. 22), or all Lancelot's contrition in Book XV, or the last message of Galahad, now almost a blessed spirit, to his father (*C* XVII. 22), or the final lament of Ector (*C* XXI. 13). In such passages, and indeed almost everywhere, we meet something which I chiefly hesitate to call 'morality' because it is so little like a code of rules. It is rather the civilization of the heart (by no means of the head), a fineness and sensitivity, a voluntary rejection of all the uglier and more vulgar impulses. We can describe it only in words derived from its own age, words which will now perhaps be mocked, such as *courtesy*, *gentleness*, *chivalry*. It makes the *Morte* a 'noble' as well as a 'joyous' history. I at any rate will never blacken the book to make it match the man.

But was the man so black? At first sight it would seem hard to deny, for he was convicted of cattle-lifting, poaching, extortion, sacrilegious robbery, attempted murder, and rape. The record suggests to Professor Vinaver a man who at the age of forty 'from being a peaceable and presumably well-to-do citizen . . . became a law-breaker'.[b]

---

[b] Op. cit., p. xvi.

And if we apply certain habitual conceptions of our own to Malory's record, this result seems inevitable. But are these conceptions possibly too local and modern? 'Citizen', 'law-breaker', and (why has that come in?) 'well-to-do'. I suspect that a man of Malory's class and time would not much have relished the titles 'peaceable' or 'citizen'; and the real question about his actions probably was for him, and should be for us, not whether they broke the law but whether they were cowardly, discourteous, treacherous, and (in a word) unknightly. It is not clear that they need have been. Our record of them comes from lawyers. In that age evidence was not scientifically sifted and accusers laid it on thick. In every county civil war exploited, and was exploited by, local feuds. Legal proceedings, whether civil or criminal, were often primarily moves in family quarrels. We need not assume that he did all the things he was accused of. But even if he did, he need not have been, by all standards, a villain. Cattle-lifting was a gentlemanly crime. If he killed other men's deer, so did the Douglas at Otterburn. A knightly ambush and encounter could be attempted murder. Rape need mean no more than abduction; from the legal point of view Lancelot committed rape when he saved Guinevere from the fire. If Malory, loving Joan Smyth *par amours*, and knowing her cuckoldy knave of a husband to be little better than a King Mark, carried her off behind him at 'a great gallop' and perhaps thus saved her from a broken head and two black eyes at home, he may have done what a good knight and a true lover ('of a sinful man') should. That he often fell below the highest standards of chivalry, we may well believe; we

‚need not believe that he fell flagrantly below them. He might, on the evidence, have been as good a knight as Tristram; for what should we think of Tristram himself if our knowledge of him were derived only from King Mark's solicitors?

Of course this picture is conjectural; but it is equally conjecture to represent him, on the strength of the records, as the sort of man who in our days becomes a 'criminal'. We don't know what he was really like, and I suppose we never shall.

II. This Paradox, like the next two, of course involves the assumption that differences between Malory's text and the extant MSS. of his originals are due to Malory. I think this is very probably so. I agree with Professor Vinaver that it is monstrous to set out by assuming that Malory had no spark of originality and therefore to trace everything in which he differs from those MSS. to a hypothetical, lost, intermediary. But probability is not certainty. We cannot be absolutely sure that any given passage, peculiar to Malory, or even any given omission, was his own. Everything I say about Paradoxes II, III, and IV must be understood with this *caveat*.

There are fewer marvels in Malory than in the corresponding French romances. There are, to be sure, at least two places where he introduces a marvel which they lack. But one of these seems to me[c] to be almost certainly the (not unhappy) result of a graphic error. In *C* XVII. 19 the *sword* 'arose great and marvellous and was full of

[c] Vinaver (op. cit., p. 1569 n. on 1027, 30–32) prefers a different explanation.

great heat that many men fell for dread'. In the French it was a wind (*ung vent*) that so arose. I suppose that either Malory or the scribe of the French MS. he was using, having the sword in his head from the preceding passage, wrote it here, intending to write *wind*. The other is in *C*. IV. 6, where a sudden, presumably miraculous light of torches in Malory replaces the French text's ordinary arrival of torches carried by ladies. But this, or both these, amount to nothing against the opposite instances. No one disputes that Malory's text naturalizes, negatively, by the omission of wonders, and positively, by introducing practical, mundane details. When Arthur defeats Damas he makes proper legal arrangements for the righting of the wrongs Damas has done: 'I will that ye give unto your brother all the whole manor with the appurtenance, under this form, that Sir Ontzlake hold the manor of you, and yearly to give you a palfrey' (*C* IV. 12). Similarly (in *C* VII. 35) the defeated knights swear homage and fealty to Gareth 'to hold of him for evermore'. King Anguysh sending Marhaus to Cornwall, assures him that his expenses will be amply covered (*C* VIII. 4). When Tristram bleeds over the lady's bed in *C* VIII. 14, we are told the extent of damage almost as if Malory had made up the laundry list – 'both the over-sheet and the nether-sheet and the pillows and the head-sheet'. Mordred explains at length, and very sensibly, why young knights are at a disadvantage on horseback (*C*. IX. 4). Lancelot's habit of talking in his sleep is noted (*C* XI. 8). Best of all, we are told exactly how much it had cost the Queen (£20,000) to send out knights in search of him (*C* XII. 9).

The Paradox here is not very strong, for it turns on the contrast between Malory's supposed intentions and the known effect of his work. For, clearly, even if we know what he did, we can only guess what he intended. It is possible to imagine a burly, commonsensible man who was always trying to turn the faerie world of the romances into something much more earthy and realistic. Accepting that picture, we may smile at the 'success by failure', the happy frustration of his vain labour which has made his book for centuries the chief delight of all who love the 'fairy way of writing'. But a quite different picture is equally possible. If you write fairy-tales and receive letters from your child readers, you will find that children are always asking the sort of questions that Malory is always answering. A simple and serious delight in marvellous narrative most emphatically does not involve any indifference to mundane details. The more seriously you take the story the more you want to tie everything up and to know how people got from one place to another, and what they had to eat, and how all outstanding issues were settled. Neglect of these points, whether in writer or reader, means that the whole thing is merely conventional or playful. Multiplication of marvels goes with the same attitude. Those who love them, as alone they can be loved, for their suggestiveness, their quality, will not increase their number. Two enchanters, two ghosts, two ferlies are always half as impressive as one. Every supposedly naturalistic change that Malory made in the story might proceed from a far fuller belief and a more profound delight in it than the French authors had ever known. He would not be the less English for that.

Once more, I ask no one to choose between these two pictures. Either, as it seems to me, will fit the facts. We shall never know which is true.

III. The excellent remarks of Professor Vinaver on what I have called Interwoven or Polyphonic narrative[d] will have made it clear to all readers that this is a real technique, not, as an earlier generation supposed, a mere muddle or an accidental by-product of conflation. It is a technique not peculiar to medieval prose romance. We find it fully developed over long stretches of Ovid's *Metamorphoses*. The rudiments of it are there in parts of *Beowulf*. The epic poets of Italy took it over from the romance, and Spenser took it over from them. Sidney re-wrote the *Arcadia* to make it more polyphonic. Milton seems to have toyed with the idea of using it for a great epic; he certainly acknowledged that to depart from Aristotelian unity in a narrative might be an enriching of art.[e]

Quite clearly the method continued to be used for centuries, not in blind obedience to tradition but because it gave pleasure. Dante selected this feature of chivalrous romance for special praise: *Arturi regis ambages pulcerrime*.[f] Tasso confesses that all knights and ladies prefer it; everyone reads Ariosto, and no one reads Trissino.[g] He even records how his father discovered by sad experience that 'unity of action gave little pleasure'.[h] The vogue of the Polyphonic in fact lasted longer than that of the modern novelistic technique has yet done. It would be interesting to analyse, and perhaps not difficult to account for, the pleasure it gave. But that would be too long a digression. What matters for the moment is that it

---

[d] Op. cit., pp. xlviii–liii.
[e] *Reason of Church Government*, Preface, Book 2.
[f] *De Vulgari Eloquentia*, I. x. 2.
[g] *Discorsi Poetici*, II.
[h] *Apologia in difesa della Ger. Lib.*

did please and can please still. To the present day no one enjoys Malory's book who does not enjoy its *ambages*, its interweaving.

For it is certainly interwoven. Arthur has a war against five kings. To repair his losses he must make new knights. His selection sends Bagdemagus, malcontent, from the court, and the story of his wanderings crosses the latter end of Merlin's story. Arthur meanwhile has got involved in the affairs of Damas and Ontzlake, which in their turn involve both him and Accolon in the machinations of Morgan, which lead to the banishment of her son Uwain, which leads to his joint errantry with Gawain, which brings them both (now in the company of Marhaus) to those three damsels at the river-head who fork the story into three (*C* IV. 4–19) . . . and so on. Those who dislike this sort of thing will not much like Malory.

Yet it may be, as Professor Vinaver concludes,[i] that Malory 'strongly disliked' it himself. Certainly the evidence that he constantly simplified is irresistible. Whether he wanted to simplify still further and get rid of the Polyphonic altogether, or whether he wanted to go just as far as he has gone and liked the degree of Polyphony which survives under his treatment, we do not know. If he wanted to get rid of it altogether, he has undoubtedly failed. To anyone who comes to this work fresh from modern literature its Polyphonic character will be at first one of the most noticeable things about it. And the work will be liked, where it is liked, not despite of this peculiarity but (in part) because of it.

[i] Op. cit., p. lii.

IV. This Paradox involves us in two subjects: Malory's treatment of the holy quest, and the connexion, if any, between it and other matters in his text.

Professor Vinaver's view on the first subject depends on the interpretation of a great many different passages. I shall refer to them both by the Book and Chapter of Caxton's edition and by the page and line of the Professor's (which I indicate by the letter $W$). They fall into four classes.

1. A passage[j] held to indicate Malory's 'confidence in the unfailing merits of Arthurian chivalry' ($W$ 1524). This is $C$ xvi. 3 ($W$ 946.18) where a Hermit in the French text condemns the Round Table for *luxure* and *orgueil*; but in Malory, for 'sin and wickedness'. I cannot myself see that the substitution of the general for the particular makes the condemnation less severe.

2. Passages where Malory substitutes the worldly for the religious. Thus in $C$ xvi. 3 ($W$ 945.10) the dying Uwain in the French asks that prayer be made for his soul; in Malory he asks to be remembered to Arthur and the court, 'and for brotherhood, think on me'. (This phrase itself might imply a request for prayers, but I would not press that.) Again, in $C$ xvi. 6 ($W$ 955.9) Bors, surprisingly, and without authority from the French, says that he who achieves the Grail will win 'much earthly worship'. Both these, and especially the latter, are strong evidence for Professor Vinaver's view: if it is felt that they are sufficient to colour the whole narrative, then that view will be unassailable. Two other passages which might be quoted here seem to me, on the other hand, to rank as 'worldly' only if

---

[j] At least I think this must be the passage Vinaver has in mind on p. 1524.

we adopt standards of worldliness which are almost intolerably severe. In *C* XIII. 19 (*W* 896.11) Malory allows the contrite Lancelot to be 'somewhat comforted' when day breaks and he hears the birds sing. In the French (which is finely imagined) the morning and the birds directly produce the conviction of God's anger, which in Malory comes home to Lancelot only when he realizes that has lost his horse and his armour. This is certainly very practical, homely, English, and (in a word) Malorian; but it does not for me empty the scene of all religious significance. Again in *C* XVII. 13 (*W* 1011.31–1012.1) Malory's Lancelot (not his French equivalent) after a month of fasting on board ship with no one but a dead lady for company 'was somewhat weary of the ship' and went ashore 'to play him'. (Middle English *play* in such a context is of course a very mild word; we should have said 'to stretch his legs' or 'to relax'.) Now I think a man might have done that and yet be a very good sort of penitent on the whole. Both passages, indeed, are for me specimens of that Malorian realism which brings the story to life; they make Lancelot, not a stained-glass figure, but a real man, though a contrite one. It is proper, however, to point out that the difference between Professor Vinaver and myself may be simply the same difference there was between the French originals and Malory, the difference between the hard lines and rigid schematization of Latin thought, and the softening, compromising temper of us islanders. (For some say our best Christians are all Pelagians, and our best atheists all Puritans, at heart.)

3. The third class is, for me, the hardest to feel sure about. In *C* XIII. 14 (*W* 886.18) the qualification for success in the holy quest is, in the French, *chevaillerie celestiale*; in

the English, 'virtuous living'. In *C* XIII. 13 (*W* 891.32) it is again, for Malory, 'knightly deeds and virtuous living'; for the French author it is service to the Creator, defence of our Holy Church, and the offering to Christ of the treasure (one's soul) which has been entrusted to one. In *C* XVI. 6 (*W* 956.2) Bors is praised in the French for his 'religious', in Malory for his 'stable', life. In *C* XVI. 13 (*W* 968.11) Lionel is condemned by the French author because *n'a an soi nule vertu de Nostre Seignor qui en estant le tiegne*; by Malory, because 'he is a murderer and doth contrary to the order of knighthood'. These are I think the strongest specimens. That in *C* XV. 5 (*W* 931.25) seems to me weak. It is true that the motive which Malory gives Lancelot for joining in a certain fray is, as Professor Vinaver claims, incongruous with the Quest; but then Malory is fully aware of this and in the very next chapter (*C* XV. 6; *W* 933.32–934.4) makes his recluse tell Lancelot that such 'bobaunce and pride of the world' must be abandoned. The insertion of both these passages by Malory would seem to emphasize the very point which, it is claimed, he was ignoring. We might perhaps add *C* XVI. 17 (*W* 974.15–17) where the edifying mutual forgiveness of Bors and his brother is also peculiar to Malory.

But the earlier passages remain, and I will not for a moment dispute that they all indicate an important change made by Malory and affecting his version throughout. The question is how we are to define it. At first sight I am tempted to say that where the originals used specifically religious, Malory uses ethical, concepts: *virtuous* for *celestial*, *knightly* and *virtuous* for the offering of the heart to Christ, *stable* for *religious*. This certainly means that the choice before Malory's knights is not that between 'religion' in the technical sense and active life in the world. They are to go on being knights (*C* XIII. 20; *W* 899.1–5); just as the soldiers who came to the Baptist were told to go on being soldiers.[k] Malory in fact holds the same view as Langland and Gower and many other English medieval moralists. No man need leave the Order to which he has been called, but every man must begin really to fulfil the functions for which that Order exists. The recall is not from knighthood to the cloister, but from knighthood as it has come to be (full of 'sin and wickedness') to a knighthood as it was intended to be, grounded in 'patience and humility' (*C* XVI. 3; *W* 945–47). Admittedly, then, the story is ethical, as against mystical. But we must not say 'ethical, as against religious', for the ethical claim and the attempted ethical response, when prompted by a vision, purged by confession and penance, supported and corrected, at every turn by voices, miracles, and spiritual counsels, is precisely the religious as it most commonly appears in secular vocations. And *stability* (perseverance to the end, or consistency) is of course essential.

4. Finally, we have those passages which exalt the supremacy of Lancelot over all other knights. There may be some difference of opinion as to which we should include in this class. I certainly would not include *C* XVII. 22 (*W* 1035.11–12) where Galahad, almost at the threshold of Heaven, sends to his father a message bidding him 'remember of this unstable world'. The words are full of knightly courtesy, filial duty, and Christian charity, but of course they are a warning and (by delicatest implication) a reproof. It is Galahad whom they exalt. Nor do I find

[k] Luke iii. 14.

much 'rehabilitation' of Lancelot in Malory's insertion at the end of *C* XVII. 23 (*W* 1036.19–1037.7). Lancelot does not relate the adventures of the Grail *simpliciter*, but those 'that he had seen'. Bors had seen, and Bors told, what Lancelot had not seen. One would expect the surviving knights each to contribute to the report which Arthur naturally demanded. And the passage repeats Galahad's message, with its grave implication. Another doubtful place is *C* XVI. 1 (*W* 941.20–22). Here Gawain says that 'if one thing were not' (surely beyond all doubt the 'one thing' is his adultery?) Lancelot would be matchless. But as things are, far from rising (for purposes of this Quest) to the level of Galahad, Perceval, and Bors, Lancelot 'is as we be', is just like the rest of us, *nous autres*, Ectors and Gawains – 'but if he take the more pain on him'.[/] I cannot imagine a better way of making us feel how Lancelot has sunk than thus to let us hear lesser men exclaiming that at least he's no better than they.

The passages on which the Vinaverian view must finally rest are those where Malory deliberately inserts the praise of Lancelot. A damsel in *C* XIII. 5 (*W* 863.30), a hermit in *C* XV. 4 (*W* 930.14), and a second hermit in *C* XVI. 5 (*W* 948.27–28) all remind us that Lancelot was the best knight, for a sinful man, that ever lived. The reservation is of course important; but in spite of it, I am prepared to admit that all these passages may be meant to blunt us for the edge of the abasement which Lancelot undergoes in the French text. But it also seems to me equally possible

---

[/] I don't believe this means 'even though he takes'. Rather 'unless he were to take'; i.e. he is (and will remain) like us unless he should take more pains than he's taking at present.

that they were intended to have – and for me they have – a very different effect. It is a question of what may be called the logic of the imagination. If one wanted to exhibit in a novel the theme that intellectual achievements were no passport to heaven, one would not choose for one's protagonist some mediocrity who has 'got a good second'. Only a fool would labour to show the failure, on the highest level, of pretensions which were doubtfully adequate even on their own. Obviously one would build one's protagonist up to the stature of a Porson, a Sherrington, or a Mahaffy. If you want to show that one sort of achievement is inferior to, even incommensurable with, another, then of course the more splendid (in its own kind) your specimen is, the more impressive its failure (in another kind) will be. Every word said in praise of Lancelot as a good knight 'of a sinful man' – as the bravest, most courteous, most faithful in his love, but not seriously hitherto attempting that perfection of chastity and all other virtues which the Christian law demands of the knight, in his own fashion, no less than of the contemplative – serves all the more to drive home the moral of the whole story, makes it all the clearer that with the Quest we have entered a region where even what is best and greatest by the common standards of the world 'falls into abatement and low price'.[1]

But, as before, I end in uncertainty. I am sure that Malory's handling has not on me the effect, and therefore need not have been meant to have the effect, which Professor Vinaver supposes. I know it has the opposite effect on me. I cannot rule out the possibility that it was intended to have this opposite effect. I do not claim to know that it was.

So much for his treatment of the Quest. As regards its relation to other parts of his work, I feel a little more confident. It appears to me to be unmistakably linked with the *Morte*. Before the Quest begins, before Galahad is begotten, when the Grail first appears before Lancelot in the house of Pelles, Malory inserts the prophecy that 'when this rich thing goeth about, the Round Table shall be broken for a season'. (*C* XI. 2; *W* 793.32–36). I do not know what to make of 'for a season', and how right (as often) Caxton was to omit it! But it is Malory who has introduced, even if Caxton perfected, the note of doom: the dreadful hint that the best is fatal to the good. Then in the Quest itself (*C* XIII. 20; *W* 897.27–28) Lancelot promises 'by the faith of his body' never to come in Guinevere's 'fellowship' again if he can avoid it. Then, when the Quest is over, almost immediately, Lancelot 'forgat the promise and the perfection that he made in the Quest'. This is in the French; but as if this were not enough, Malory must add that this was the inadequately repented 'bosom-sin' which had led him to fail in that attempt (*C* XVIII. 1; *W* 1045.12–16). Notice too that in thus forgetting his promise Lancelot is verifying the diagnosis ('not stable, but...likely to turn again') made upon him by the hermit in *C* XVI. 5 – a passage, so far as we know, of Malory's own making. The connexion here, if unintended, is singularly fortunate. But Malory still feels he has not done enough. Returning to *C* XVIII. 1, we find a dialogue between Lancelot and Guinevere inserted (*W* 1045.30–1048.14) in which he almost begs the terrible woman to release him, pleading, 'I was but late in the quest', confessing that 'privy thoughts to return to your love' were the lime-twigs he could not escape, trying to make her

understand that such experiences 'may not be lightly forgotten'. Then later (*C* XIX. 10–12) we have what is perhaps
the greatest of all passages peculiar to Malory, the healing
of Sir Urry. Here Lancelot is proved by infallible signs to
be in one sense (he knows too well in what and how limited a sense) the best knight of the world. Hence, while
all praise him to the skies, he can only weep like a beaten
child. As he failed on the Quest, so (for the same reason)
he is failing now. In him, its highest specimen, the whole
Round Table is failing; on it and him, as the result of his
illicit love, the prophecies begin to be fulfilled. They are,
no doubt, worked out through a tangle of human motives,
the spite of Agravain and Mordred, the assumption of the
blood-feud by Gawain. Of course. The fulfilment of the
prophecies about Oedipus came about through seemingly
free agents obeying human motives. That is how prophecies are fulfilled in good stories; no one ever suggested that
the motivation somehow abolishes the connexion between
the prediction and the event. And when all is nearly over
and the doom worked out, Lancelot again recalls to us
the source of the whole tragedy: 'For in the quest of the
Sangreal I had forsaken the vanities of the world had not
your love been' (*C* XXI. 9; *W* 1253.14–15).

And still, though I cannot see how any reader fails to
see the connexion, I cannot be certain whether Malory
himself saw it or not.

5. Finally, did Malory write one book or eight? Close
study of the Winchester MS. has convinced Professor Vinaver that he wrote eight; instead of the *Morte
Darthur* we have the 'Works' of Malory, and inconsisten-
cies between them no longer matter – indeed, no longer
exist, for independent worlds of invention cannot be

inconsistent with one another. This view has been seriously criticized by Mr D. S. Brewer.[m] He points out that the eight 'works' are full of backward and forward references, their order not alterable, and 'bridge' passages often supplied. I think I should be on Mr Brewer's side in this question, if I were not bogged down in a preliminary doubt as to what precisely the question is.

I believe I know fairly well what we mean if we say, '*Pickwick* is one work, but *Pickwick* and *Great Expectations* are two works'. We mean that within *Pickwick*, as within *Great Expectations*, there are characters that continue or recur, and that there are causal connexions, and the later parts presuppose the earlier; whereas there are no common characters and no causal connexions shared by both. But ask me the same questions about *Barchester Towers* and *The Last Chronicle*; already a shade of ambiguity has crept in. Now go a step further. What of *Paradise Lost* and *Paradise Regained*? Here there are characters common to both, and the later poem presupposes and recalls events in the earlier. Satan's temptation of Christ presupposes his rebellion against God and his expulsion from Heaven. And if Satan, and the whole story, were as purely Milton's invention as Archdeacon Grantly is Trollope's, the two poems would stand in the same not very easily defined relation as the two novels. Actually, however, Satan's career with all its causal and chronological structure already exists in the Fathers and in popular belief, before Milton sets pen to paper, and continues to exist whether he wants us to treat *Regained* as a sequel or as a wholly separate poem. Presupposals of events in *Paradise Lost*, and backward

[m] 'Form in the Morte Darthur'. *Medium Aevum* xxi (1952), pp. 14–24.

references, are bound to occur. It may be impossible to say whether a given instance of them illustrates the unity of the two poems or whether it merely exhibits at one point the external, pre-existing, non-Miltonic unity of the matter he worked on. Hence we may generalize: wherever there is a matter (historical or legendary) previous and external to the author's activity, the question 'One work or many?' loses a good deal of its meaning. And of course Malory's matter was of this kind.

On top of this a special difficulty arises from the fact that Malory was a medieval author. If it were possible to question him directly, in what form should we put our question? It would be no use asking him how many books he thought he had written; he would think we meant the material volumes or 'quairs'. If we asked him, 'How many tales?' he might enumerate more than eight. Such expressions as 'Thus endeth the tale of...' (*C* II. 19; *W* 92.22), or 'the adventure of' (*C* III. 8; *W* 108.28) or 'the quest of' (*C* III. 11; *W* 113.34) occur within the Vinaverian units. If we talked to him about 'artistic unity', he would not understand. We might finally, in desperation, try to find out whether he was at all worried at the appearance in one passage of some knight whose death had been recorded in an earlier passage. He would, I feel certain, simply refer us to 'the French book' as his authority. For the difficulty between Malory and us would not be merely linguistic. We should by the very form of our questions be presupposing concepts his mind was not furnished with. Did any Middle English author conceive clearly that he was writing fiction, a single work of fiction, which should obey the laws of its own inner unity but need not cohere with anything else in the world? I cannot believe it. They are all, even Chaucer, handing on, embellishing, expanding, or abridging a matter received from some source. They feel free to illuminate it at any number of points with their own vivid imagination, and even to correct what seems to them improbable, improper, or unedifying. But whatever their own degree of actual belief or of scepticism (were they clearly aware of either? did they for the most part even raise such questions?) they all proceed as if they were more or less historians; unscholarly, decorating, and emotional historians to be sure, like Livy or Plutarch, but (by and large) historians still. I do not for a moment believe that Malory had any intention either of writing a single 'work' or of writing many 'works' as we should understand the expressions. He was telling us about Arthur and the knights. Of course his matter was one – the same king, the same court. Of course his matter was many – they had had many adventures.

The choice we try to force upon Malory is really a choice for us. It is our imagination, not his, that makes the work one or eight or fifty. We can read it either way. We can read it now one way, now another. We partly make what we read.

*

As will be seen, the examination of all five Paradoxes produces in me varying degrees of doubt (weakest as regards the Third, strongest as regards the Second and Fifth) about Professor Vinaver's idea of Malory's intentions; but it produces no confidence in any alternative theory. The net result is that Malory eludes me. Perhaps, then, I shall be able to find him in his style, for they say that a man's style is himself. Unfortunately, Malory turns out to have not a style, but styles. The inverted and alliterative language of the Roman War has little likeness to the limpid, unobtrusive prose in which we follow the adventures of knights errant. And we know why. The one is from the Alliterative *Morte*, the other renders, and copies as closely as English can, the style of the French prose romances. In both, Malory writes such a style as he has most lately read. And we cannot say that this subjection to the model is a prentice weakness which he outgrew in his maturity. At the very end, as soon as the Stanzaic *Morte* comes before him, the tell-tale features, the tags, inversions, and alliterations, creep into his prose: 'while we thus in holes us hide' – 'that was wary and wise' – 'droop and dare' – 'shred them down as sheep in a fold' (*C* xx. 19; *W* 1211–12). And when he leaves his original altogether to reflect upon the story (*C* xviii. 25; *W* 1119–20), we have a style different from all these. There are more (ultimately) Latin derivatives close together (*constrain, divers, negligence, stability,* and *rasure*), and doublets like 'bring forth fruit and flourish', 'springeth and flourisheth', 'arase and deface', 'deface and lay apart'. This is quite unlike the prose used in his own (or what we take to be his own) additions to the narrative parts, especially those dialogues which he inserts more freely as he nears the end. These are no doubt admirable; but who, on purely internal evidence, could have picked them out (as almost anyone could pick out the alliterative passage about the dream in *C* v. 4)? They may be better than the surrounding prose which reproduces the French, but they are all of a piece with it. Malory's greatest original passages arise when he is most completely absorbed in the story and realizes the

characters so fully that they begin to talk for him of their
own accord; but they talk a language he has largely learned
from his sources. The very ease with which he wanders
away from this style into that of some inferior source or
into a language of his own (which he may have thought
'higher') suggests that he hardly knows what he is doing.
Thus, while in one sense it would be monstrous to say
that he 'has no style' (he has written prose as musical, as
forthright, as poignant, as was ever heard in England) it
would be true in another. He has no style of his own, no
characteristic manner. (If you were searching all literature for a man who might be described as 'the opposite
of Pater', Malory would be a strong candidate.) In a style
or styles so varied, everywhere so indebted to others, and
perhaps most original precisely where it is most indebted,
one cannot hopefully seek *l'homme même*. Here also Malory vanishes into a mist.

And this result neither surprises nor disappoints me. I
have called this essay 'The English prose *Morte*', because
I think we may deceive ourselves by such expressions as
'Malory's *Morte Darthur*' or 'The Works of Sir Thomas
Malory'. They sound so dangerously like 'Browning's *Sor-
dello*' or 'The Works of Jane Austen'. But there is no real
parallel. Our familiar concept of 'author-and-his-book' is
foiled by the composite works of the Middle Ages. Even
in *Troilus and Crisyede*, where the whole is much shorter
and the last worker's additions are much larger and known
more certainly, we are foiled. We can sort out the Boccaccian and the Chaucerian passages. But not the Boccaccian
and the Chaucerian element. For of course the surviving Boccaccio is modified by the interpolated Chaucer,
and the Chaucer modified (this is less often stressed)

by the Boccaccio. In the end we cannot really say that either author, nor even in what proportion each author, is responsible for the total effect. The prose *Morte* is very much more complicated. Whatever Malory's intentions – if he had any intentions – may have been, it is agreed on all hands that he has changed the tale very little. From the nature of the case he could not have changed it much. It is too vast, too filled with its own strong life, to be much affected by alterations so comparatively short and sporadic as his. This does not mean that his contribution is of negligible value. Like so many medieval authors (like, for example, the poet of *Cleanness* and *Patience*), at point after point he adds vividness, throws some figure into bolder relief, cuts away an excrescence, or sweetens some motive that he rightly found odious.[n] The process may be described as 'touching up'. But there is no question of a great artist giving to a pupil's work those strokes of genius 'which make all the difference'. Rather, a deft pupil has added touches here and there to a work which, in its majestic entirety, he could never have conceived; and from which his own skill has been chiefly learned. Though he has in fact improved it, it was (by our standards, not by those of the Middle Ages) rather cheek of him to try. But even if he had done harm, he would not have done much harm.

If some people find it distressing to have a work which cannot be assigned to any single author, let me remind them that in another art we are familiar with this sort of thing. I am thinking of a great cathedral, where Saxon, Norman, Gothic, Renaissance, and Georgian elements all

---

[n] E.g., at *C* VIII. 9 (*W* 385.6–8) where he turns Tristram from a cad into an ordinary amorous young man.

co-exist, and all grow together into something strange and admirable which none of its successive builders intended or foresaw. Under Malory's work lies that of the French prose romancers; under theirs, that of Chrétien, Wace, and other poets; under that, Geoffrey, and perhaps the Breton *lais*; deepest of all, who knows what fragments of Celtic myth or actual British history? Malory is only the last of many restorers, improvers, demolitionists; if you will, of misunderstanders. Meanwhile, the great cathedral of words stands solidly before us and imposes on us a meaning which is largely independent of their varying and perhaps incompatible purposes. Who, if any, first saw or intended the tragic and ironic parallel between Mordred's begetting and Galahad's? Or the necessity that the Grail should bring not peace but a sword? Or the three-storied effect inevitably produced by the intermediate position of the good knights between the villains like Mark and the perfect knights like Percivale? Or the deep suggestiveness of Arthur's relation to that dark family (Morgan, Morgause, and the rest) from whom he emerges, who lie in wait for him, and who mysteriously return in his last hour to take him away?

I said just now that Malory was only the last of the makers of the *Morte*. I should have said, last but one (or even last but two). It follows from the view I am trying to put that Caxton's text is not most usefully regarded as a corruption. He touched up Malory as Malory touched up his predecessors and by the same right. The greatest service that he did the old fabric was one of demolition. Most unluckily (and probably, as Professor Vinaver thinks, early in his career) Malory had come across the Alliterative *Morte*. It is not a first-class poem, not comparable in epic quality to the battle scenes of Laȝamon, and it treats the dullest and most incredible part of the whole Arthurian legend. It is far easier to suspend one's disbelief in enchantments than in vast contradictions of known history scrawled across a whole continent; and a narrative of unbroken military successes, dull even when true, is insufferable when feigned. It is defeat, or (as in the *Iliad*) discords within one of the armies, that we need for epic. Malory swallowed this poem almost whole, except that by separating it from the *Morte* he deprived it of the tragic close and the moral judgement[0] which had saved it from total paltriness. He also surrendered his style without resistance to the influence of the alliterative metre, which, degenerate even in the original, becomes in prose a noisy rumble. Caxton wisely abridged the whole dreary business, and removed (he might well have used the knife more boldly) some of the traces of the metre. Thus where Winchester's (and no doubt Malory's) text read

Now fecche em, seyde sir Pryamus, my vyall that hangys by the gurdyll of my haynxman, for hit is full of the floure of the four good watyrs that passis from Paradyse, the mykill fruyte in fallys that at one day fede shall us all. . . .

Caxton gives

And Priamus took from his page a vial full of the four waters that came out of Paradise.

Notice that Caxton has made it much more Malorian, more like the best and most typical parts of Malory, than

---

[0] Alliterative *Morte* 3393–3402, ed. E. Brock (Early English Text Society, 1865).

Malory himself had done. This is 'forcing a man to be free',[2] making him himself (*C* v. 10; *W* 234.11–14). Again in *C* v. 8 (*W* 219.16–17) we owe to Caxton 'the ground trembled and dindled' instead of 'all the vale dyndled'. The division into chapters, if sometimes unskilfully done, has made the book everywhere more readable. The rubrics he prefixed to the chapters have become as much part of its beauty as the glosses of the *Ancient Mariner*'s. Sometimes, as in 'how Lancelot fell to his old love again', they direct us unerringly to the pith of what follows (*C* XVIII. 1); again and again they are evocative in the highest degree.

I am not of course suggesting that Caxton's share in the final effect is remotely comparable to Malory's; only that he too, in his degree, has helped a little, and that it is no misfortune if his text has counted for so much in the English imagination. That is why I have usually quoted not only from Caxton but even from Caxton edited by Pollard; the household book.[3] I enjoy my cathedral as it has stood the test of time and demand no restoration. I have no more wish to discard Caxton for Malory than to discard Malory for the French romances.

It would distress me if anyone took this to imply the slightest depreciation of Professor Vinaver's great edition. It is an indispensable work of which English scholarship may well be proud, and my own debts to it will be obvious. Indeed the view I have taken allows me to give Professor Vinaver a place higher, in my opinion, than scholarship of itself could claim. I hesitated a while ago whether to call Malory last but one, or last but two, of the many who worked at the prose *Morte*. For has not Professor Vinaver some right to be numbered among them? He has not, naturally, allowed himself the liberties of a Malory or even of a Caxton. His chisel has touched no stone of the building. But he has made a new approach, and one which many modern pilgrims will find more congenial. His book smacks of our own century as Caxton's smacked of his. The division into eight romances, and above all the title, *The Works* of Malory, whether right or wrong (or neither), makes it far more digestible by contemporary critical conceptions than the old *Morte*. The *Works*, the Complete Works – that is what our libraries are used to. Already Malory fits more comfortably on the shelf beside the 'works' of everyone else. And the mere look of the pages – the paragraphing and the inverted commas – acclimatizes the book still further. Beyond question, Professor Vinaver has shown the cathedral from a new angle; placed the modern pilgrim where he will enjoy it best. And now that his edition is deservedly reaching the stage of cheap reprints, it may in turn become the household book; until perhaps *alter Achilles*, some second Vinaver (a little cold to the first one as he is a little cold to Caxton) recalls his generation to the long forgotten book of 1485 or even to the French, and someone like myself puts in a plea for what will then be the old, the traditional, 'Works of Malory'. And all these preferences will be legitimate and none of them 'right' or 'wrong'. The cathedral of words is so large that everyone can find in it the work of his favourite period; and here, as you could not do in a real cathedral, you can always strip that favourite work of later accretions without pulling the whole thing down. What you must not do is to call those bits 'the' or 'the real' cathedral. They might have been. The whole might have been designed by one man and finished in one style. But that is not what happened. Though every part of it was made by a man, the whole has rather grown than been made. Such things have a kind of existence that is almost midway between the works of art and those of nature.

# 41

# Leone Ebreo, *The Philosophy of Love (Dialoghi d'Amore)*, trans. J. Friedeberg-Seeley and Jean H. Barnes, intro. Cecil Roth (London: Soncino Press, 1937)

~

Judah Abrabanel, or Leone Ebreo, as his gentile friends called him, physician to Don Gonsalvo de Cordoba, reputed friend of Pico della Mirandola, and Platonic theologian, is a figure not perhaps sufficiently familiar to English students of the Renaissance.[1] The catalogue of one great library reveals only the Spanish version of the *Dialogues of Love*; and the present translation – indeed any translation – of the Italian text is to be welcomed.

The *Dialogues*, written apparently as early as 1502, are of equal interest to the literary historian and to the philosopher as a document of that mode of thought which is loosely called 'Renaissance Platonism'. The title is somewhat misleading, as may be gauged by Ficino's list of *summi theologi*,[2] which includes, along with Plato and Pythagoras, names such as Zoroaster, Orpheus and Trismegistus.[3] The physics of the school came from Aristotle and the Stoics: its pneumatology is in the direct line of descent from the semi-philosophical paganism which

Review published in *The Times Literary Supplement* (15 January 1938), p. 36. Leone Ebreo (*c.* 1465–*c.* 1523) was a Portuguese poet and philosopher.

St Augustine attempted to strangle in the *De Civitate*, but which escaped his grip to survive into the Middle Ages; and Oriental elements are present, perhaps from the outset, certainly in the sixteenth century.

It is something very different from Platonism as Jowett and Bosanquet understood the term, though perhaps it does no more violence to the spirit of Plato in one direction than academic and secularizing idealists have done in another.[4] Its vitality carried it far into the seventeenth century, and the philosophy of Locke is partly to be understood as a reaction against it. Without some insight into this unsystematic yet strangely homogeneous effort of thought and imagination and some sympathy for its picture of the universe – a universe packed, as it were, to bursting with anthropomorphic life and tingling with desire – no real understanding of Renaissance art and poetry is possible.

Abrabanel's place in this tradition is among the moderates. He may claim, and justly, to 'have discussed the love of the universe more widely than Plato in the Symposium',[5] but he shows no taste at all for the rankly magical elements we find in Ficino or even for the milder occultism of Henry More.[6] He has a great deal to say about the gods, but it is all in the way of allegorical interpretation, and that at such length that the pupil in the *Dialogues* marvels to see 'so many meanings' drawn out of the myths 'and each nobler than the last'. In this respect the whole of the second Dialogue is an important reminder of something we easily forget – that the gods were never, to the men of that age, devils (as to the Fathers) nor figments (as to the Augustans), but always something more: planets, elements or moral allegories. He has much, too, to tell us

of angels and intelligences, but it is all about their relations
to God and to the system of things, and not about their
possible contacts with one another or with human individuals. He writes, in fact, as a genuine theologian, and
on the theological side a permanent value may be claimed
for his work.

The editors of this translation tell us that Spinoza
'according to a view which has recently gained ground',
may have derived from the *Dialogues* 'his doctrine of
the Intellectual Love of God'.[7] If such a view is gain-
ing ground, this is surely to be deplored: for what
is most important in Abrabanel is his difference from
Spinoza. Professor Nygren has emphasized the antag-
onism between systems based on Eros, the love of the
lower for the higher, with an unmoved mover, an unlov-
ing Beloved, as the Highest of all, and those based on
Agape, the love of higher for lower, where the Highest is
a god conceived as purposive and capable of interfering
in history.[8] Philosophy, and specially Greek philosophy,
inclines to the former: religious experience, and specially
Jewish and Christian experience, to the latter. Spinoza
walked the Eros road as far as any man has ever done:
Abrabanel, with equal temptation to do so, obstinately
refuses it, and his central problem is how to combine his
philosophical conception of God as the Beloved with his
religious conception of God as the Lover. He has two
methods of doing so. One is to argue that Eros in practice is Agape, that love for the end or the Higher must
work to raise the lower, since the perfection of the lower
somehow or other (he is timid, though immovable, on this
point) contributes to the perfection of the end. The other
is to introduce within the Deity itself distinctions between

God as self-loved, and God as self-lover, united to beget Love, which bring him to the verge of Trinitarianism.

In true Platonic style the author has put all this forward in the form of conversations between a lover (Philo) and his mistress (Sophia). The latter, despite her name, is not an allegorical figure, and remains, in philosophy, a mere pupil to the end. Most often the two speakers are not dramatically conceived, but there are some interludes of high comedy. The lady's determination to keep Philo off the subject of his love for her and on the subject of love in general (for he tends to stray in both directions) is well conceived. The translation is, on the whole, readable and dignified, but sometimes betrays an uncertainty about English idiom.

# 42

## E. K. Chambers, *Sir Thomas Wyatt and Some Collected Studies* (London: Sidgwick and Jackson, 1933)

~

Of the six essays in this volume the only two which are here printed for the first time fall outside the scope of *Medium Aevum*; of the remaining four all except one are concerned with medieval literature. The short paper entitled *Some Points in the Grail Legend* is, perhaps, the most controversial. Sir Edmund Chambers criticizes the theories of Nutt, Miss Weston, Loomis, and Brown, and advances one of his own.[1] His criticisms are generally simple and cogent pleas of 'not proven'. He 'rejects Miss Weston *in toto*' on the very rational ground that there is after all no evidence (except the suspect claims of *modern* occultists) for the cult of Attis in Britain, and that the ritual parallels are imperfect.[2] All this seems to be a legitimate use of Occam's razor.

It is not, however, very easy to see how those who have followed the argument can be expected, a moment later, to welcome Sir Edmund's own suggestion that the Grail story dramatizes the ritual of succession in certain forms of early kingship. The 'Shilluk tribe of the White Nile' and the Persians in Herodotus, who are cited as examples, seem to labour under the same disadvantage as the

Review published in *Medium Aevum*, vol. 3 (October 1934), pp. 237–40.

cult of Attis.[3] The author would no doubt claim that the succession-ritual, in varying forms, is widely diffused: but the same may be said for the rituals of fertility.

The next essay – that on *Sir Thomas Malory* – is partly appreciative, partly biographical, and partly controversial. The appreciative passages are as admirable as readers of Sir Edmund Chambers will have learned to expect – masterpieces of what we must unhappily begin to call the older tradition, the tradition so wide that it includes both Raleigh and Mackail. The author is not afraid of evocative quotation, nor even of retelling Malory's story at some length. I am aware that many dislike this kind of thing: for my own part, I anticipate with very little pleasure the day when it will be finally silenced by the steady tramp of the thesis-mongers.

On the controversial side I find this essay a little ambiguous. The name of Professor Vinaver appears only once, and then in a footnote which ominously glosses the statement that Malory's treatment of his sources is an intricate subject and that the available evidence 'has not always been wisely used'.[4] It is not clear whether we are referred to Professor Vinaver for an account of the evidence, or for one more example of its unwise use.

If I understand both scholars aright, Sir Edmund Chambers' disagreement with Professor Vinaver is not very great. Both are agreed that Malory's treatment of the Grail story is unsatisfactory and even irrelevant. Sir Edmund maintains that the true catastrophe of Malory's story has nothing to do with the clash between Corbenic and Camelot; Professor Vinaver says the same thing in almost the same words.[5]

They differ, however, in their explanation of Malory's failure. For Professor Vinaver, Malory is, perhaps, misunderstanding, or at least following half-heartedly, a work of Cistercian mysticism; for Sir Edmund, Malory has simply stumbled on an inferior version as his source, which lacks the 'mystery' of Chrétien, the 'melancholy' of *Perlesvaus*, and the 'humanity' of Wolfram.[6] In strict logic the two views are not incompatible: but we shall probably neither err nor offend if we suspect in the English writer a profound lack of sympathy with Professor Vinaver's (or M. Gilson's) implied estimate of the 'French book' at this point.[7] Sir Edmund is a little impatient with the whole thing; his heart, he frankly admits, 'goes down the hill with Gawain'. In other words, he *really* feels as Professor Vinaver supposes Malory to have felt.

Did Malory really feel so? It is possible for our reading of an author to become what we may call 'source-ridden', so that we no longer see his book as it is in itself, but only as it contrasts with its sources. This is clearly an injustice to the author, for we are preserving in their original form elements which he has transmuted, and even elements which he rejected. It is as though we ate all the raw ingredients of a pudding along with the pudding itself: such an eating is emphatically not the pudding's proof. If we wish to know how far Malory's Grail is a success, we must sooner or later read it as if we knew nothing about its sources. When it is thus read, I think we shall find that while there are structural weaknesses and confusions of plot, there are no confusions of sentiment and no 'false issue'. Let any man sit down and read, in this spirit, the last four chapters of Book XIII, and he will see that Malory fully understands the condemnation and the contrition of Launcelot. His heart has not the slightest tendency to go downhill with Gawain: and Professor Vinaver could have found in Malory a wish to spare Launcelot only because he turned to Malory with a memory, too full and too recent, of other versions where Launcelot was even more severely treated. Malory has no doubt at all that Launcelot is to be condemned – by the highest standards and in the long run: that Corbenic is above Camelot – in the long run. But this is quite compatible with his praise of Camelot (that is, of love and of Guenevere) in other passages.

I cannot share Sir Edmund Chambers' suspicion that Malory does not 'see his way clearly through the queer spiritual tangle' of courtly love.[8] Malory is simply in agreement with Andreas Capellanus' double doctrine: that, on the one hand, *nullum in mundo bonum vel curialitas exercetur nisi ex amoris fonte derivetur*, while, one the other hand, love is a mortal sin.[9] He is in agreement with Chaucer's praise of love in the earlier books of *Troilus*, and equally with Chaucer's rejection of love at the end of *Troilus*. The apparent inconsistency results from the fact that the medieval writers are using a triple scale of values where their modern critics are using only a double one.

Professor Vinaver sees a simple dichotomy of worldly and spiritual (of Corbenic and Camelot) and assumes that Malory must be simply *for* the one and *against* the other: the only problem being to find out which. Sir Edmund Chambers has a dichotomy of good and bad (both in the 'human' sense), and, wishing Malory to play out a purely secular tragedy between these in the Shakespearian or modern way, regards the intrusion of any third term as a confusion of the issue. But Malory has a three-storeyed mind – a scale of bad–good–best (Mark–Launcelot–Galahad) which, if read backwards, becomes of course good–bad–worst. It will be seen that the middle term may appear sometimes as 'good' and sometimes as 'bad', without any inconsistency. He is thus perfectly serious about the nobility of Launcelot and of courtly love – the 'old love' so much more faithful and patient than 'love nowadays': and he is equally serious about the yet higher law which cuts across the courtly world in the Grail books. Launcelot rises so high on the natural plane that he must face the alternative of rising yet higher to the supernatural, or of falling. He fails to meet the higher claim: he 'falls to his love again', 'forgets the promise and the perfection'; is discovered, forced into blood feud with his best friend, and drags down the whole structure of Britain with him.

It is quite true, as Sir Edmund Chambers says, that the catastrophe is brought about by 'the familiar conflict between human love and human loyalty'; but this does not mean that the Grail episode is irrelevant. It is an essential part of the tragedy of Launcelot (perhaps the first truly tragic hero in our literature) that he should have been given the chance of escaping from this human level on which the tragedy is foredoomed, and should have failed to take it. To remove from the story the account of his last efforts at escape and of his relapse (xviii i–ii) would be a tasteless over-simplification. To be sure, Malory is a simple man in the sense that he is not analytical. But the sentiments which he presents, without analysis, are in themselves complex and delicate; as we may see from the beautiful episode of Sir Urre, which Sir Edmund quotes.

The third item in the book is a reprint of the introduction to the Sidgwick and Jackson *Early English Lyrics* of

1907. Those who remember, as the present writer remembers, making their first acquaintance with the subject by means of this essay, must always regard it with a sort of piety that almost precludes criticism. From such an abundance of happy quotation, unobtrusive argument, and critical sensibility it would be idle, perhaps impertinent, to select particular passages for praise: but I cannot leave it without reflecting how much nonsense about the Renaissance might have remained unuttered if everyone had noticed the statement that the Provençal *chanson d'amour* 'may be said to have fixed the type of literary romantic sentiment from the Canzoniere of Petrarch to *The Angel in the House*'. This seems – if we omit the possibly ambiguous word 'romantic' – to be one of those rare propositions in literary history which are entirely true, and yet important.

# 43

## M. Pauline Parker,
## *The Allegory of the* Faerie Queene
## (Oxford: Clarendon Press, 1960)

~

This is a sane book and well written. If it is at times more eloquent than the sullen fashion of the moment allows, what matter? *Multa renascentur.*[1] The author finds the key to *F. Q.* in theology 'not dogmatic but ascetic and moral'; claims (I think, rightly) that Spenser was no Puritan; soft-pedals his Platonism; relegates the historical allegory to a short appendix: and produces (p. 10) an interesting interpretation of 'as Aristotle hath devised'.[2] As might be expected, she is especially happy on Spenser's images of good and evil; but I could have wished for more about that whole iconography of pageant and emblem through which his moral theology was mediated.

It will always be disputed how far we can trust to logic in the interpretation of Spenser. If A in the story symbolizes α in the real world and B symbolizes β, are the relations of A and B within the story to be interpreted as symbols of those between α and β in the world? Clearly, we must not go the whole hog. Otherwise, since Belphoebe 'is' Elizabeth and is begotten by the Sun, the Sun will 'be' Henry VIII; which is nonsense. The author is well aware that 'there are moments when the story is only a story'

Review published in *The Cambridge Review*, vol. 81 (11 June 1960), pp. 643, 645.

(p. 158), but she trusts the logical method further than I. Thus she believes that the combat between Guyon and Britomart must represent some sort of opposition between Temperance and Chastity. Again, following Kitchin,[3] she takes the Dwarf in Book 1 to be Natural Reason. Logically, a case can be made for this. But not imaginatively. I will never believe that so elusive and unimpressive a figure stands for so high an abstraction. When logic suggests anything contrary to the actual *quality* of Spenser's images – their immediate impact on the eye and the emotion – logic is, I believe, misleading us.

A few points on detail may be noted.

*Othava rima* is not 'two alternatively rhyming quatrains followed by a couplet' (p. 24). On p. 141 the author writes as if she had momentarily forgotten the normal Latin meaning of *impotentia*. 'Weakness', without further qualification, is not enough and might seriously mislead a student. 'Loss of self-control' is the correct rendering. Cf. *P. L.* ii, 156.[4]

Old Meliboe's maxim (vi, ix, 30) is a *locus communis* in Europe ever since Boethius wrote the *De Consolatione*. *Falls of Princes* (p. 296) should be *Fall of Princes*.[5]

I must not end without praising the almost Johnsonism finality of certain sentences. For critics (like myself) who jib at Talus there is the unanswerable reply 'it is highly desirable that unshakeable justice should be attended by irresistible strength' (p. 9). The principle behind modern methods of reading is stated in the form 'If there is to be a meaning it shall be ours' (p. 28). And of Spenser in general we read, 'No poet has less to say about great cities'.

# 44

## John Vyvyan, *Shakespeare and the Rose of Love* (London: Chatto and Windus, 1960)

~

This book ought to have been longer, for the author has given himself room only to expound, and not to defend, his thesis. He maintains that Shakespeare was deeply influenced, if not by the *Romance of the Rose* itself, at any rate by the medieval conception of love. This seems probable. But it is also his 'aim to uncover a little of the meaning that the heroine, as a love-symbol, has in Shakespeare' (p. 182). *Symbol* is not here used vaguely – Mr Vyvyan is too good a writer so to use it – as a synonym for 'instance' or 'type'. The heroine 'is in her second nature, the allegorical figure either of love itself or of the beauty by which love is awakened' (p. 20); 'Sylvia is a personification' (p. 112); 'the duality of Shakespearian heroines is a principle' (p. 66). All this seems to me like putting a man on his trial before a *prima facie* case has been made out.

If we started by knowing that Shakespeare's plays were allegorical, we might well accept Mr Vyvyan's interpretation. But he really makes no attempt to convince us that there is any allegory. He assumes it, as Fulgentius assumed it in Virgil or St Augustine in Genesis.[1] That he can make out an allegory is no sufficient proof. It is impossible for the wit of man to devise a story which the wit of some

Review published in *The Listener*, vol. 64 (7 July 1960), p. 30.

other man cannot allegorize. The author does not, to my mind, show that the plays will either read or act better if we accept his theory. He does not show how such a 'duality' could have helped Shakespeare. On the contrary, we are told that 'when drama is allegory, compromise is inevitable' (p. 131), so that the theory is as much an excuse for bad scenes as an explanation of good ones.

I do not conclude that the book has no value. The author's analyses of individual plays are always interesting and often draw our attention to neglected points. But we are left saying 'This may be so, but there is still no evidence that it is'. Surely Mr Vyvyan must have foreseen, and ought to have rebutted one very obvious answer to his question (p. 188) 'Why is Shakespearian allegory so elusive?' We are promised another volume which will investigate Shakespeare's debt to Plato. I look forward to this with interest, but I hope the existence of the debt will be established before its character is investigated. No inquirer needs to use Occam's razor more vigorously than the literary critic.

# PART VI
# MILTON AND LATER ENGLISH LITERATURE

~

*Over seventy years after it was first published, Lewis's* A Preface to Paradise Lost *(1942) remains a seminal work. In it, he introduced the term 'secondary epic' to literary criticism, distinguishing Virgil's literary creation from Homer's oral composition, and he argued that any epic after the* Aeneid *had to take as its subject a single great theme. 'Secondary epic' became so embedded as a literary term that W. H. Auden could use it without explanation as the title to one of his poems. Two of the reviews reprinted here add detail to that famous study of Milton. The rest reflect Lewis's interests in later English literature. However much he may have disliked 'modernism', he was yet interested in modern literature and modern approaches, and so while authors such as Boswell, Collins, Arnold, Rossetti, Morris, and even Rider Haggard are represented, we also find engagement with the poetry of Yeats and the literary criticism of Harold Bloom.*

# 45

## Logan Pearsall Smith, *Milton and his Modern Critics* (London: Oxford University Press, 1940)

~

*The request that Lewis review Logan Pearsall Smith's* Milton and his Modern Critics *was timely.* Milton had long been *one of Lewis's favourite poets, and in Hilary Term 1937 he gave a series of lectures in the Oxford School of English on 'Milton and the Epic Tradition'. But nothing had intensified Lewis's appreciation of Milton as much as the lectures on* Comus *his friend, Charles Williams, gave to the University of Oxford in February 1940. Then, about the time Lewis was asked to review Logan Pearsall Smith's book, he was invited to give three talks on Milton to University College in North Wales. The book that resulted from those talks in December 1941 was* A Preface to Paradise Lost *(1942). In the meantime, Charles Williams included much of his* Comus *lectures in an introduction to* The English Poems of John Milton *(1940). When Lewis read that introduction he not only dedicated* A Preface to Paradise Lost *to Charles Williams, but wrote a dedicatory letter in which he insisted that Williams's introduction amounted to 'the recovery of a true critical tradition after more than a hundred years of laborious misunderstanding' (p. v).*

Review published in *The Cambridge Review* (21 February 1941), p. 280.

\* \* \*

The two purposes of this book are to flay alive the critics whom Mr. Pearsall Smith happily calls Miltonoclasts
(such as Mr. Eliot and Dr Leavis)[1] and to defend Milton.[2]
The flaying alive is well done, if you like that kind of
thing; it is the old style of 'culinary coolness', and very
unlike the spluttering brutality of most modern polemics.
But the defence of Milton has made me very uneasy.
Dr Leavis attacks Milton from the ground of a poetic
theory which makes poetry one of the highest ventures
of consciousness in search of its adjustment with reality.
Mr. Pearsall Smith, urbane, delicate, and sophisticated,
and at bottom (I think) quite sceptical about the possibility of truth and the majesty of moral virtue, admits that
'what the Muses *think* is of little interest' to him, concedes
to Miss Macaulay that Milton had an 'exotic, monstrous
mind', and is satisfied with a defence of Milton which turns
on the 'charm' and 'enchantment' of his words.[3] *Non tali
auxilio nec defensoribus istis*.[4]

If Mr. Pearsall Smith, to whose books I owe much
delight and knowledge, will forgive me for saying so, he
is playing straight into his enemies' hands. If anything
could make Dr Leavis more certain that Milton is not a
great poet, Mr. Pearsall Smith's book is that thing. His
defence would anger the real Milton much more than
Dr Leavis's attack. Milton's robust Renaissance theory
of poetry is very much closer to Dr Leavis than either
of them is to that of Mr. Pearsall Smith. The paradox
is that Mr. Pearsall Smith really agrees with Dr Leavis's
view of Milton; he thinks that Milton has nothing of
real moment to say, and so does Dr Leavis. The only

difference is that Mr. Pearsall Smith thinks this doesn't matter.

Compared with a real Miltonist, such as Mr. Charles Williams shows himself to be in his preface to the poet's works in *The World's Classics*, they are both in the same camp – both people who have simply failed to see what is in *Paradise Lost*.[5] And there are reasons for avoiding it. In one or other of the 'states of being' which it delineates, every reader finds himself;[6] [the one] in which we most commonly find ourselves is indicated by the romantic special pleading for Satan. Of course Satan *is* like Milton: but equally like Dr Leavis, Mr. Pearsall Smith, Mr. Williams, and myself. Fallen men and fallen angels *are* very alike. This cosmic coxcomb who 'thought himself impaired', this egoist who can never utter ten lines without getting back to himself and his film star's 'sense of injured merit', who hardly ever says anything that is *quite* true, this great sulker with his rants and melodrama and eternal inferiority complex, is simply Everyman in one of his worst moments.[7]

Over against him, as Mr. Williams shows, stands the hierarchical pattern of reality, the dignity and joy of unequal loves, of ruling and obeying, the humility of [a] derived being which knows it is derived and is happy in the fact. For the whole poem is what Mr. Williams would call an 'appearance of Byzantium', an assertion of Order, a grand illustration of the speech on 'Degree' which Shakespeare put into the mouth of Ulysses.[8] So far from being a remote or 'escapist' work it is relevant to every reader at almost every moment.

It would be impertinent to accuse any one contemporary by name of deliberately evading this relevance, but I find it hard to explain the resentment with which Milton is attacked and the almost patronizing fashion in which he is defended except on the hypothesis of a widespread wish not to see what is there. And indeed we all have, if not good, yet cogent, motives for not looking at, say, the war in heaven too steadily: that Satanic ridiculousness at which even Deity *must* laugh, and that moment (Mr. Williams is very great on this) when the whole world becomes a 'blaze of eyes',[9] have a meaning that no one receives without disquiet. Keats was quite right: 'there is death' in the poem;[10] death and life, both the fullest sense. All this Dr Leavis and Mr. Pearsall Smith *equally* ignore. After that, it makes very little difference that one should call Milton a good, and the other, a bad, poet. But it makes some. I think it would be easier for Dr Leavis some day to read Milton aright than for Mr. Pearsall Smith, who thinks he is on Milton's side already. I do not mean to be insolent; but a great matter is at stake.[11]

# 46

## Douglas Bush, Paradise Lost *in Our Time: Some Comments* (London: Cornell University Press, 1945)

~

In this book Dr Bush publishes his Messenger Lectures of 1944.[1] It is packed with good meat, and its zest and wit (do not miss the excellent application of Johnson's 'Was ever poet so trusted before?' on p. 9) are a pleasing proof that the author's spirit has not been broken by his late gigantic labours for the *Oxford History of English Literature*.[2]

Dr Bush's first chapter is (almost inevitably) devoted to an account of that controversy which at present divides opinion about Milton in England. He both summarises and contributes. Of his contribution, since I am myself on his side, I cannot claim to be a neutral judge. If I wished any points added to his summary (and especially for the benefit of his American audience) they would be these. (1) That Dr Leavis, for fidelity of observation and consistency of thought, is in a different class from the other Miltono-clasts. You may disagree with his judgement, but he keeps his eye on the object and knows exactly what he would be at. Some of his colleagues, in my opinion, do not.

(2) That the debate is not between two, but between three parties. The school of Pearsall Smith and that of Charles Williams are as opposed to one another as either

Published in *The Oxford Magazine*, vol. 65 (13 February 1947), pp. 215–17.

is to that of Dr Leavis.³ If they find themselves sometimes joining in an attack on the same enemy, this is almost an accident, on noticing that both tend to exclaim fervently *haud tali auxilio!*⁴ On the other hand, Williams and Dr Leavis are united by certain serious demands. I suspect that Milton himself, with his grave Renaissance doctrine of the poet's office, would be equally repelled by the naturalism of Dr Leavis and the aestheticism of Pearsall Smith, thinking the one barbaric and the other frivolous. The conflict is thus extremely complicated, and something more than the reputation of a particular poet is involved. Milton's poetry is, at the moment, a touchstone which reveals divergent tendencies of great importance in our own culture.

The bulk of Dr Bush's literary criticism comes in his third and fourth chapters. The third deals with the 'characters and drama' of *Paradise Lost*, and the fourth examines its 'poetic texture' mainly by detailed analysis of particular passages. In such analysis no two critics ever wholly agree, but I have learned much from this chapter. Dr Bush rightly points out how small variations within the self-imposed limits of a stylised art may, in the actual reading, have a value equivalent to that of the most violent and obvious devices in a looser manner. He adds that 'there are always critics who, seeing the surface of the ocean smooth, take it for a pond'.⁵

The second chapter, on 'Religious and Ethical Principles', is the most original in the book. In the attempt to classify Milton's thought Dr Bush goes behind the popular (and perhaps not very useful) antitheses of Puritan and Humanist, or Puritan and Anglican. For him the important contrast is that between thinkers who regard Reason, and thinkers who regard Will, as the basis of Law (whether

Divine or human) – if you will, between Rationalists and Dynamists. In Theology the supreme example of Rationalism would be Hooker;[6] his conception of the law of Nature has been characterized by Professor d'Entrèves as implying 'that this law has a value and a meaning apart from God Himself – *licet Deus non esset*'.[7]

The extreme instance of Dynamism would be Paley.[8] In Politics the convinced Rationalists (Aristotle and the Scholastics) are few and come only at the peaks of a culture: the Dynamists, from Hobbes to Hitler, are innumerable. Dr Bush's contention is that Milton stood with Hooker and the Cambridge Platonists on the Rationalist side and, like them, based his Theology on the *de jure*, not the *de facto*, sovereignty of God. This would put an even sharper chasm than has yet been acknowledged between his thought and that of orthodox Puritanism, which was usually dynamistic and anti-intellectual.

Dr Bush brings evidence to support his view, but his case requires fuller development than the limits of a lecture allowed him to give it. For my own part, I am still only willing to be convinced. Both types of thought seem to be represented in Milton. Nor do I quite understand why Dr Bush thinks it 'quaint' (p. 40) that Mr. Murry should bring against Milton charges 'essentially the same as those brought against Whichcote by his quondam tutor, the Calvinist Anthony Tuckney'.[9] If Milton is really a Rationalist (in the sense defined above) surely this is just what we ought to expect? At no stage in his career has Mr. Murry been a Rationalist in any sense; at no stage would he have been safe among our ancestors from the imputation of 'enthusiasm'. Nothing can be more alien to most characteristically modern modes of thought – Barthian,

Marxist, or Bergsonian-Shavian – than an interest in that which has authority *de jure*.

English readers will be a little puzzled at the 'semi-official' character which Dr Bush attributes to the *Oxford Book of Verse* (p. 23) and to the *Times Literary Supplement* (p. 25). Our constitution knows (as yet) no office to which either could be even semi-attached. The statement (p. 39) that for certain seventeenth-century thinkers 'God and nature are one', even with the qualification which Dr Bush gives it, seems to me simply false. But no book is without a careless sentence – or, more strictly, no prose book – and we may be grateful for what Dr Bush has given us. My own gratitude takes the form of a wish that he may hereafter deal more fully with some of the points touched on in these lectures.

# 47

## H. W. Garrod, *Collins*
## (Oxford: Clarendon Press, 1928)

~

'I was chidden for being academic... I was speaking to
an academy'. The second sentence is Professor Garrod's
unanswerable defence, and it is also the key to his whole
book, and to his earlier book on Keats. His method is that
of the enlightened scholiast: to read his *Collins* is like reading one's own copy of Collins enriched with marginalia,
as though from an etesian borrowing.

Eschewing generalization, he takes the odes to pieces,
stanza by stanza, and often line by line, and examines them
with the determination (too rare in English criticism) of
understanding what every sentence means: and when the
result of this process is to reveal incurable confusion in
the poet, the scholiast does not spare the moderate and
considered rebuke.

The reader will gather that Professor Garrod, as against
the romantics, agrees with Dante's stern dictum – it is a
disgrace for a poet to hide under '*figura o colore rettorico*'
that which, when stripped of its ornaments, cannot exhibit
a clear meaning to the prose consciousness.[1] However we
may quarrel with this doctrine in its universal application,
it is certainly applicable to a poet like Collins. The result
of its application may, for the moment, be chilling to the

Published in *The Oxford Magazine*, vol. 47 (16 May 1929), p. 633 on the
English poet William Collins (1721–1759).

poet's admirers, but we hardly deny the critic's plea that the good can be adequately praised only by a separation of the less good, and if we are honest with ourselves we shall be constantly made aware, in reading these criticisms, how slovenly and unawakened our own reading of the poets has often been. The book is naturally provocative and controversial.

Everyone will have his own say about some of the professor's suggested emendations, and I, for one, will go to the stake in defence of the passage quoted from W. P. Ker on p. 49.[2] The earlier chapters, which are the most important for the general history of the early romantics, bristle with challenges. Whether Thomas Warton, the elder, was really as poor a poet as Professor Garrod thinks – whether a movement in poetry is necessarily shallow because it is not preluded by 'the crash of thrones'[3] – whether Swinburne was really 'not inferior' to Tennyson 'in the music of verse'[4] – but it is impossible within the limits of a review to attack these questions. That we inevitably raise them is a testimony to the abundant interest of the book, and a proof, if proof were needed, that Professor Garrod's coolness has nothing to do with dullness.

# 48

## Hugh Kingsmill, *Matthew Arnold*
## (London: Duckworth, 1928)

≈

I am beginning to wonder whether biography, in our own time, may not replace the novel as the dominant form – the literary centre of this age towards which writers gravitate as inevitably as they gravitated to allegory in the later Middle Ages or to drama in the reign of James I. What has been illustrated by a few men of genius has always this tendency to attract literary 'casuals' who imagine that they have thus found the secret.

The occasion of these remarks is Mr Hugh Kingsmill's *Matthew Arnold*. Mr Kingsmill, after an introduction in which we are shown 'Frank Harris ... brooding over ladies' underwear at the editorial desk' (a few lines lower down 'Murry suddenly looked very old') proceeds to disassociate himself from the contemporary reaction in favour of the Victorians.[1] He dislikes most heartily the period he has chosen to write about.

Oddly enough he dislikes Arnold just as heartily. 'I am aware', he writes, 'that so far neither Matt. nor I have found each other congenial companions'.[2] For one thing Matthew Arnold was not added 'to the list of George Sand's victims', and though Mr Kingsmill tries to notice this oversight 'without wasting regrets', he never

Review published in The *Oxford Magazine*, vol. 47 (15 September 1928), p. 177.

really forgives him.[3] Again, Matthew Arnold wrote *Sohrab* 'with hardly a hint of any relation between Thomas and Matthew Arnold on the one hand, and Rustum and Sohrab on the other...any conscious or unconscious recognition on Arnold's part of the likeness between his fate and Sohrab's'.[4] This, to Mr Kingsmill, is most intolerable and not to be endured.

If after two hundred odd pages of this sort of stuff the reader is tempted to ask why Mr Kingsmill, hating Arnold, hating the Nineteenth Century, and hating poetry, has found it necessary to write the life of Arnold, he will find his answer in a cautionary tale on page 54. Mr Kingsmill knows a man who read *David Copperfield* without investigating the private life of Dickens; so naturally when he had seen Micawber shipped off to Australia – and not knowing that Dickens didn't get on with his wife – he shipped his own son off to Australia where the young man didn't do half so well as Micawber. So that's what you get if you don't study biography. The blurb on the inside of the jacket justly remarks that Mr Kingsmill writes 'with unusual courage'.

# 49

## Evelyn Waugh, *Rossetti: His Life and Works*
## (London: Duckworth, 1928)

~

Mr Evelyn Waugh is a courageous writer. He is opposed
to 'period' biographies – those char-a-banc trips in time
when literary tourists bring home 'a present from Victo-
rialand'. He is also opposed to certain elements in contemporary aesthetic theory. Holding such views, he has
ventured to test them where the strain is greatest.

Rossetti, with his self-deception, his avarice, and his
table turning, seems almost designed to tempt the biographer to an abstract Stracheyan 'humour'. Rossetti's
work – the painting so literary, the poetry so steeped in
facile 'Weltanschauung',[1] and both so erotic – invites the
surgery of the 'pure' school of criticism. Yet Mr Waugh
has resisted both solicitations. The result is an interesting, if not perfectly successful, book. On the theoretical
side Mr Waugh's case is this: if you cannot fit things like
the *Beata Beatrix* into the 'pure' theory, and if, none the
less, amidst the emotions which they apparently arouse (I
am taking the author's word for it), there remains something not to be accounted for by vicarious sexuality, human
sympathy, literary associations, and the like, what is to be
done?[2]

Review published in *The Oxford Magazine*, vol. 47 (25 October 1928),
pp. 66, 69 (unsigned).

At present, he can hardly pass beyond the iteration of his question. Wonder, however, is 'broken knowledge': and Mr Waugh is wondering very hard about matters on which the prevalent modes of thought do not encourage him to wonder. That is a merit not to be passed over. On the biographical side his work is much firmer. He has failed, I think, to make us see the early days of the PRB.[3] as they must have appeared to the actors themselves: we are left with the feeling that it was funny, but we know that it was not funny from the inside. On the whole, however, Mr Waugh's picture is convincing. The 'minor characters' are particularly good – Madox Brown, Millais, and, above all, Ruskin.

Mr Waugh had every temptation to exploit Ruskin as a comic prig: he might thus have flattered the vulgar appetite for funny old Victorians and at the same time displayed one passage of his own hero's life in a more favourable light. Yet the real Ruskin is allowed to pass across the stage, and, in so doing, to confirm our confidence in the author's good sense and insight. We look forward with interest to Mr Waugh's next book.

# 50

# Boswell's bugbear: Sir John Hawkins, *The Life of Samuel Johnson*, ed. Bertram Hylton Davis (London: Cape, 1961)

~

For many of us Sir John Hawkins has long been an invisible character in the wings about whom Boswell, on the stage, makes rude remarks. Our hearts leaped up when we heard of this edition of *The Life of Samuel Johnson*. But alas! B. H. Davis has given us only a 'processed' Hawkins: abridged and in modernised spelling. I would rather have done my own abridging.

We must not blame Mr Davis for not doing what he did not attempt, or perhaps was not allowed, to do. The disappointment remains. If this venture helps to discourage (what is long overdue) a new edition of the full text, it will be a disaster.

Mr Davis labours in his introduction to defend Hawkins from Boswell's charge of 'dark, uncharitable conjecture'. He thinks Hawkins's account of Johnson's marriage 'forthright' and Boswell's 'sentimentilised', and adds that the marriage 'was not an ideal one'.[1]

I cannot recall anyone who said it was, but I do not know on what evidence Hawkins can be pronounced, in this matter, 'closer to the truth' than Boswell. Neither biographer had ever seen Johnson and Tetty together.

Review published in *The Sunday Telegraph*, no. 61 (1 April 1961), p. 8.
John Hawkins (1719–1789) was a friend of Samuel Johnson.

Hawkins, without using the opprobrious word, gives us to understand that his marriage was purely mercenary. It may have been. But how could Hawkins know something about another man's heart which many a man does not perfectly know even about his own?

So with his more notorious comment on Johnson's expressions of grief for Tetty's death: 'If this fondness was not dissembled, it was a lesson he had learned by rote'. It is, I suppose, just possible that a very queer man should be dissembling – and more possible that he might be deceiving himself – in private prayers and jottings intended for no eye but his own. But again, Hawkins has no evidence: he is merely 'inclined to think'.[2]

It is the same throughout. Like all the great denigrators – like Tacitus, Saint-Simon, and Strachey – Hawkins relies heavily on suppositions which cannot be either verified or refuted. 'It is conjectured', 'Can it be supposed?' 'We must doubt', are the staple of his logic.

Even a confession of ignorance can be used to insinuate nastiness: 'How far his conversations with Savage might induce him to delight in tavern society, which is often a temptation to greater enormities than excessive drinking, cannot now be known'.[3]

In many such passages one almost feels that Hawkins was born before his time. With Freud to help him, with neo-Georgians for readers and some great Victorian for his victim, might he not have been a popular author?

All this may suggest a positive enmity to Johnson on Hawkins's part, but my diagnosis would be different. Admittedly there was much in Johnson that displeased him: his earlier politics, his indolence and procrastination,

the disorder of his life and dress, his legacy to his servant Frank (Hawkins seems never to have met Hodge,
his cat), his promiscuous charities. Johnson's unwearied
indulgence to the quarrelsome lame dogs who made his
household is, for Hawkins, 'pusillanimity'; his vulnera-
bility by comparison, a weakness of nature. In a word,
'Johnson could not be said to be a staid man'.[4]

Hawkins was eminently staid: Boswell mentions 'the
rigid formality of his manners'. But his feeling towards
Johnson is not hatred; it is tranquil disapproval *de haut
en bas*.

This disapproval extends to almost everyone Hawkins
mentions with the exception of Cave and Thrale.[5] Cave is
odd, because Hawkins regards professional authorship as
a sort of prostitution, and one might have supposed that
if those who write for periodicals are prostitutes, editors
must be procurers.

It was, presumably Cave's 'staidness' that redeemed
him. What Hawkins could not bear were people like Field-
ing and Smollett – or Goldsmith, whom he calls an 'idiot'
for using an interview with a nobleman to advance his
brother's interests instead of his own.[6]

Hawkins, then, is as pure a specimen of the cold prig
as we are ever likely to meet: but his book is very well
worth reading. Partly for a vein of comedy which the
author never suspected, but partly also on less discred-
itable grounds.

He has, after all, a great deal to tell us. He records
the famous speech beginning 'As soon as I enter the door
of a tavern'.[7] He gives us Johnson's reply to the baronet
who said that, if his circumstances allowed, he would have

settled £500 a year on him: 'Sir, if the first peer in England were to make me such an offer I would show him the way downstairs'.[8]

He has preserved the schoolboy's opinion that oracles ceased when the monasteries were dissolved. And he has valuable information to give us about the Ivy Lane Club, the possible theological background of Johnson's prayers for the dead, his later religious history (he read Nonconformist divines) and his last illness.

Contemporaries censured Hawkins for writing like a lawyer. It would be truer to say that his style, especially in the earlier pages, smells more of the 17th and the 18th century: the same long sentences sometime recalled to the main road with a recapitulatory 'I say'.

Yet every now and then he strikes out something good – Johnson's 'disquisitive propensity', a playhouse 'encircled with an halo of brothels', Johnson 'where he had reason to expect learning never showed mercy to ignorance', and 'the succession of knave to knave and fool to fool is hereditary and interminable'.[9] Once, by an astonishing anticipation, we reach pure Macaulay: 'the deep-mouthed rancour of Pulteney and the yelping pertinacity of Pitt'.[10]

Like all Johnsoniana the book leaves us with an increased respect for both Johnson and Boswell. For Boswell, because he is so incomparably the best of reporters: for Johnson, because he comes so unmistakably through them all. How many other men in all history have his double reality – real to our intellect (we believe him to be historical), but also as real to our imaginations as Mr Pickwick or Mr Woodhouse?

# 51

# Poetry and exegesis: Harold Bloom, *The Visionary Company: A Reading of English Romantic Poetry* (London: Faber, 1962)

∾

This is one of the most difficult books I have ever read: harder than *Romans* and ten times harder than Aristotle. In such a case vanity whispers that the fault lies with the author: prudence and the desire to be just ask whether it may not be one's own. Perhaps the best I can do is to cite a few of the expressions which puzzled me and leave the reader to judge.

'They perform for us the work of the ideal metaphysician or therapeutic idealist, which is the role our need has assigned to the modern poet'.[1] Have we here two alternative characterisations of the same work or two works of which a poet must do one or the other? Is a therapeutic idealist one who heals by idealism or one who is idealistic about healing? And in what sense is *idealist* used? 'The apocalyptic ambition . . . is to humanise nature and to naturalise the imagination'.[2] Naturalising the imagination might surely mean a good many different things? 'Poems of iconic response'.[3] Response to images (and images in what sense?) or a response (to something or other) which expresses itself in images? 'Awakening from experience into a visionary reality.' But if the vision is experienced,

Reviewed in *Encounter*, vol. 20 (June 1963), pp. 74–6.

those who achieve it have not emerged from experience. If not, the process is surely to be described not as wakening but as losing consciousness? 'An imagination ... so predicated against the Harlot Mystery'.[4] I can make no sense at all of *predicated* in this context.

Sometimes by a small emendation I can hammer out a meaning, but I don't know for sure whether it is Mr Bloom's. 'The Miltonic belief that the sexual entrance was wider, was in fact an entire body entering into an entire body'. The natural implication of *was* is 'used to be, but isn't now'; and since *Paradise Lost* is all about a great change in the nature of man, the suggestion is irresistible. But then Milton says nothing of the sort about pre-Lapsarian copulation between humans. In the previous paragraph, however, Mr Bloom has been talking about angelic amours ('total they mix'). I can therefore make sense if I emend *was* to 'is for creatures extremely different from us'. But if that is what he meant, how could he have written *was?*

Sometimes the difficulty is that Mr Bloom seems to be saying what is simply untrue about matters of fact which he must know perfectly well. Thus we are told that the Ancient Mariner 'is a haunter of wedding feasts'.[5] I can find no evidence for this in the text. An impulse points out to him the man to whom he must tell his story, and the particular hearer on this occasion happens to be a wedding-guest. The Mariner's own preference (which anyway has nothing to do with the matter) is 'a goodly company' going to an ordinary service.

The book is occupied almost entirely with exegesis; with expositions of what various poets have to say abstracted from the poetry itself. Mr Bloom is not to be blamed if, in such treatment, the very great differences of poetic achievement between the works he deals with slip out of sight. It can't be helped. If the exegesis is correct, it may in the long run do more than criticism to promote good reading.

The first and largest study is of Blake. Mr Bloom is very anxious to separate him from occult tradition and 'the swamp of Neoplatonism'; the names of Porphyry, Taylor, and Kathleen Raine do not appear in the index. He finds in Blake many ironies which have not, I think, been seen before.

To my mind Blake overshadows the rest of the work too much. I think Mr Bloom sees the other romantics far too much in terms of the anthroposophy (so to call it) he found in Blake. Hence, while his exegesis of Blake, if correct, clarifies Blake's poems, his exegesis of the *Prelude* seems to me to make dark what was clear enough already.

Mr Bloom thinks better than I of *Laodamia* as poetry;[6] yet to call the ghost 'a puritan' and to speak of 'denied sensuality' is surely to misunderstand. The ghost, because he is a ghost, can never give his wife what she really wants. It is death, not Wordsworth, that denies sensuality. This poem, like the *Comedy* and *Pearl*, arises from taking seriously the belief in transmortal life.[7] All three poets are too mature for the consolatory fantasy that this could simply restore an old happiness unchanged. Beatrice turns from Dante *all'eterna fontana*.[8] The father–child relation is as ruthlessly transformed in *Pearl* as eroticism is in *Laodamia*. We accept the negation in Dante because it is swallowed up in the glowing and positive vision at the end. We can make shift to endure it in *Pearl* because the New Jerusalem is something more than an abstraction. But poor Wordsworth has nothing to set against it but 'moral babble'. He has attempted a task hopelessly beyond his powers.

In *Kubla Khan* surely *momently* ('a mighty fountain momently was forced') must mean not 'momentarily', as Mr Bloom wants, but 'moment by moment'? How else could it resemble 'fast thick pants'? And 'the thresher's flail' also suggests repetition.

# 52

## The Sagas and modern life – Morris, Mr Yeats, and the originals: Dorothy M. Hoare, *The Works of Morris and of Yeats in Relation to Early Saga Literature* (Cambridge University Press, 1937)

~

'And yet one hesitates', says Miss Hoare on page 145 of her scholarly essay. It is timely and honestly said, and it is on a certain hesitation that much of the value of her book depends. Her task has been to compare certain works by Morris and Mr Yeats with their Icelandic or Irish originals and to explain the differences between them.

Such studies encourage a confusion between changes of kind and losses of value, as when we see Pope condemned for being unlike Theocritus, or Tennyson for being unlike Malory. But Miss Hoare, for the most part, has escaped this disease. Her final judgement on 'Sigurd the Volsung' perhaps assumes that what is 'more in the nature of tragedy' (like the Saga) must differ from what is less tragic simply as better differs from worse: and her excellent account of Mr. Stephen's 'Deirdre' is sometimes less concerned to establish the goodness either of the ectype or of the archetype than to praise both for their similarity.[1]

Review published in *The Times Literary Supplement* (29 May 1937), p. 409 (unsigned).

315

In general, however, the author cannot be accused of thus mixing questions. Her belief that the medieval originals are not only different from but also better than the corresponding pieces by Morris and Mr Yeats, is conscious and explicit: to defend it is part of her purpose. The initial difficulty – how things, on Miss Hoare's own showing, so unlike can be arranged in a unilinear series of value – has not been solved: but in other respects her position is clear. The old texts have a 'fierce active response to life', reveal 'actuality' and treat of 'feelings at the root of human nature'; the modern versions, on the other hand, exist at a 'remove from actuality' and 'seek to evade life'. Such expressions as 'a bias away from reality', 'unable to face distasteful facts', 'escape from life', 'without significance and reality', 'away from reality to vagueness and dream', recur in her pages with monotonous, but perhaps unavoidable, frequency.[2]

If this were all that Miss Hoare had to offer, her book would be less interesting than it is. The theory of literature implied would not be new nor very profound; and that sense of the words 'reality' and 'life' which excludes such emotional experience as that expressed in *The Shadowy Waters*,[3] or even our emotions about the imagined past, would need further definition. To cry for the moon is, after all, a commoner experience for most of us than to suffocate a wife or to be turned out into a thunderstorm by our pelican daughters: it also lasts longer. But here Miss Hoare's invaluable hesitation saves her from dullness. The most interesting characteristic of her book – the thing most useful to others in her predicament and fullest of promise for her own future as a critic – is the discrepancy between her actual literary experience and her implicit literary theory. Her very choice of subjects reveals it; and so does the fact that her most 'emotive' pages of criticism are devoted to Morris's prose romances and to *The Shadowy Waters* itself. Of this she admits with truthful reluctance that 'one can abandon oneself to it for a time'. Similarly, after complaining that *The Life and Death of Jason* 'is never strung up to intolerable pitch' (why should it be?) and sadly lacks 'rawness and fierceness of passion', she frankly adds that 'somehow' – the word is significant – 'somehow . . . one reads, and reads to the end'.[4] It is 'only when the end has been reached' that Miss Hoare discovers its defects; only, in other words, when she passes from imaginative experience to literary theories.

To praise a critic for honesty will seem damnation by faint praise only to those who have never tried very hard either at honesty or criticism; but it is a great thing to remain true to the facts under a severe strain.

Of Mr Yeats posterity will judge. Of Morris we can only say that Miss Hoare should read him again, with less submission to a narrow theory of literature. His real theme is very difficult to describe, but it is 'actual' enough. Morris himself does not state it philosophically. We may say, if we will, that it becomes explicit in *The House of the Wolfings* when the hero has to choose between immortality and mortal life with 'the kindreds', or again in *The Glittering Plain* where we reach the land of the everliving only to long for our escape from it.[5] But in so far as these stories pose a question and give an answer they are not typical. More characteristic is the strange poise of the Argonauts between 'formless and wailing thoughts' and the recurrent business of sail-mending, launching, and camping:[6] or the knight who carries with him to the well of life, and back, the resolution to be a good king in his own small country. But we cannot, in the long run, thus disengage characters or episodes. From the whole atmosphere of each tale arises our awareness that something which has made the vast unnoticed background to much of our experience is at last being given expression. We recognise (it is no other poet's theme) the endless hithering and thithering of natural desire, the irrepressible thirst for immortality, and its inevitable recoil to the familiar – the sweet familiar whose very sweetness must once more reawake the rebel passion. Morris may build a world in some ways happier than the real one; but happiness puts as stern a question as misery. It is this dialectic of desire, presented with no solution, no lies, no panacea, which gives him his peculiar bittersweet quality, and also his solidity. He has faced the fact. There are greater writers than Morris. You can go on from him to all manner of subtleties and sublimities which he does not offer: but you cannot go behind him.

Fortunately Miss Hoare has a real appreciation of romantic literature which the mistaken scruples of her literary conscience cannot wholly suppress. She is free from the usual misunderstandings of Morris's prose style, and sensitive to that quality in him which she happily describes as 'cleared and cool' – his triumph over 'turmoil and muddle', and his 'mature, autumnal quiet'. She sees that his romance is 'not entirely an airy thing' but full of 'actual vivid sights and sounds'.[7]

Her account of Mr Yeats's earlier manner is not unsympathetic, and she has good things to say about its characteristic rhythms. Perhaps by underemphasizing the element of *believed* occultism in his work (she touches the subject only once) she is led to neglect that important cleavage between him and Morris which results from the difference between fantasy known for such by author and reader alike and that which is not truly fantasy at all, being fact for the author and error for most readers. Both, no doubt, would be flights from reality on Miss Hoare's view; but surely not flights of the same kind or of the same significance.

On Morris's real defects as a translator Miss Hoare has much that is valuable to say. Certainly *whenso* and *were* or *ware* have overtones for us which the style of the sagas probably had not for their first hearers. It is a nice question whether their translator should give his readers what they would have got if they had been medieval Icelanders or what they would get if they now knew how to read Icelandic. Morris is as much in love with the language as with the stories – its influence on his original prose is considerable – and he is tempted by the second ideal; and, though he does not succeed, his methods are reasonable in so far as Icelandic strikes the modern ear as an archaic speech. The problem becomes most acute in the translation of *Kenningar*. We cannot, in a literary version, sit on the fence and say with Miss Hoare 'ships (lit. sail-steeds)'. If we write *twigsbane*, *wormsbed* and *Odin's ransom* we produce an oddity which the original had not: if we write 'fire', 'gold' and 'eye' we are omitting its most obvious characteristics.

Miss Hoare's account of the Icelandic sagas is attractive and duly praises 'the barrenness and coolness of the expression' and the 'way in which things are *not* said'.[8] One may venture to doubt whether either the behaviour of the heroes or the style owe as much to nature and as little to art as her words sometimes suggest. No noble tradition of speech or conduct is likely to be 'natural' except in the sense in which everything is natural. On p. 46 there is a slight ambiguity: the uninstructed reader would infer that Birdalone comes in *The Well at the World's End* and not in *The Water of the Wondrous Isles*.[9] And the same reader might be even more misled when on p. 54 Miss Hoare says that Morris's 'they tilted over a wain' (for *þeir tjölduþu vagu*) suggests 'a kind of leisure wrestling'.

# 53

## Haggard rides again: Morton Cohen, *Rider Haggard: His Life and Works* (London: Hutchinson, 1960)

~

I hope Mr. Cohen's excellent *Rider Haggard: His Life and Works* will move people to reconsider the whole Haggard question. For there really is a problem here. The vices of his style are inexcusable; the vapidity (and frequency) of his reflections, hard to bear. But it is no longer any good pretending that his best work was merely an ephemeral and commercial success. It has not passed away like the works of Ouida, Mrs Oliphant, Stanley Weyman, or Max Pemberton.[1] It has survived the whole climate of opinion which once made its imperialism and vague pieties acceptable. The promised time 'when the Rudyards cease from Kipling and the Haggards are no more' has failed to arrive.[2] Obstinately, scandalously, Haggard continues to be read and re-read. Why?

The significant fact for me is the feeling we have as we close *King Solomon's Mines*, or, still more, *She*. 'If only . . .' are the words that rise to our lips. If only we could have had this very same story told by a Stevenson, a Tolkien, or a William Golding. If only, *faute de mieux*, we were even allowed to re-write it ourselves!

Reviewed in *Time and Tide*, vol. 41 (3 September 2960), pp. 1044–5.

Note, the very same story. It is not the construction that is faulty. From the move of the first pawn to the final checkmate, Haggard usually plays like a master. His openings – what story in the world opens better than *She*? – are full of alluring promise, and his catastrophes triumphantly keep it.

The lack of detailed character-study is not a fault at all. An adventure story neither needs nor admits it. Even in real life, adventures tend to obliterate fine shades. Hardship and danger strip us down to the bare moral essentials. The distinction between shirker and helper, brave and cowardly, trusty and treacherous, overrides everything else. 'Character' in the novelist's sense is a flower that expands fully where people are safe, fed, dry, and warmed. That adventure stories remind us of this is one of their merits.

The real defects of Haggard are two. First, he can't write. Or rather (I learned from Mr. Cohen) won't.[3] Won't be bothered. Hence the *clichés*, jocosities, frothy eloquence. When he speaks through the mouth of Quatermain he makes some play with the unliterary character of the simple hunter. It never dawned on him that what he wrote in his own person was a great deal worse – 'literary' in the most damning sense of the word.

Secondly, the intellectual defects. No one after reading Mr. Cohen can believe that Haggard was out of touch with reality. Apparently his agriculture and sociological works are a solid meal of hard-won facts and of conclusions firmly drawn. When he decided that the only hope for the land lay in a scheme which flouted all his political preferences and shattered all his treasured hopes for his own class and his own family, he recommended that scheme without flinching.

Here lies the true greatness of the man; what Mr. Cohen calls his 'overall sturdiness'. Even as an author he can sometimes be shrewd – as when in *She* Allan Quartermain neither succumbs to the charms of Ayesha nor believes her 'tall' autobiographical stories. By making Quartermain keep his head Haggard shows that he can keep his own.

But though Haggard had sense, he was ludicrously unaware of his limitations. He attempts to philosophise. Again and again in his stories we see a commonplace intelligence, armed (or hampered) with an eclectic outfit of vaguely Christian, theosophical, and spiritualistic notions, trying to say something profound about that fatal subject 'Life'. This is seen at its embarrassing worst whenever Ayesha speaks. If she was really Wisdom's daughter, she did not take after her parents. Her thought is of the regrettable type called 'Higher'.

What keeps us reading in spite of all these defects is of course the story itself, the myth. Haggard is the text-book case of the mythopoeic gift pure and simple – isolated, as if for inspection, from nearly all those more specifically literary powers with which it so fortunately co-exists in, say, *The Ancient Mariner*, *Dr Jekyll and Mr. Hyde*, or *The Lord of the Rings*. To make matters even clearer, in Haggard himself the mythopoeic power seems to have grown less as the literary art improved. *Ayesha* is not such good myth as *She*, but is better written.

This gift, when it exists, in full measure, is irresistible. We can say of this, as Aristotle did of metaphor, 'no man can learn it from another'.[4] It is the work that Kipling called 'the daemon'.[5] It triumphs over all obstacles and makes us tolerate all faults. It is quite unaffected by any foolish notions which the author himself, after the daemon has left him, may entertain about his own myths. He knows no more about them than any other man. It was silly of Haggard to treasure a belief that there was, in a factual sense, 'something in' his myths. But we, as readers, need not concern ourselves with that at all.

The mythical status of *She* is indisputable. As we all know, Jung went to it for the embodiment of an archetype. But even Jung did not, I think, get to the centre. If his view were right, the myth ought to function only for those to whom Ayesha is a powerfully erotic image. And she is not so for all who love *She*. To myself, for example, Ayesha or any other tragedy Queen – any tall, crowned, stormy, deep-breasted contralto with thunder in her brow and lightnings in her eye – is one of the most effective anti-aphrodisiacs in the world. Ultimately the life of the myth is elsewhere.

The story of Ayesha is not an escape, but it is about escape; about an attempt at the great escape, daringly made and terribly frustrated. The closest relative, perhaps its child, is Morris's *Well at the World's End*, which came ten years later. Both stories externalise the same psychological forces; our irreconcilable reluctance to die, our craving for an immortality in the flesh, our empirical knowledge that this is impossible, our intermittent awareness that it is not even really desirable, and (octaves deeper than all these) a very primitive feeling that the attempt, if it could be made, would be unlawful and would call down

the vengeance of the gods. In both books the wild, trans-
porting, and (we feel) forbidden hope is aroused. When
fruition seems almost in sight, terrifying disasters shat-
ter our dream. Haggard's version is better than Morris's.
Morris makes his heroine too human, too wholesome.
Haggard, truer to our feelings, surrounds the lonely she-
Prometheus with terror and misery.

Haggard's best work will survive because it is based on
an appeal well above high-water mark. The fullest tides
of fashion cannot demolish it. A great myth is relevant as
long as humanity lasts. It will always work, on those who
can receive it, the same catharsis.

Haggard will last, but so will the hatred of Haggard.
The vindictiveness with which adverse critics attacked him
in his own day had, no doubt, some local and temporary
causes. His own truculence was one. Another was the natural jealousy of the gigadibs who can produce only a *succès
d'estime* for the writer who produces 'popular' – but also
living and viable – work. The author of a *Gorboduc* always
has a keen eye for the faults of a *Tamburlaine*.[6] But there
was, and there always will be, a deeper cause. No one is
indifferent to the mythopoeic. You either love it or else
hate it 'with a perfect hatred'.

This hatred comes in part from a reluctance to meet
Archetypes; it is an involuntary witness to their disquieting
vitality. Partly it springs from an uneasy awareness that
most 'popular' fiction, if only it embodies a real myth, *is*
so very much more serious than what is generally called
'serious' literature. For it deals with the permanent and
inevitable, whereas an hour's shelling, or perhaps a ten
mile walk, or even a dose of salts, might annihilate many

of the problems in which the characters of a refined and subtle novel are entangled. Read James' letters and see what happened to him for some weeks after the war broke out in 1914. He presently builds up the Jamesian world again; but for a time it seemed to have 'left not a wrack behind'.[7]

# NOTES

## 1 The idea of an 'English School'

1. Francis Bacon, *Novum Organum* (1620), Book 1, section 23: 'The difference between idols of a human mind and the ideas of a divine one is certainly not slight: that is, between certain empty beliefs and the true signatures and marks impressed upon creation as it is found.'
2. John Henry Newman, *The Idea of a University* (1852).
3. Roger Ascham (*c.* 1515–1568), best known for *The Schole-master* (1570), a treatise on teaching.
4. Ovid, *Ars Amatoria*, Book 3, line 397: 'There is no desire for that which is unknown.'
5. Goethe, *Faust* (1808; 1832), Section 87, line 1348: Mephistopheles is describing himself: 'I am part of the part who once was all.'
6. Thomas Gray (1716–1771), English poet and scholar.
7. George Chapman (*c.* 1559–1634) published translations of the *Iliad* and *Odyssey* in 1616. The translation of the *Iliad* by Alexander Pope (1688–1744) was published between 1715 and 1720, and his translation of Homer's *Odyssey* appeared in 1726.
8. Marsilio Ficino (1433–1499), Italian Renaissance philosopher and humanist.
9. *The Greek Anthology* is a collection of 6,000 short elegaic poems by more than 300 writers (seventh century BC–tenth century AD).
10. This seems to be a Catholic aphorism of unknown origin. (Cf., for example, St Thomas Aquinas, *Summa Theologiae*,

part 1, question 75, article 5) The translation is: 'Whatever is received is received according to the manner of the one who receives.'

11. Virgil, *Aeneid*, Book 7, line 172, which Lewis translated in *A Preface to Paradise Lost* (1942), chapter 6, as 'awful with woods and sanctity of elder days'; see A. T. Reyes (ed.), *C. S. Lewis's Lost Aeneid* (London and New Haven: Yale University Press, 2011), p. 159.

12. Virgil, Book 8, line 323, explaining the name 'Latium' ('because it had been hidden on these shores.').

13. Matthew Arnold, 'The Function of Criticism at the Present Time' in *Essays in Critcism* (London: Macmillan, 1865), p. 35.

14. This is a Latin translation of a fragment from Euripides' lost play *Telephus*. Agamemnon is speaking to Menelaus: 'Sparta has fallen as your portion' (the phrase continues: *hanc exorna* – 'therefore, it is yours to provide for').

15. The English Faculty of Oxford University voted, by a significant majority, to abolish compulsory Anglo-Saxon from its undergraduate syllabus in 2000.

## 2 Our English syllabus

1. William Shakespeare, *As You Like It*, Act 3, scene 2, lines 283–5.

2. John Milton, *Of Education* (1644), paragraph 1.

3. Artistotle, *Nicomachean Ethics*, Book 10, section 7.

4. Geoffrey Chaucer, *Parlement of Foules* (1343?–1400), line 1.

## 3 Image and imagination

1. *Collected Letters* III, pp. 1522–3.

2. A reference to the aesthetic philosophy of Benedetto Croce (1866–1952). Cf. the final sentence of 'Image and Imagination'.

3. H. W. B. Joseph, *Introduction to Logic* (Oxford: Clarendon Press, 1916). LCM = 'Least Common Multiple' in Mathematical Logic.

4. Keats, 'Ode to a Nightingale':

> ... The same that oft-times hath
> Charm'd magic casements, opening on the
>   foam
> Of perilous seas, in faery lands forlorn.

5. By Robert Browning (1855).

6. *Esse* = reality; *percipi* = appearance.

7. 'The souls of the just', from the Book of Wisdom, chapter 3, verse 1: 'But the souls of the just are in God's hand; no torment will touch them' (RSV).

8. Thomas Rymer (*c.* 1643–1713), scholar with a particular interest in Aristotle's *Poetics*.

9. William Wordsworth, 'Letter to John Wilson' in N. C. Smith (ed.), *Wordsworth's Literary Criticism* (London: Oxford University Press, 1905), p. 8.

### 4 *Arundell Esdaile*, The Sources of English Literature

1. Charles Edward Sayle (1864–1924), a librarian at the University of Cambridge.

### 5 *W. P. Ker*, Form and Style in Poetry

1. There are at least two passages in George Macdonald's work that bear a close similarity to the passage Lewis ascribes to MacDonald, and which he quotes in a number of places: 'God is easy to please but hard to satisfy.' In the 1867 essay, 'The Imagination: Its Function and Its Culture', in *A Dish of Orts* (1903) we find: 'The right teacher would have his pupil

easy to please, but ill to satisfy; ready to enjoy, unready to embrace; keen to discover beauty, slow to say, "Here I will dwell".' In George Macdonald, *Donal Grant* (1883) chapter 46, we find: 'The maister's jist as easy to please as he's ill to saitisfee.'

Lewis almost certainly got the actual words from G. K. Chesterton. In his Introduction to Greville MacDonald's *George MacDonald and His Wife* (1924), Chesterton rephrased the passage from *Donal Grant* as: 'Carlyle could never have said anything so subtle and simple as MacDonald's saying that God is easy to please and hard to satisfy.' Lewis quoted these words again in *George MacDonald: An Anthology* (1947) and in *Mere Christianity* (1952), Book 4, chapter 9: 'As a great Christian writer (George MacDonald) pointed out... "God is easy to please, but hard to satisfy."'

2. W. P. Ker, *Epic and Romance: Essays on Medieval Literature* (London: Macmillan, 1897).

3. Lady Raleigh (= Lucy Gertrude Jackson Raleigh) (ed.), *The Letters of Sir Walter Raleigh (1897–1922)*, 2 vols. (London: Methuen, 1926), vol. 1, p. 192: 'I like your severe and withal judicial treatment of Romance. It is a new view, that Romance was a kind of plague spoiling a fine native development. I wish that your book may be a starting-point of a new literary movement.'

4. W. P. Ker (ed.), *Essays of John Dryden*, 2 vols. (Oxford: Oxford University Press, 1900).

5. The Literary Forms, in verse and prose, are usually considered to be: Poetry, Drama, Epic, Legend, Myth, Ballad, and Folktales. In chapter 1, on 'Form and Style' Ker said: 'The commonest meaning of "form" in poetry is perhaps that of metrical pattern or form... The poet gives poetical shape to his thoughts and experience... like an artist in the kitchen pouring hot jelly into a mold to cool and

stiffen' (pp. 95–6). Cf. Lewis's essay, 'Sometimes Fairy Stories May Say Best What's to be Said' in *Of This and Other Worlds* (1982) in which he said of writing the Narnian stories: 'In the Author's mind there bubbles up every now and then the material for a story. For me it invariably begins with mental pictures. This ferment leads to nothing unless it is accompanied with the longing for a Form: verse or prose, short story, novel, play or what not...It is now a thing inside him pawing to get out. He longs to see the bubbling stuff pouring into that Form as the housewife longs to see the new jam pouring into the clean jam jar' (pp. 57–8).

## 6 *Denis de Rougemont,* Poetry and Society *and Claude Chavasse* The Bride of Christ

1. Writing to his brother on 29 March 1940, Lewis said: 'The other thing I've been busy on this week is a book called *L'Amour et l'Occident* by one Denis de Rougement, apparently a French Protestant wh. I have to review. It contains a thoroughly bad historical thesis about medieval love, and an absolutely first class *moral* thesis about the utter incompatibility of *l'amour passion* with Christian marriage, happiness, or even enjoyable physical sexuality. He's a corker of a man, tho' with some bogus elements in him. I've written to him today.' (*Collected Letters II*, p. 379.)

2. In a strict sense, the Gyges fallacy is the argument deployed by Glaukon in Book 2 of Plato's *Republic*, in which he says that everyone will be unjust given the opportunity. To illustrate this, Glaukon uses the story of King Gyges of Lydia and his invisible ring, adapted from Herodotus' account. Socrates then attempts to expose this argument as a fallacy. Lewis, however, uses the term 'Gyges fallacy' idiosyncratically, simply because he is thinking of the 'invisible

man' example, and Gyges' ring had the power of making its wearer invisible. In fact, Lewis's fallacy is a variant on what is more commonly known as the *post hoc, ergo propter hoc* fallacy (i.e., given this fact, therefore because of this fact), in which the two premises of a syllogism are true but are followed by an unwarranted conclusion. (For example: I am carrying garlic, so that vampires do not attack me. Vampires have not attacked me. Therefore, carrying garlic works as a way of warding off vampires.)

3. An *Alba* is a Provençal troubadour poem about the parting of lovers at dawn.

4. Molière, *Le Misanthrope*, Act 1, scene 2, line 41: 'I prefer my darling.'

5. In *The Four Loves* (1960), chapter 1, Lewis wrote: 'St John's saying that God is love has long been balanced in my mind against the remark of a modern author (M. de Rougemont) that "love ceases to be a demon only when he ceases to be a god"; which of course can be re-stated in the form "begins to be a demon the moment he begins to be a god." This balance seems to me an indispensable safeguard. If we ignore it the truth that God is love may slyly come to mean for us the converse, that love is God.'

## 7 *Oliver Elton (1861–1945): an obituary*

1. O. Elton, *A Survey of English Literature*, vol. III (London: E. Arnold, 1920), p. 51.

2. *Ibid.*, p. vi.

3. 'Now the German and the Englishman are not in the least alike ... They are, in everything good and evil, more unlike than any other two men we can take at random from the great European family. They are opposite from the roots of their history, nay, of their geography' (G. K. Chesterton, *The Anatomy of Tyranny*, chapter 4: 'The Escape of Folly').

See *The Collected Works of G. K. Chesterton*, vol. v (San Francisco: Ignatius Press, 1987), p. 270.

4. George Saintsbury (1845–1933), literary historian and critic.

5. Thomas Warton (1728–1790), literary historian and critic, best known for his three-volume work, *The History of English Poetry*, published between 1774 and 1781.

6. Clio was Muse of History in Classical mythology.

7. From William Wordsworth, *The Excursion*, Book 1: 'The Wanderer', lines 105–6:

> The high and tender Muses shall accept
> With gracious smile, deliberately
>    pleased...

## 8 *Howard Rollin Patch*, The Other World, According to Descriptions in Medieval Literature

1. 'On Fairy-Stories', pp. 119–20: 'Students of folk-lore are apt to get off their own proper track, or to express themselves in a misleading "shorthand"...They are inclined to say that any two stories that are built round the same folklore motive, or are made up of a generally similar combination of such motives, are "the same stories."...Statements of that kind may express...some element of truth; but they are not true in a fairy-story sense, they are not true in art or literature. It is precisely the colouring, the atmosphere, the unclassifiable individual details of a story, and above all the general purport that informs with life the undissected bones of the plot, that really count.'

2. James Russell Lowell, 'Chaucer', in *My Study Windows* (London: Walter Scott, 1886), p. 234: 'Love, beauty, passion, nature, art, life, the natural and theological virtues – there is nothing beyond his power to disenchant.'

3. Alexander Pope, *An Essay on Criticism* (1711), Part 2, line 256.

## 9 *Werner Schwarz*, Principles and Problems of Biblical Translation

1. Much of Lewis's thought on translations of the Bible are found in his *English Literature in the Sixteenth Century*, Book 2, section 1, 'Drab Age Prose – Religious Controversy and Translation.'
2. LXX is the Septuagint, the Greek version of the Hebrew Bible or the Old Testament.
3. The *Letter of Aristeas*, probably written in the mid-second century BC, describes the translation of the Hebrew Scriptures into Greek during the reign of Ptolemy II Philadelphos. It is considered partly mythical.
4. Philo (20 BC–AD 50) was a Hellenistic Jewish philosopher from Alexandria. *De Vita Mosis* = *On the Life of Moses*.
5. St Augustine, City of God, Book 18, chapter 43: 'If there seems no agreement, we must trust that there is a prophetic depth there.'
6. *Ibid.*, chapter 44: 'translated so much later'.
7. *Ibid.*: The Holy Spirit 'spoke one prophecy through the prophet Jonah, the other through the 70 translators'.
8. Johann Reuchlin (1455–1522), German humanist and Hebraist.
9. John Colet (1467–1519), English theologian. He was, among other preferments, Dean of St Paul's Cathedral, London from 1505 to 1519.
10. Jacobus Latomus (1475–1544), Flemish scholar and opponent of Martin Luther.
11. '...I might well be able to praise and describe myself as a servant and evangelist...' Luther's full sentence is as follows: 'I have received my gospel not from men but from

heaven only, by our Lord Jesus Christ, so that I might well be able to praise and describe myself as a servant and evangelist, as I shall do in future.' The quotation appears in a letter to Frederick the Wise of Saxony, from Martin Luther, dated 5 March 1522. For the full translation of the letter, see Preserved Smith, *The Life and Letters of Martin Luther*, ed. Robert Blackhouse (London: Hodder and Stoughton, 1993), pp. 133–6.

12. Cicero, *De Legibus*, Book 3, chapter 16, section 36: 'He was stirring up a tempest in a teapot.'

13. *Vetus Latina* ('Old Latin') were older Latin translations of the Bible, before the version by St Jerome.

14. Martial, *Epigrams*, Book 2, epigram 86, lines 9–10: 'It is disgraceful to make difficulties from trifles, and to labour over nonsense is stupid.'

### 10  *Tragic ends: George Steiner,* The Death of Tragedy

1. In the Preface to William Wordsworth and Samuel Taylor Coleridge, *Lyrical Ballads, With a Few Other Poems* (1798) Wordsworth wrote: 'There will also be found in these volumes little of what is usually called poetic diction; as much pains has been taken to avoid it as is ordinarily taken to produce it; this has been done for the reason already alleged, to bring my language near to the language of men.'

2. W. B. Yeats, *The Countess Cathleen* (1895), Scene 5: 'And God the herdsman goads them on behind, / And I am broken by their passing feet.'

3. Aristotle, *Politics*, Book 3, section 11.

4. *Paradise Lost*, Book 2, line 1051.

5. *The Death of Tragedy*, pp. 43, 88, 138.

6. *Ibid.*, p. 9.

7. *Ibid.*, pp. 5, 10.

8. By Pierre Corneille in 1637 and by Jean Racine in 1689, respectively.

9. An English surname derived from Cumbria, first recorded in the fifteenth century.

10. 'Comprehensive world view'.

11. Richard Wagner's *Ring of the Nibelungen* (1876), a cycle of four operas: *Das Rheingold*, *Die Walküre*, *Siegfried*, and *Götterdämmerung*.

12. Oceanus is one of the Titans in John Keats's *The Fall of Hyperion* (1856).

13. S. Spencer and B. Millington (eds.), *Selected Letters of Richard Wagner* (London: Dent, 1987), p. 307 (Letter to August Röckel of 25 January 1854).

14. See 'The Funeral of a Great Myth' in Lewis's *Christian Reflections* (1967): 'If popular Evolutionism were (as it imagines itself to be) not a Myth but the intellectually legitimate result of the scientific theorem on the public mind, it would arrive *after* that theorem had become widely known. We should have the theorem known first of all to a few, then adopted by all the scientists, then spreading to all men of general education, then beginning to affect poetry and the arts, and so finally percolating to the mass of the people. In fact, however, we find something quite different. The clearest and finest poetic expressions of the Myth come before [Charles Darwin's] *Origin of Species* was published (1859) and long before it had established itself as a scientific orthodoxy' (pp. 105–6).

## 11 *Eros on the loose: David Loth,* The Erotic in Literature

1. *The Erotic in Literature*, p. 189, citing John Lothrop Motley, *The Rise of the Dutch Republic*, 3 vols. (London: John Chapman, 1856).

2. Charles Lamb, 'Witches and Other Night Fears' (1821).
3. Samuel Taylor Coleridge, 'Dejection: An Ode' (1802).
4. John Sparrow, 'Regina v. Penguin Books', *Encounter*, vol. 63 (February 1962), pp. 35–43.
5. *The Erotic in Literature*, p. 11.
6. *Ibid.*, p. 12.
7. *Ibid.*, p. 159.
8. John Ford, *'Tis Pity She's a Whore* (1633).
9. *The Erotic in Literature*, p. 181.
10. *Ibid.*, p. 97.
11. *The Erotic in Literature*, p. 43. The story of Judah and Tamar is told in Genesis, chapter 38, verses 1–30.
12. *Ibid.*
13. *Ibid.*, p. 75.
14. Dante, *Inferno*, Canto 25, line 116. Both *aidoia* and *pudenda* mean 'the shameful parts'.

## 12 *Who gaf me drink?: Owen Barfield,* Romanticism Comes of Age

1. F. L. Cross and E. A. Livingstone (eds.), *The Oxford Dictionary of the Christian Church*, third revised edition (Oxford: Oxford University Press, 2005), pp. 76–77.
2. David Gwilym James, *Scepticism and Poetry: An Essay on the Poetic Imagination* (London: Allen and Unwin, 1937).
3. *Romanticism Comes of Age*, p. 18.
4. Samuel Taylor Coleridge, *Biographia Literatia* (1817). This work of philosophical autobiography and Romantic literary criticism was essential to Lewis's and Barfield's thoughts on Imagination. See the distinction between Fantasy and Imagination in Lewis's 'On Three Ways of Writing for Children' in *Of This and Other Worlds* (1982), and the two chapters on 'Imagination and Fancy' in Owen Barfield's

*What Coleridge Thought* (Middletown, Connecticut: Wesleyan University Press, 1972).

5. Dante, *Purgatorio*, Canto 7, lines 7–8: 'e per null' altro rio / lo ciel perdei che per non aver fé'. 'I came short of Heaven / For no default, save that I had not faith.'

6. *Romanticism Comes of Age*, p. 34.

7. G. K. Chesterton, *Orthodoxy* (1909), chapter 1: 'I did try to be original; but I only succeeded in inventing all by myself an inferior copy of the existing traditions of civilized religion. The man from the yacht thought he was the first to find England; I thought I was the first to find Europe. I did try to found a heresy of my own; and when I had put the last touches to it, I discovered that it was orthodoxy.'

8. *Romanticism Comes of Age*, p. 60.

9. Geoffrey Chaucer, *Troilus and Criseyde*, Book 2, line 651.


## *13 G. A. L. Burgeon*, This Ever Diverse Pair

1. Walter de la Mare (1873–1956), English poet and author.

2. Lewis has misremembered the title of James Hogg, *The Private Memoirs and Confessions of a Justified Sinner* (1824).

3. Colossians, chapter 3, verses 9–10: 'Lie not one to another, seeing that ye have put off the old man with his deeds; and have put on the new man...' (AV); cf. Ephesians, chapter 4, verses 20–4.

4. George Meredith, *Modern Love*, Sonnet 43, lines 14–15.

5. *This Ever Diverse Pair*, p. 72.

6. 'Condescendingly'.

7. *This Ever Diverse Pair*, chapter 5, 'Rhematophobia [= fear of the spoken word']', p. 50: 'Generally speaking, it is the meaning of words and the tone in which they are spoken which are the cause of pain. I have only lately realised that mere words, as such, irrespective of tone or meaning, mere quantity of utterance apart altogether from the quality, can

inflict as much pain as a rebuff or a cold reply to an affectionate question.'

## *14  A world for children: J. R. R. Tolkien,*
## The Hobbit: or There and Back Again

1. *Flatland* (1884) is by Edwin A. Abbott, *Phantastes* by George MacDonald (1858).
2. *The Hobbit: or There and Back Again* (1937), chapter 1.
3. *Ibid.*, chapter 15.

## *15  Professor Tolkien's hobbit: J. R. R. Tolkien,*
## The Hobbit: or There and Back Again

1. In Kenneth Grahame, *The Wind in the Willows* (1908).
2. *The Hobbit: or There and Back Again* (1937), chapter 3.

## *16  The gods return to earth: J. R. R. Tolkien,*
## The Fellowship of the Ring

1. William Blake, *Songs of Innocence* (1789).
2. 'One Ring to Bind Them', *New Statesman and Nation*, vol. 48 (18 September 1954), p. 331.
3. 'On Fairy-stories', pp. 122 ff.
4. *The Fellowship of the Ring*, 'Prologue.'
5. 'On Fairy-stories', p. 148: 'It is plain that I do not accept the tone of scorn or pity with which "Escape" is now so often used ... In what the misusers of Escape are fond of calling Real Life, Escape is evidently as a rule very practical, and may even be heroic ... Why should a man be scorned, if, finding himself in prison, he tries to get out and go home? Or, if, when he cannot do so, he thinks and talks about other topics than jailers and prison-walls. The world outside has not become less real because the prisoner cannot see it. In

using Escape in this way the critics have chosen the wrong word, and, what is more, they are confusing, not always by sincere error, the Escape of the Prisoner with the Flight of the Deserter.'

6. Charlotte Brontë and her brother Branwell in 1834 created the imaginary country of Angria. The stories were first published as *Legends of Angria*, compiled from the early writings of Charlotte Brontë by Fannie E. Ratchford with the collaboration of William Clyde DeVane (New Haven: Yale University Press, 1933).

7. *Furioso* = *Orlando Furioso* by Ludovico Ariosto (1532). William Morris wrote *Water of the Wondrous Isles* (1897).

8. *The Fellowship of the Ring*, Book 1, chapter 2.

## 17   *The dethronement of power: J. R. R. Tolkien,* The Two Towers *and J. R. R. Tolkien,* The Return of the King

1. *The Two Towers*, Book 3, chapter 2.

2. 'On Fairy-Stories', p. 135: 'A real taste for fairy-stories was wakened by philology on the threshold of manhood, and quickened to full life by war.'

3. *The Two Towers*, Book 3, chapter 2.

4. *Ibid.*, chapter 4.

5. *Ibid.*

6. *Ibid.*, Book 4, chapter 10.

7. *Ibid.*, Book 3, chapter 4.

8. *Ibid.*, Book 3, chapter 2.

9. 'On Fairy-stories', p. 146: 'Recovery ... is a re-gaining ... of a clear view ... I might venture to say "seeing things as we are (or were) meant to see them" – as things apart from ourselves. We need ... to clean our windows; so that the things seen clearly may be freed from the drab blur of triteness or familiarity.'

## 18 Preface from Essays Presented to Charles Williams

1. These are, respectively, Dorothy Sayers, C. S. Lewis and J. R. R. Tolkien, Owen Barfield, Fr Gervase Mathew, and Major W. H. Lewis.

2. 'Ambrosian Nights': a series of articles by John Wilson *et al.* from *Blackwood's Magazine* (1822–1835).

3. Hugo Dyson (1896–1975), Fellow in English at Merton College, Oxford, and a member of the Inklings.

4. R. W. Chapman (1881–1960) of the Oxford University Press, best known for his editions of Jane Austen's novels and Samuel Johnson's letters.

5. Neville Coghill (1899–1980), Professor of English Literature at Oxford and a member of the Inklings.

6. Psalm 17, verse 10: 'They [the wicked] are inclosed in their own fat: with their mouth they speak proudly' (AV).

7. From Edmund Burke, *Reflections on the Revolution in France* (1790).

8. Alexander Pope, *Essay on Man*, Epistle 4, line 379 (1734).

9. 'Esemplastic' = 'unifying', coined by Samuel Taylor Coleridge in *Biographia Literaria* (1817).

10. Proverbs 27, verse 6: 'Faithful are the wounds of a friend . . .' (AV).

11. 'The Two-Sided Man', from *Kim* (1908), chapter 8.

12. 'What do I know?': motto from Montaigne's *Essays* (1595), Book 2, chapter 12.

13. i.e., Doubting Thomas, the Disciple initially sceptical of the Resurrection of Christ.

14. Jonah, chapters 1–2.

15. 2 Kings, chapter 2, verse 24.

16. P. V. M. Benecke (1868–1944), Fellow of Magdalen College, Oxford, who taught Classics and Theology.

### 19 *A sacred poem: Charles Williams,* Taliessin Through Logres

1. *Taliessin Through Logres,* 'The Calling of Arthur', 26.
2. *Ibid.,* 'The Star of Percivale', 4.
3. *Ibid.,* 'The Sister of Percivale', 22.
4. *Ibid.,* 'Lamorack and the Queen Morgause of Orkney', 10–12.
5. Abraham Cowley (1618–1667), who tried to assimilate the Pindaric ode into the English poetic tradition.
6. *Ibid.,* 'Taliessin in the School of the Poets', 42.
7. Charles Williams, *He Came Down from Heaven* (London: Heinemann, 1938).
8. *Ibid.,* p. 17.
9. *Taliessin Through Logres,* 'Lamorack and the Queen Morgause of Orkney', 21–3.
10. *Ibid.,* 'The Vision of the Empire', η, 6, 4–8.
11. *He Came Down from Heaven,* p. 18.
12. *Taliessin Through Logres,* 'The Vision of the Empire', θ, 33.
13. *Ibid.,* θ, 2.
14. *He Came Down from Heaven,* pp. 83–114.
15. *Taliessin Through Logres,* 'The Vision of the Empire, β, 11–17.
16. *He Came Down from Heaven,* 'The Theology of Romantic Love', p. 91ff.
17. *Ibid.,* 'The Practice of Substituted Love', pp. 114–33.
18. *Ibid.,* p. 115.
19. Charles Williams, *Descent into Hell* (London: Faber, 1937).
20. *Taliessin Through Logres,* 'Bors to Elayne: on the King's Coins', 80–4.
21. *Ibid.,* 38, 40.
22. *Ibid.,* 'The Crowning of Arthur', 59.
23. *Ibid.,* 'The Vision of the Empire', α, 6; α, 16.
24. *Ibid.,* α, 10.

25. *Ibid.*, δ, 5; ε, 17.
26. *Ibid.*, θ, 9; ἡγεμονικόν-authoritative part of the soul.
27. *Ibid.*, 'Mount Badon', 36, 41.
28. *Ibid.*, 48, 50.
29. George Meredith, 'Lucifer in Starlight', line 14 (1883).
30. *Taliessin Through Logres*, 'Taliessin's Return to Logres', 9–12.
31. *Ibid.*, 'The Vision of the Empire', α, 8.
32. 'Each thing is one, but appears to be many in association with actions.... '
33. *Ibid.*, 'Taliessin in the School of the Poets', 52–5.
34. Charles Williams, *Many Dimensions* (London: Faber, 1931).
35. Charles Williams, *The Greater Trumps* (London: Faber, 1932).
36. 'For HUMPHREY MILFORD / Under Whom We Observed / An Appearance of / BYZANTIUM.' Sir Humphrey Milford (1877–1952) managed Oxford University Press in London from 1913 to 1945.
37. *Taliessin Through Logres*, 'The Coming of Palomides', 62.
38. *Ibid.*, 'Palomides Before his Christening', 20.
39. *Ibid.*, 'The Coming of Palomides', 57–8.
40. *Ibid.*, 'Taliessin in the School of the Poets', 65–6.
41. *Ibid.*, 'The Last Voyage', 15–16.
42. *Ibid.*, 'The Crowning of Arthur', 43–7.
43. *Ibid.*, 'The Vision of the Empire', θ, 32–5.
44. *Ibid.*, 'Bors to Elayne: on the King's Coins', 20.
45. *Ibid.*, 'The Departure of Merlin', 21–4.
46. Johann Wolfgang von Goethe, *Faust*, Part 2 (1832), Act 1, scene 5, paragraph 6855; Percy Bysshe Shelley, *Prometheus Unbound* (1820), Act 4; Jacob Böhme, *The Way to Christ* (1623), Book 1.
47. *Taliessin Through Logres*, 'The Vision of the Empire', γ, 6.
48. *Ibid.*, 'The Son of Lancelot', 207.
49. *Ibid.*, 9, 30, 32–3.

50. *Ibid.*, 'Bors to Elayne: on the King's Coins', 94–7.
51. E. Vinaver (1899–1979), author of the standard edition of Malory.
52. *Taliessin Through Logres*, 'The Son of Lancelot', 188–91.
53. Blaise Pascal, *Pensées* (1670; trans. 1688), Section 5, 353.
54. *Taliessin Through Logres*, 'The Coming of Galahad', 23.


## 20  *Charles Williams,* Taliessin Through Logres

1. Following the publication of the second volume of Charles Williams' Arthurian poems, *The Region of the Summer Stars* (London: Editions Poetry London, 1944), Oxford University Press reissued *Taliessin Through Logres*.
2. *Taliessin Through Logres*, 'The Vision of the Empire', β, 13–14.
3. On Logres, see further the comments at the end of this review.
4. 'In his own manner'.
5. *Taliessin Through Logres*, 'The Vision of the Empire', β, 20; 'Lamorack and the Queen Morgause of Orkney', 23.
6. *Ibid.*, 52.
7. *Ibid.*, 'Prologue', II, 2.
8. T. S. Eliot, 'Hamlet', *Selected Essays* (London: Faber, 1932; third enlarged edition, 1951), p. 145.
9. *Taliessin Through Logres*, 'The Crowning of Arthur', 59. ἄπειρον = boundless; πέρας = limit, boundary.
10. *Ibid.*, 'The Coming of Palomides', 57–58.
11. Dante, *La Vita Nuova* (1295), section 2: 'Behold a deity stronger than I.'
12. *Taliessin Through Logres*, 'Taliessin's Return to Logres', 32.
13. *Ibid.*, 'The Vision of the Empire', γ, 2.
14. *Ibid.*, 'The Calling of Arthur', 26.
15. *Pervigilium Veneris* ('A Vigil for Venus'), Latin poem, perhaps of the late fourth century AD.

16. Virgil, *Aeneid*, Book 3, line 505: 'Let that care fall to our descendants.'

## 21  *Charles Walter Stansby Williams (1886–1945)*

1. Charles Williams, *Taliessin Through Logres* (1938), 'The Crowning of Arthur', 45.

## 22  A Lectionary of Christian Prose from the Second Century to the Twentieth Century, *ed. A. C. Bouquet*

1. *A Lectionary of Christian Prose from the Second Century to the Twentieth Century*, p. xxii.
2. *Ibid.*, p. xvii.
3. *Ibid.*, pp. xvii–xxi.
4. Henry Scott Holland (1847–1918), Professor of Divinity at Oxford.
5. George Berkeley (1685–1753), theologian and philosopher.
6. Justin Martyr (*c.* AD 100–165), *Second Apology*, chapter 13.
7. Friedrich von Hügel (1852–1925), Austrian theologian; Frederick William Robertson (1816–1853), English minister; Benjamin Jowett (1817–1893), English theologian and Classical scholar.

## 23  The Oxford Book of Christian Verse, *ed. Lord David Cecil*

1. Richard Rolle (1290–1349), religious writer; Ruth Pitter (1897–1992), poet and close friend of C. S. Lewis.
2. *The Oxford Book of Christian Verse*, p. 69: St Robert Southwell (*c.* 1561–1591), 'Time Go by Turns'.
3. *Ibid.*, p. 140: George Herbert (1593–1633), 'The Temper'.
4. *Ibid.*, p. 350: William Cowper (1731–1800), 'The Lord Will Happiness Divine'.

5. *Ibid.*, p. 478: 'Christina Rossetti (1830–1894), 'I Will Accept'.

6. From Peter Abelard (1079–1142), *O Quanta Qualia*.

7. John Mason Neale (1818–1866), Anglican author and hymn-writer.

8. *Oxford Book of Christian Verse*, p. 502: Gerard Manley Hopkins (1844–1889), 'Thou art indeed just'.

9. George Herbert, *The Temple* (1633), 'Denial', lines 16–18.

10. *Oxford Book of Christian Verse*, p. 3: Anonymous. 'The Shepherd Upon the Hill'.

11. Anonymous, 'Quia Amore Langueo', Arthur Quiller-Couch (ed.), *The Oxford Book of English Verse* (Oxford: Clarendon Press,1919), p. 94.

12. *Oxford Book of Christian Verse*, p.155: George Herbert, 'The Pulley'.

13. *Ibid.*, p. 453: Coventry Patmore (1823–1896), 'Legum Tuam Dilexi'.

14. *Ibid.*, p. 514: Francis Thompson (1859–1907), 'The Hound of Heaven'.

15. William Dunbar (*c.* 1465–*c.* 1520), 'On the Nativity of Christ', lines 1–2: 'Hevins, distil your balmy schouris!'; Christopher Smart, *Hymns and Spiritual Songs* (1765).

16. *Oxford Book of Christian Verse*, p. 356: Augustus Montague Toplady (1740–1778), 'Deathless Principle, Arise'.

17. 'The Will of Jupiter': *Aeneid*, Book 4, line 614.

18. Torquato Tasso, *Gerusalemme Liberata* (1580); William Davenant, *Gondibert* (1651); Abraham Cowley, *Davideis* (1656).

19. An epic on Christ's life by Marco Girolamo Vida (1535).

20. William Cowper, *The Castaway* (1803).

21. Isaac Watts (1674–1748); Charles Wesley (1707–1788).

22. Nahum Tate (1652–1715) and Nicholas Brady (1659–1726), 'Through all the changing scenes of life', lines 21–2.

23. E. M. W. Tillyard (1889–1962), specialist on Shakespeare and Milton.

24. Amos, Chapter 6, verse 1: 'Woe to them that are at ease in Zion' (AV).

25. 'Supreme One'.

26. *Oxford Book of Christian Verse*, p. 7: Anonymous, 'Mary and her Child'.

27. 'Tell, my tongue': the first line of a well-known Roman Catholic hymn.

28. T. S. Eliot, *The Journey of the Magi* (1927), line 31.

29. *Oxford Book of Christian Verse*, p. 502: Gerard Manley Hopkins, 'Thou art indeed just'.

30. *Ibid.*, p. 538: Fredegond Shove (1889–1949), 'The New Ghost'.

31. Hymns from the Psalms and non-biblical sources used in Morning and Evening Prayer.

32. *Oxford Book of Christian Verse*, pp. 136–7; 510 (Thompson); 540 (Ruth Pitter, 'Help, Good Shepherd').

### 24 *Dorothy L. Sayers,* The Mind of the Maker

1. *The Mind of the Maker*, p. vi. Sayers used the quotation from *The Destiny of Man* (1937, English edition) by the Russian philosopher N. Berdyaev (1874–1948) as an epigraph to her book.

2. *The Mind of the Maker*, p. 63.

3. *Ibid.*, p. 66.

4. *Ibid.*, p. 72.

### 25 *Selected sermons:* A Selection from the Occasional Sermons of Ronald Arbuthnott Knox, *ed. Evelyn Waugh*

1. Ronald Knox, *Essays in Satire* (London: Sheed and Ward, 1928); Ronald Knox, *The New Testament of Our Lord and*

*Saviour Jesus Christ: Newly Translated from the Vulgate Latin* (London: Burns, Oates, and Washbourne, 1945); *The New Testament in Basic English*, translated by S. H. Hooke (Cambridge: Cambridge University Press, 1941).

2. 'Saving your presence'.

3. This was a specially printed book of only 550 copies.

4. The quotation is from *A Selection from the Occasional Sermons*, p. 61. On the preaching of St John Fisher (1469–1535), see Lewis's *English Literature in the Sixteenth Century*, Book 2, chapter 1, pp. 161–3. On Jeremy Taylor (1613–1667), see *Collected Letters II*, pp. 4–5. Frederick William Faber (1814–1863), British hymn writer and theologian, presided over the London Oratory, 1849–63. Hugh Latimer (*c.* 1485–1555), one of the three Oxford Martyrs of Anglicanism, was burnt at the stake in 1555.

5. *A Selection from the Occasional Sermons*, p. 45.

6. *Ibid.*, pp. 84, 101.

7. *Ibid.*, p. 35.

8. Lady Julian of Norwich (*c.* 1342–*c.*1416), *Revelations of Divine Love*, Sixth Revelation, chapter 14.

9. *A Selection from the Occasional Sermons*, p. 102: 'It was as something guessed at, not as something seen, that the Divine Hand stretched out to receive their sacrifice'.

10. *Ibid.* p. 25.

11. *Ibid.*, p. 84.

12. *Ibid.*, p. 44.

## 26 *Foreword to Joy Davidman*, Smoke on the Mountain

1. David Wesley Soper (ed.), *These Found the Way: Thirteen Converts to Protestant Christianity* (Philadelphia: Westminster Press, 1950). In the biography attached to Joy Davidman's essay, 'The Longest Way Round', she says on page

12 that in 1939 she spent six months in Hollywood as a junior screen writer for MGM, occupying her time by 'writing half a dozen scripts which no one ever read, and by playing with the M-G-M lion, then a cub'.

2. Joy Davidman, *Letter to a Comrade* (Yale: Yale University Press, 1938).

3. Soper, *These Found the Way*, p. 16.

4. *Ibid.*

5. Charles Lamb, *Essays of Elia* (1823), 'A Chapter on Ears': 'I am for the time – rapt above earth, And possess joys not promised at my birth'.

6. *Letter to a Comrade*, 'Jewess to Aryan', p. 83, line 16.

7. 1 Kings, chapter 18, verse 21.

8. *Letter to a Comrade*, 'Jewess to Aryan', p. 83, lines 8–9.

9. Psalm 19, verses 5–9 (Coverdale translation).

10. See Lewis's treatment of Psalm 19 in *Reflections on the Psalms* (1958), chapter 6.

11. Samuel Johnson, *The Idler* (1758–1760), vol. 1, p. 169: 'Among the calamities of war may be justly numbered the diminution of the love of truth by the falsehoods which interest dictates and credulity encourages. A peace will equally leave the warrior and the relater of wars destitute of employment; and I know not whether more is to be dreaded from streets filled with soldiers accustomed to plunder or from garrets filled with scribblers accustomed to lie.'

12. *Smoke on the Mountain* (1953), chapter 9, p. 101.

13. *Ibid.*, chapter 4, p. 54.

14. John Bunyan, *The Pilgrim's Progress*, (1678), First Part.

15. *Smoke on the Mountain*, 'Introduction', p. 20.

16. *Ibid.*, chapter 6, p. 72.


*28 Odysseus sails again:* The Odyssey, *trans. R. Fitzgerald*

1. Hafiz (1325/6–1389/90), a Persian lyric poet.

2. George Chapman (*c.* 1559–1634), Alexander Pope (1688–1744), and William Morris (1834–1896) had all translated Homer's *Iliad* and *Odyssey*.

3. Stephen Vincent Benét (1898–1943), American poet and novelist. Benét had written the foreword to Joy Davidman's poetry collection, *Letter to a Comrade* (New Haven: Yale University Press, 1938).

4. *Odyssey*, Book 1, line 14.

5. *Ibid.*, line 36.

6. *Ibid.*, Book 6, line 58.

7. *Ibid.*, Book 4, lines 441–2.

8. *Ibid.*, Book 7, lines 84–91.

9. *Ibid.*, Book 21, lines 8–16.

10. *Ibid.*, Book 5, line 37.


## 29 *Ajax and others: John Jones,* On Aristotle and Greek Tragedy

1. *On Aristotle and Greek Tragedy*, p. 15. *Hamartia*, sometimes translated 'tragic flaw', more generally means 'error' or 'mistake'.

2. *Ibid.*, p. 34.

3. *Ibid.*, p. 49.

4. *Ibid. Praxis* = 'Action' or 'Actual life'. *Muthos* = 'Plot' or 'Story'.

5. *Ibid.*, pp. 86, 128.

6. *Ibid.*, pp. 114, 129.


## 30 Lucretius

1. J. K. Fotheringham (ed.), *Eusebii Pamphili Chronici Canones* (London: Humphrey Milford, 1923), p. 231, under the 171st Olympiad.

2. Plutarch (first century AD), 'Against Colotes' (= *Moralia* 1107 ff.).

3. *De Rerum Natura*, Book 3, lines 27–8: 'A certain divine joy and trembling falls upon me at such moments'.
4. *Ibid.*, Book 1, line 629: 'nature, the female-creator of things'; Book 1, line 1: 'joy of men or gods'.
5. 'Dissatisfaction with the world'.
6. On Lucretius's influence on the thinking of C. S. Lewis, see T. LaPrade, '*Percipit Atque Horror*: C. S. Lewis's Lost Essay and Notes on Lucretius', unpublished MA thesis, University of North Carolina at Chapel Hill (2010).

## 31 *T. R. Henn*, Longinus and English Criticism

1. Longinus (first century AD), author of *De Sublimitate* ('On the Sublime').
2. 'As a cloud'.
3. 'Elevation of thought'.
4. 'To treat so great a matter so carelessly': Terence, *Andria*, Act 1, scene 5.

## 32 *Helen M. Barrett*, Boethius: Some Aspects of his Times and Works

1. *Boethius: Some Aspects of his Times and Works*, p. vii.
2. Hermann Usener (1834–1905), German professor of Classics.
3. *Anedoton Holderi* is an anonymous work of the sixth century AD, edited by Usener in 1877. *De Fide Catholica* (On the Catholic Faith) is a treatise by Boethius.
4. Theodoric (*c.* 454–526), king of the Ostrogoths and ruler of Italy.
5. 'The always unpunished greed of the barbarians'; 'eager for the death of all'. Cassiodorus (*c.* 490–*c.* 585) was a late Roman historian and statesman.

6. Thomas Hodgkin (1831–1913), British historian with an interest in late antiquity. On Cyprian and Opilio, see *De Consolatione*, Book 1, part 4.

7. Aristides, fifth-century BC Athenian politician, nicknamed 'The Just'.

8. *De Consolatione*, Book 4, part 6: 'that divine reason'; 'inherent in things that move'.

9. 'Evil, therefore, is nothing'.

10. *De Consolatione*, Book 3, part 12: 'There is nothing which, keeping to its nature, would try to contravene God'; 'that there was no nature of evil'.

11. Boethius, 'A Treatise Against Eutyches and Nestorius', Part 1: 'Nature is the specific difference giving form to any object.'

12. About the same time that Lewis was writing this review, he was composing *The Screwtape Letters* (1942) in which he has Screwtape say, in Letter 15: 'The humans live in time but our Enemy [God] destines them to eternity. He therefore, I believe, wants them to attend chiefly to two things, to eternity itself, and to that point of time which they call the Present. For the Present is the point at which time touches eternity. Of the present moment, and of it only, humans have an experience analogous to the experience which our Enemy has of reality as a whole; in it alone freedom and actuality are offered them.'

13. *Et pressus gravibus colla catenis*: 'And weighed down by heavy chains on the neck'; *ipsa loci facies*: 'The very appearance of the place'; *exilium* = 'exile'; *patria* = 'homeland'.

14. St Thomas More, *A Dialogue of Comfort against Tribulation* (1553).

15. 'Spear and sword' (*contum gladiumque*) is a quotation from Juvenal, Satire 10, lines 20–2.

16. 'We are condemned to death and to proscription'. Boethius, *The Theological Tractates*, with an English translation by H. F. Stewart and E. K. Rand (Loeb edition).

17. '[The highest good] rules all boldly and arranges all pleas-antly'; cf. Book of Wisdom, chapter 8, verse 1, describing wisdom: 'She spans the world in power from end to end and gently orders all things' (RSV).
18. St Thomas More, *A Godly Meditation* (1534), line 7: 'Little by little to throw off the world completely'.

### 33 *Ruth Mohl,* The Three Estates in Medieval and Renaissance Literature

1. *The Three Estates in Medieval and Renaissance Literature*, chapter 1, p. 1.
2. *Ibid.*, chapter 2, pp. 5–6.
3. *Ibid.*, p. 11.
4. *Ibid.*, chapter 7, p. 339.
5. John Lydgate, *Troy Book* (1412–20) translated by Guido delle Colonne, *The Siege of Thebes* (1287).
6. D. Laing (ed.), *The Poetical Works of Sir David Lyndsay*, 3 vols. (Edinburgh: W. Paterson, 1879), vol. I: 'The Dreme', lines 169 ff.; Robert Henryson, *Orpheus and Eurydice* (*c.* 1508).
7. Thomas More (1478–1535) and Thomas Elyot (1490–1546) were English humanists.
8. *Boke of Nurture* (*c.* 1460–1470).
9. Jacobus de Cessolis (*c.* 1250–*c.* 1322).
10. *Confessio Amantis*, Prologue, 529–33: 'And natheles yet som men wryte / And sein that fortune is to wyte / And som men holde oppinion / That it is constellacion / Which causeth al that a man doth.'
11. Cf. C. S. Lewis, *The Discarded Image* (1964), chapter 5, pp. 103–4: 'Astrology is not specifically medieval. The Middle Ages inherited it from antiquity and bequeathed it to the Renaissance. The statement that the medieval Church frowned upon this discipline is often taken in a sense that

makes it untrue. Orthodox theologians could accept the theory that the planets had an effect on events and on psychology, and, much more, on plants and minerals. It was not against this that the Church fought. She found against three of its offshoots. (1) Against the lucrative, and politically undesirable, practice of astrologically grounded predictions. (2) Against astrological determinism. The doctrine of influences could be carried so far as to exclude free will. Against this determinism, theology had to make a defence... The propensity can be resisted; hence the wise man will overrule the stars...(3) Against practices that might seem to imply or encourage the worship of planets.'

12. 'Influence of the planets'; '*Dream of Scipio* (*Somnium Scipionis*)-Cicero, *Republic*, Book 6. See *The Discarded Image*, chapter 3, pp. 23–8.

## 34 *J. W. H. Atkins*, English Literary Criticism: The Medieval Phase

1. James Boswell, *The Life of Samuel Johnson*, ed. George Birkbeck Hill, 6 vols. (Oxford University Press, 1934), vol. III, 13 April 1778, p. 279: 'Langton said to me afterwards, that he could repeat Johnson's conversation before dinner, as Johnson had said that he could repeat a complete chapter of "The Natural History of Iceland," from the Danish of *Harrebow*, the whole of which was exactly thus: Chap. LXXII. *Concerning snakes*. "There are no snakes to be met with throughout the whole island."'

2. Giovanni Boccaccio, *De Genealogia Gentilium* ('On the Genealogy of the Gods of the Gentiles') (1472).

3. John Barbour (1320–1395), author of *The Bruce* on Robert Bruce, King of Scotland, and his follower James Douglas, with a celebrated account of Bannockburn.

## 35 *Arthuriana:* Arthurian Literature in the Middle Ages, *ed. R. S. Loomis*

1. Jean Frappier (1900–1974), author of *Chrétien de Troyes: l'homme et l'œuvre* (Paris : Hatier-Boivin, 1957).
2. Charles Augustin Sainte-Beuve (1804–1869), literary critic.
3. Karl Lachmann (1793–1851) argued that when manuscripts commit the same error, they had similar origins.
4. Joseph Bédier (1864–1938), French medievalist; Eilhart von Oberge, twelfth-century German poet; Béroul, twelfth-century Norman poet.
5. Percevale is one of Arthur's knights.
6. Lewis was under the impression that the essay on *Gawain and the Green Knight* (pp. 528–40) was by the editor, Roger Sherman Loomis. It is by his wife, Laura Hibbard Loomis.
7. See Lewis's essay 'The Anthropological Approach' in Walter Hooper (ed.), *Selected Literary Essays* (Cambridge University Press, 1969), pp. 301–11.
8. The Green Knight's real name.
9. J. S. P. Tatlock, 'Laȝamon's Poetic Style and its Relation', *The Manly Anniversary Studies in Language and Literature* (University of Chicago Press, 1923), pp. 3–11. On Laȝamon's *Brut*, see Lewis's 'Introduction' to the *Brut* in this volume.
10. On Wace (*c.* 1115–*c.* 1183), see Lewis's 'The Genesis of a Medieval Book' in Walter Hooper (ed.), *Studies in Medieval and Renaissance Literature*, (Cambridge University Press, 1966), pp. 18–40.
11. Horace, Odes, Book 1, poem 1, line 28: *crambe repetita*: 'stale repetitions'.
12. 'The brutality of English newspapers', a phrase from Matthew Arnold, *Essays in Criticism*, 'The Literary Influence of Academies' (London: Macmillan, 1865).

## 37 *Andreas Capellanus*, The Art of Courtly Love

1. *The Art of Courtly Love*, p. 3. Robert Bossuat (1888–1968) was a French philologist and specialist in medieval literature.
2. *The Dove's Neck-Ring* is a discussion of the nature of love by the Andalusian lawyer and scholar Ibn Hazm (994–1064).
3. *The Art of Courtly Love*, p. 9.
4. *Ibid.*, p. vii.

## 38 *Rhyme and reason: Dorothy L. Sayers*, The Poetry of Search and the Poetry of Statement

1. Dorothy Sayers translated *The Divine Comedy* in three volumes for Penguin Classics (1949–62), the last completed by her friend Barbara Reynolds.
2. Henry Francis Cary (1772–1844) began translating Dante when he was an undergraduate at Christ Church, Oxford (BA 1794). His translation of the *Inferno* in blank verse was published in 1805–6, while his immensely popular translation of the whole of *The Divine Comedy* in blank verse was published as *The Vision: or Hell, Purgatory and Paradise of Dante*, translated in three volumes (1814–19). In her paper, 'On Translating The *Divina Commedia*', Dorothy Sayers said: '[Cary] was the first great English "vulgariser" of Dante, who translated him into the Miltonic blank verse which was in his time, the recognised medium for any long and important English narrative poem' (p. 93).
3. *Hell*, Canto 21, line 139: 'He promptly made a bugle of his breech.'
4. *Ibid.*, Canto 22, line 7: 'sometimes with trumpets, sometimes with bells'; *The Poetry of Search and the Poetry of Statement*, chapter 5, pp. 103–4.

### 39 *Alan M. F. Gunn*, The Mirror of Love

1. Jean de Meun (*c*. 1240–*c*. 1305), one of the authors of the *Romance of the Rose*.
2. Alexander Pope, *An Essay on Criticism*, Part 2, line 34.
3. 'By a leap'.
4. 'Pleasant and fitting both their use will be
    When time and mode and measure do agree . . .'.
5. 'The lower parts should be ruled'; 'the earthly things are governed'.

### 40 The English prose *Morte*

1. William Shakespeare, *Twelfth Night*, Act 1, scene 1, line 13.
2. Jean-Jacques Rousseau, *The Social Contract* (1762), Book 1, chapter 7.
3. A. W. Pollard (ed.), *Le Morte Darthur: Sir Thomas Malory's Book of King Arthur and of his Noble Knights of the Round Table*, 2 vols. (London: Macmillan, 1903).

### 41 *Leone Ebreo*, The Philosophy of Love

1. Gonsalvo de Cordoba (1453–1515), a Spanish general; Pico della Mirandola (1463–1494), Italian philosopher and humanist.
2. 'The best theologians'.
3. Zoroaster is the Greek form of the Persian religious reformer or prophet Zarathustra (alive perhaps *c*. 1000 BC). Hermes Trismegistus was the supposed author of forty-two books on Egyptian religion, of uncertain date.
4. Benjamin Jowett (1817–1893) and Bernard Bosanquet (1848–1923) were both English scholars, with particular interests in the works of Plato.
5. *The Philosophy of Love*, p. 332.

6. Henry More (1614–1687), English theologian and philosopher.

7. *The Philosophy of Love*, p. xv.

8. Anders Nygren (1890–1978), Swedish theologian known for his work *Agape and Eros* (London: SPCK, 1953, rev. edn, translated into English).

## *42* E. K. Chambers, *Sir Thomas Wyatt and Some Collected Studies*

1. See Alfred Nutt, *The Influence of Celtic upon Medieval Romance* (London: D. Nutt, 1904); Jessie Weston, *From Ritual to Romance* (New York: Peter Smith, 1941); Roger Sherman Loomis, *Celtic Myth and Arthurian Romance* (New York: Columbia University Press, 1927); Arthur Charles Lewis Brown, *Iwain: A Study in the Origins of Arthurian Romance* (Boston: Ginn, 1903).

2. *Sir Thomas Wyatt and Some Collected Studies*, p. 14.

3. *Ibid.*, p. 17.

4. On Vinaver and Malory, see Lewis's essay, 'The English Prose *Morte*', above.

5. Corbenic is the name of the castle of the Holy Grail, and Camelot refers to the castle and court of King Arthur.

6. *Perlesvaus* is a French Arthurian romance of the thirteenth century. The German poet Wolfram von Eschenbach (*c.* 1170–*c.* 1220) retold the tale of the Holy Grail in his poem *Parzival*.

7. Étienne Gilson (1884–1978), French philosopher with a particular interest in medieval philosophy.

8. Lewis's first scholarly work, *The Allegory of Love: A Study in Medieval Tradition* (1936), is a study of Courtly Love. In chapter 1, he wrote: 'Every one has heard of courtly love, and every one knows that it appears quite suddenly at the end of the eleventh century in Languedoc... The sentiment, of

course, is love, but love of a highly specialized sort, whose characteristics may be enumerated as Humility, Courtesy, Adultery, and the Religion of Love'.

9. Andreas Capellanus, *De Amore*, Book 1, section 49: 'No one exercises goodness or courtliness in the world except from a source of love'.

### 43 *M. Pauline Parker*, The Allegory of the Faerie Queene

1. Horace, *Ars Poetica*, line 70: '*Multa renascentur quæ nunc cecidere*' ('Many words now fallen into disuse will be revived').
2. Edmund Spenser, Prefatory Letter to Sir Walter Raleigh on *The Faerie Queene* (1589).
3. Presumably a reference to G. W. Kitchin, *Spenser: Faery Queen, Book 1* (Oxford: Clarendon Press, 1905).
4. I.e., *Paradise Lost*, Book 2, line 156.
5. John Lydgate, *Fall of Princes* (c. 1480).

### 44 *John Vyvyan*, Shakespeare and the Rose of Love

1. Fabius Planciades Fulgentius, late fifth-century Christian author.

### 45 *Logan Pearsall Smith*, Milton and his Modern Critics

1. See, e.g., T. S. Eliot, 'A Note on the Verse of John Milton', *Essays and Studies of the English Association*, vol. 21 (Oxford: Clarendon Press, 1936), pp. 32–40; F. R. Leavis, *Revaluation: Tradition and Development in English Poetry* (London: Chatto and Windus, 1936), pp. 43–4.
2. In *A Preface to* Paradise Lost (1942), chapter 19, Lewis wrote: 'It is not that [Dr Leavis] and I see different things when we look at *Paradise Lost*. He sees and hates the very

same that I see and love. Hence the disagreement between us tends to escape from the realm of literary criticism. We differ not about the nature of Milton's poetry, but about the nature of man, or even about the nature of joy itself.'

3. *Milton and his Modern Critics*, p. 49, 65; Rose Macaulay, *Milton* (London: Duckworth, 1934), chapter 8, p. 126.

4. Virgil, *Aeneid*, Book 2, line 521. 'Not such aid, nor such defenders (does this crisis demand)'.

5. *The English Poems of John Milton*, from the edition of H. C. Beeching, together with an 'Introduction' by Charles Williams, and a 'Reader's Guide to Milton' compiled by Walter Skeat, MA, FSA (London: Oxford University Press, 1940).

6. *Ibid.*, Charles Williams's 'Introduction', p. xiv: 'The poem is concerned with a contrast and a conflict between two states of being. But those states are not only mythological; they are human and contemporary, and thus the poem has a great deal of interest for us.'

7. *Paradise Lost*, Book 1, line 98; Book 5, line 665.

8. Charles Williams, *Taliessin Through Logres* (1938), Dedication; William Shakespeare, *Troilus and Cressida*, Act 1, scene 3, lines 83–139.

9. *The English Poems of John Milton*, 'Introduction', p. xiv.

10. Lewis mistakenly attributed the quotation to Keats. Pearsall Smith, in fact, had written (p. 20): 'Robert Bridges, in his essay on Keats . . . expressed his opinion that the best period of Keats' writing was when he fell under Milton's influence, and that in *Hyperion* "we are conscious at once of a new musical blank verse, a music both sweet and strong, alive with imagination and tenderness." All this, however, [the English critic John] Middleton Murry ignores. "There is death in Milton", he reiterates.'

11. Writing to Brother George Every on 28 January 1941, Lewis said: 'I've just written a review of Pearsall Smith's

*Milton & His Modern Critics* for the *Cambridge Review*. What a perfectly ghastly book! I hope you understand that if I thought Smith's case for Milton the real and best one, I shd. join Leavis at once. Against all that bilge Leavis & Milton and I almost stand together: and Milton wd. resent *this* defence more than the attack' (*Collected Letters II*, p. 467).

## 46 *Douglas Bush, Paradise Lost* in Our Time: Some Comments

1. At Cornell University in Ithaca, New York.
2. Lewis and Douglas Bush had agreed to write a volume each for the twelve-volume *Oxford History of English Literature* published by Oxford University Press. Bush's *English Literature in the Earlier Seventeenth Century, 1600–1660* was published in 1945, while Lewis's *English Literature in the Sixteenth Century, Excluding Drama* came out in 1954.
3. For further discussion of Logan Pearsall Smith, F. R. Leavis, and Charles Williams on Milton, see the review of Logan Pearsall Smith's *Milton and his Modern Critics* in this volume.
4. Virgil, *Aeneid*, Book 2, line 521: *Non tali auxilio nec defensoribus istis* – 'not such aid, nor such defenders (does this crisis demand)'.
5. Paradise Lost *in Our Time*, pp. 92–3.
6. See Richard Hooker, *Of the Laws of Ecclesiastical Polity* (1593), Book 1, chapter 1, v: 'They err who think that of the will of God to do this or that there is no reason besides his will.' In *The Problem of Pain* (1940), chapter 6, Lewis wrote: 'It has sometimes been asked whether God commands certain things because they are right, or whether certain things are right because God commands them. With Hooker, and against Dr Johnson, I emphatically embrace the first alternative.'

7. Alexander Passerin D'Entrèves, *The Medieval Contribution to Political Thought* (London: Oxford University Press, 1939), p. 119 (*licet Deus non esset* = 'granting that there is no God').

8. See William Paley, *The Principles of Moral and Political Philosophy* (1785).

9. Paradise Lost *in Our Time*, p. 40. See J. Middleton Murry, *Studies in Keats New and Old* (London: Oxford University Press, 1939).

## 47 H. W. Garrod, Collins

1. Dante, *Vita Nuova*, chapter 25: 'figure of speech or rhetorical flourish'.

2. *Collins*, pp. 48–9: '[Collins's] *Ode to Evening* exists . . . in two versions; that of the volume of 1746, and that printed two years later in Dodsley's *Collection* . . . The late Professor Ker, in a lecture upon *Some Romantic Fallacies*, has a comment upon these two versions which is not a little mysterious to me. To him the Dodsley version is so much better than that of 1746 as to be, in itself, "significant for the progress of the romantic movement": "In the second version," he writes, "besides the true personification in 'votaress', which is from Milton's *Maske*, there is the fresh vision and understanding of the effect of a surface of water in twilight, when all the land round it is dark, and in place of the conventional ruin that 'nods', there is the old building, church or castle, dimly seen as part of the evening light along with the large bulging hill-side. If you look into it, you will see at once that the water is to the west, the 'time-hallow'd pile' to the east, and all this is given in the fewest words, and with no vanity or insistence on the accurate rendering. The romantic fallacy is cleared away, and its place is taken by a different mode of vision and poetry."'

3. 'Crash of thrones' is a quotation from Francis Palgrave's 'Ode for the Twenty-First of June 1887'.
4. *Ibid.*, pp. 30, 43.

### 48  *Hugh Kingsmill*, Matthew Arnold

1. *Matthew Arnold*, 'Introduction', p. xi. In 1932, Kingsmill published a biography of the editor and author Frank Harris (1856–1931). John Middleton Murry (1889–1957) was an influential editor and critic.
2. *Ibid.*, p. 47.
3. *Ibid.*, p. 51.
4. *Ibid.*, p. 127.

### 49  *Evelyn Waugh*, Rossetti: His Life and Works

1. 'World-view'.
2. Rossetti's painting, *Beata Beatrix* (1864–1870) is in the Tate Gallery, London.
3. Pre-Raphaelite Brotherhood (also called 'Pre-Raphaelites'), a circle of English painters and critics, founded in 1848, that included Ford Madox Brown, John Everett Millais, Dante Gabriel Rossetti, and William Holman Hunt.

### 50  *Boswell's bugbear: Sir John Hawkins*, The Life of Samuel Johnson

1. The *Life of Samuel Johnson*, 'Introduction', pp. xvi–xxiii.
2. *Ibid.*, p. 129.
3. *The Life of Samuel Johnson*, p. 49. Richard Savage (*c.* 1697–1743) was the subject of one of the best known of Johnson's *Lives of the Poets*.
4. *The Life of Samuel Johnson*, p. 175.

5. Edward Cave (1691–1754), influential editor and publisher; Hester Thrale (1741–1821), diarist and correspondent of Samuel Johnson.
6. *The Life of Samuel Johnson*, p. 181.
7. *Ibid.*, p. 48.
8. *Ibid.*, p. 82.
9. *Ibid.*, pp. 14, 35, 43, 107.
10. *Ibid.*, p. 57.

### 51 *Poetry and exegesis: Harold Bloom,* The Visionary Company

1. *The Visionary Company*, p. 3.
2. *Ibid.*
3. *Ibid.*, p. 5.
4. *Ibid.*, p. 16.
5. *Ibid.*, p. 201.
6. By William Wordsworth (1815).
7. I.e., Dante's *Divine Comedy* and *Pearl*, a fourteenth-century English poem.
8. 'To the eternal fountain'.

### 52 *The Sagas and modern life – Morris, Mr Yeats, and the originals: Dorothy M. Hoare,* The Works of Morris and Yeats

1. *The Works of Morris and of Yeats in Relation to Early Saga Literature*, p. 76 on Morris's Sigurd the Volsung (1876); James Stephens, 'Deirdre' (1915).
2. *The Works of Morris and of Yeats in Relation to Early Saga Literature*, pp. 29, 140–4.
3. William Butler Yeats, *The Shadowy Waters* (1900).
4. *The Works of Morris and of Yeats in Relation to Early Saga Literature*, pp. 37–8 on Morris's *Life and Death of Jason* (1867).

5. *The House of the Wolfings* (1889); *The Story of the Glittering Plain* (1890); both are by Morris.
6. *The Life and Death of Jason*, Book 10, line 539.
7. *The Works of Morris and of Yeats in Relation to Early Saga Literature*, pp. 33–6.
8. *Ibid.*, pp. 6–8.
9. *The Well at the World's End* (1896); *The Water of the Wondrous Isles* (1897); both are by Morris.

## 53 Haggard rides again: Morton Cohen, Rider Haggard

1. Ouida (= Maria Louise Ramé) (1839–1908), Margaret Oliphant (1828–1897), Stanley Weyman (1855–1928), and Max Pemberton (1863–1950) were all popular authors of their day.
2. J. K. Stephen, 'To R. K.' in *Lapsus Calami* (Cambridge: Macmillan and Bowes, 1891), lines 15–16.
3. *Rider Haggard*, p. 79.
4. Aristotle, *Poetics*, Section 3, part 22.
5. Rudyard Kipling, *Something of Myself* (1935), Chapter 8, 'When your Daemon is in charge, do not try to think consciously. Drift, wait, obey'.
6. *Gorboduc* (1571), an early English tragedy; Christopher Marlowe, *Tamburlaine the Great* (1590).
7. William Shakespeare, *The Tempest*, Act 4, scene 1, line 156: 'Leave not a rack behind'.

# INDEX

367